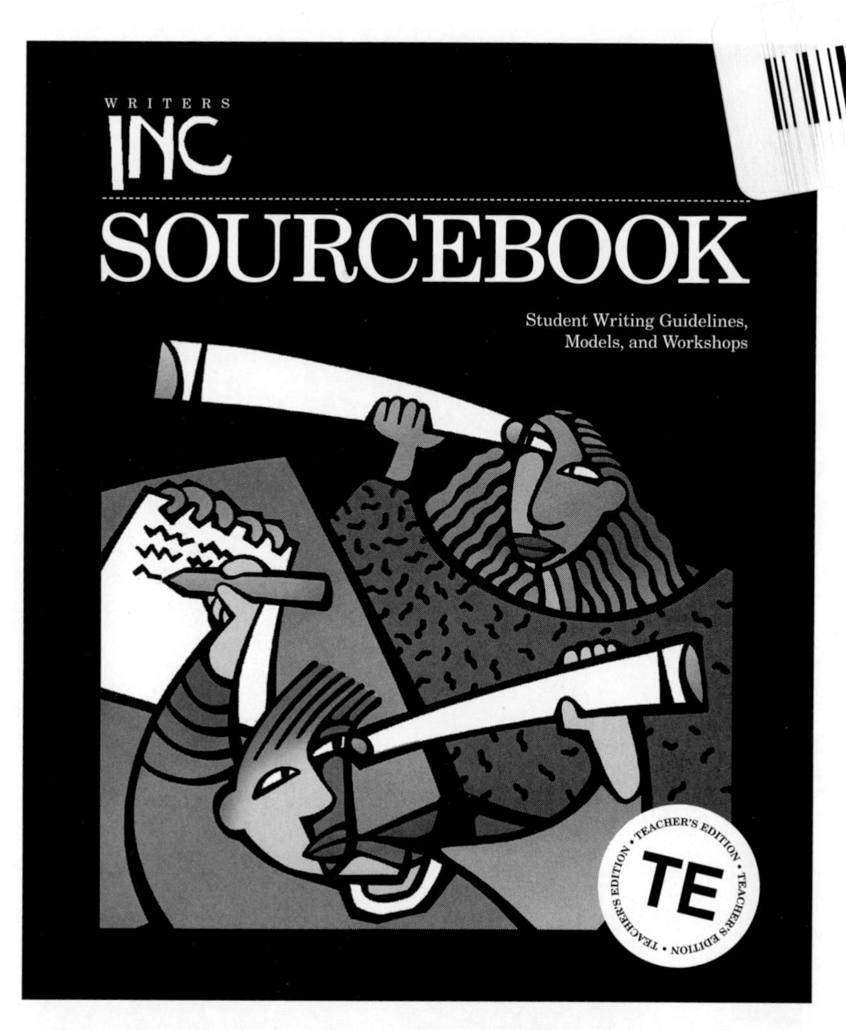

TEACHER'S EDITION FOR SOURCEBOOK 12

The Teacher's Edition of the SourceBook provides **Teacher's Notes** for each Writing Framework and **Implementation Guides and Answer Keys** for the Writing Workshops and Practical Writing Activities.

WRITE SOURCE

GREAT SOURCE EDUCATION GROUP

a Houghton Mifflin Company
Boston, Massachusetts

Authors: Pat Sebranek and Dave Kemper

Printed in the United States of America

International Standard Book Number: 0-669-38855-6

2 3 4 5 6 7 8 9 10 -RRDC- 00 99 98 97 96

Table of Contents

What is the SourceBook?

The *Writers INC SourceBook* is a wonderful companion resource to the *Writers INC* handbook. The SourceBook provides a series of important, realworld writing experiences. The handbook provides guidelines and examples that help students complete their work. Together, these two student resources make a very effective writing and learning team. (There is a separate SourceBook for each grade level, 9-12.)

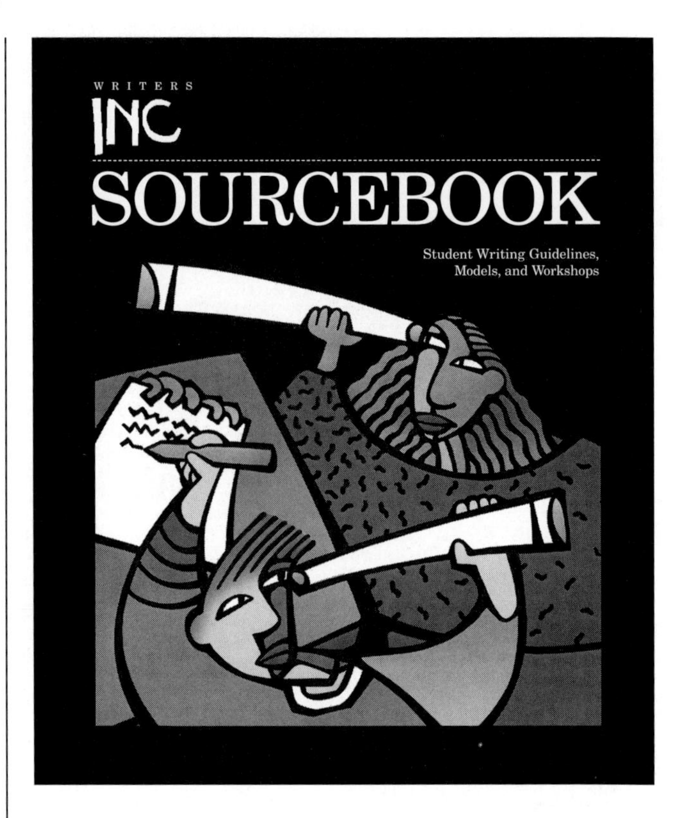

How can the SourceBook be used?

Primary Writing Resource • With the SourceBook, teachers can build an effective and comprehensive writing program by selecting writing framework activities, writing workshops, and practical writing units to implement in their classrooms.

All-School Resource • The SourceBook contains more than enough writing activities for use in the English classroom and beyond. The writing framework activities are especially well-suited for crosscurricular use. (The SourceBook and handbook can also serve as core writing and learning resources in schools developing interdisciplinary curriculums.)

Personal Reading and Writing Guide • Because of its attractive appearance, appealing models, and easy-to-follow writing guidelines, the SourceBook will "excite students to self-activity." This resource, along with the handbook, allows students in classroom workshops to progress at their own pace from one important writing project to the next.

What are the key sections in the SourceBook?

The SourceBook is divided into three major sections, each dealing with a key area of writing.

The Writing Framework • The writing framework offers a variety of real-life writing experiences, arranged according to five major categories: personal writing, subject writing, creative writing, reflective writing, and academic writing. This framework reflects the "Universe of Discourse" developed by James Moffett and addresses writing from many different points of view, including remembering, reporting, inventing, imitating, reflecting, and analyzing. Each framework activity contains a set of easy-to-follow writing guidelines plus a collection of high-interest student and professional models.

Writing Workshops • The SourceBook contains more than 60 writing workshops covering all phases of the writing process—from selecting interesting subjects to organizing writing, from advising in peer groups to editing for clarity. These workshops are designed to be used in context, when students have a need to work on a particular skill. Many of the workshops are directly tied to writing framework activities.

Practical Writing • The practical writing section contains extended units addressing basic forms of writing important both in school and later on the job. These units will work well in basic-skills classes as well as in the regular English classrooms.

Writing Framework Planning Guide

The information in this section will help you plan and implement the writing framework activities in the SourceBook. The Overview of the Writing Framework on the next two pages is of special importance since it shows how all of the writing activities in the series fit together from one level to the next. Also of importance will be the Teacher's Notes Preview page and, of course, all of the individual teacher's notes pages for the writing framework.

Overview of the Writing Framework

	9	10	11	12
Personal Writing				
	Personal Reminiscence	Reminiscence of a Person	Reminiscence of School Life	Extended Reminiscence
	Related Reminiscences	"Unpeopled" Reminiscence	Reminiscence of a Group	Personal Essay
Subject Writing				
	Description of a Person	Description of a Place	Character Profile	Case Study
	Secondhand Story	Firsthand Experience	Extended Experience	Historical Profile
	Eyewitness Account	Interview Report	Observation Report	Venture Report
	Summary Report from Single Source	Compiled Report from Multiple Interviews	Compiled Report from Multiple Sources	Personal Research Report
Creative Writing				
	Fictionalized Journal Entry	Fictionalized Memory	Fiction from Fact	Fictionalized Imitation
	Character Sketch	Patterned Fiction	Uncharted Fiction	Genre Writing
	Memory Poem	Patterned Poetry	Found Poetry	Statement Through Poetry
	Dialogue Writing	Monologue Writing	Ad Script	Playwriting
Reflective Writing				
	Essay of Illustration	Essay of Explanation	Essay of Experience	Essay of Reflection
	Dialogue of Ideas	Essay of Opposing Ideas	Satiric Essay	Essay of Speculation
	Response to Reading	Personal Review	Limited Literary Analysis	Extended Literary Analysis
	Pet Peeve	Editorial	Personal Commentary	Position Paper
Academic Writing				
	Essay of Information	Essay to Compare	Essay of Definition	Problem/Solution Essay
	Essay to Explain a Process	Cause/Effect Essay	Essay of Argumentation	Essay of Evaluation
	*Paragraph Writing	*The Traditional Essay	*The Essay Test	*Impromptu Writing
	*The Summary	*The Précis	*The Paraphrase	*The Abstract

* These extended units, as well as a sequence of letter-writing and on-the-job writing activities, can be found in the Practical Writing sections of the SourceBook.

A Closer Look at the Framework

Each activity in the writing framework is arranged into one of five categories. The categories progress from personal to public writing, building a variety of skills and strategies along the way.

Personal Writing: Remembering and Sharing

Students will write memory pieces from a number of different points of view. They will be asked to reminisce about their own experiences, other people, groups, school life, and so on. In the final memory piece, students will develop an extended reminiscence in which they explore a past phase (extended period of time) in their lives. The focus in this section is on looking into the past and sharing what is discovered.

Subject Writing: Searching and Reporting

Once students have become familiar and comfortable with writing about themselves and others from memories, they will move to writing that focuses on collecting information about more public subjects. Students will be asked to write descriptions, reports, profiles, eyewitness accounts, and experience papers much like a professional journalist. During this process they will practice observing, interviewing, researching, focusing, and compiling information. The focus here is looking into and reporting on subjects that are of current interest to the students.

Creative Writing: Inventing and Imitating

Students will also be given ample opportunities to create dialogue, stories, poems, and scripts, beginning with a fictionalized journal entry and ending with a one-act play. In the process, they will experience a wide variety of forms and strategies useful in other areas of writing. The focus here is inventing, taking memories and experiences and reshaping them into creative pieces.

Reflective Writing: Reflecting and Speculating

Students will next have the opportunity to utilize the strategies employed during personal, subject, and creative writing to bring their ideas, feelings, and memories together in a variety of reflective forms. Students will begin in ninth grade with a basic essay in which a story illustrates a point and end in twelfth grade with a fairly complex position paper. The focus here is developing reflective essays in a variety of contexts.

Academic Writing: Informing and Analyzing

Even though any of the writing activities in the framework can be used throughout the curriculum, those in the academic category are probably used most often. Students will be given opportunities to interpret, define, compare and contrast, argue, analyze, propose solutions, consider cause and effect, and evaluate. In addition, students will encounter more traditional forms of writing in extended units on paragraph writing, the traditional essay, the essay test, impromptu writing, and so on. The focus here is shaping informed, coherent, and clear essays of information.

Overview of the Framework Design

Each writing framework is designed to be efficient and user-friendly for both the teacher and student. Each page of teacher's notes in the section is divided into clear, well-labeled categories. Each student-guidelines page in the SourceBook is presented in a clear, step-by-step fashion. All models contain an introduction and helpful margin notes.

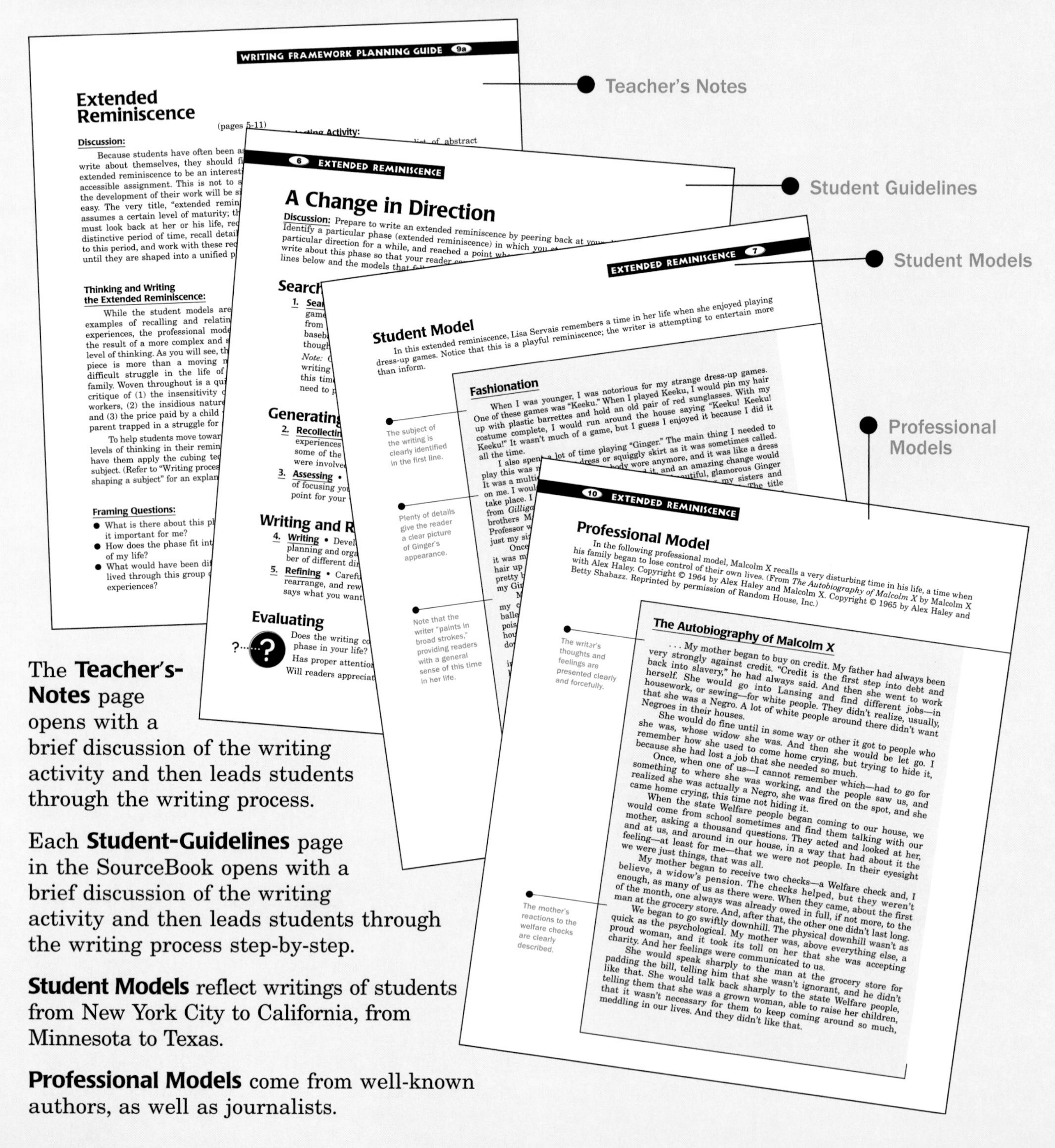

The **Teacher's-Notes** page opens with a brief discussion of the writing activity and then leads students through the writing process.

Each **Student-Guidelines** page in the SourceBook opens with a brief discussion of the writing activity and then leads students through the writing process step-by-step.

Student Models reflect writings of students from New York City to California, from Minnesota to Texas.

Professional Models come from well-known authors, as well as journalists.

Teacher's Notes Preview

The "Teacher's Notes" for each framework writing activity offer advice, insights, options, and a mini-index of related activities to help teachers implement and enrich their students' work.

Additional activities offer planning options.

The focused assignment offers teachers and students a real-world writing option.

The opening remarks establish a starting point for planning and implementing.

"Framing Questions" help students establish a frame for their work.

WRITING FRAMEWORK PLANNING GUIDE 9a

Extended Reminiscence

(pages 5-11)

Discussion:

Because students have often been asked to write about themselves, they should find the extended reminiscence to be an interesting and accessible assignment. This is not to say that the development of their work will be simple or easy. The very title, "extended reminiscence," assumes a certain level of maturity; the writer must look back at her or his life, recognize a distinctive period of time, recall details related to this period, and work with these recollections until they are shaped into a unified paper.

Thinking and Writing the Extended Reminiscence:

While the student models are very good examples of recalling and relating extended experiences, the professional model is clearly the result of a more complex and sophisticated level of thinking. As you will see, the Malcolm X piece is more than a moving memory of a difficult struggle in the life of the writer's family. Woven throughout is a quiet but strong critique of (1) the insensitivity of the welfare workers, (2) the insidious nature of prejudice, and (3) the price paid by a child who watches a parent trapped in a struggle for survival.

To help students move toward more complex levels of thinking in their reminiscence writing, have them apply the cubing technique to their subject. (Refer to "Writing process, Guidelines for shaping a subject" for an explanation.)

Framing Questions:

- What is there about this phase that makes it important for me?
- How does the phase fit into the big picture of my life?
- What would have been different if I hadn't lived through this group of related experiences?

Selecting Activity:

Provide students with a list of abstract qualities like *love, fear, security, disappointment,* etc. Then have them think, write freely, and/or discuss times in their lives when they experienced any or all of these feelings. Ideas for writing should emerge from this activity.

Real-World Writing Option:

Assignment: Write a related reminiscence about a time in your childhood when it was your goal to be a doctor, a nurse, a teacher, an actor or actress, etc.
Subject: Your choice
Purpose: To explore and share an important time in your life
Audience: Classmates
Form: Related reminiscence
Voice: Informal

Related Activities:

Writing Framework: Additional Model
"There Was a Time . . . ," pp. 39-40

Writing Workshops
"Focus Pocus," pp. 176-177
"Like a Train on Smooth Tracks," pp. 189-190
"Voice Choice," pp. 196-197

***Writers INC* References**

Clincher sentence
Memory details
Metaphor, Writing
Quickguides, Reminiscence writing
Reminiscence, Writing
Writing, About an event

Helpful handbook cross-references are also listed.

The "Related Activities" index shows complementing workshops and practical writing activities in the SourceBook.

Implementing the Framework Activities

The guidelines that follow will help teachers carry out a basic framework activity as a class-wide project. (If the frameworks are used in a writing workshop, teachers may simply have copies of the writing guidelines and models available for students to use on an individual basis.)

Planning

1. Gain a clear understanding of the framework activity by previewing the "Teacher's Notes," the writing guidelines, and the related models.

2. Review all of the "Related Activities" listed in the "Teacher's Notes" for possible inclusion in the activity.

Introducing the Activity

3. Introduce the activity by implementing any combination of the following . . .
   - ask students to review the writing guidelines.
   - have them read and react to one or more of the writing models.
   - discuss and/or display the "Framing Questions" to help students establish a frame for their work.
   - implement the "Selecting Activity."
   - offer a related writing prompt for an introductory exploratory writing.

Facilitating the Students' Work

4. To help students carry out their work . . .
   - guide them in their searching, selecting, generating, and writing as outlined in the writing guidelines.
   - provide opportunities for them to write, read, and share in class.
   - consider implementing one of the workshops listed under "Related Activities."
   - identify relevant handbook pages.

Closing Out the Activity

5. To bring the writing activity to an effective close . . .
   - ask students to conduct peer revising and editing sessions.
   - have them share (and evaluate) finished products.
   - encourage students to submit their work for publication.
   - challenge them to write additional pieces related to this framework.

Grade 12 Activities and Outcomes

The activities in the grade 12 framework provide students with a wide variety of opportunities to re-create and connect past incidents, to describe other people and events, to generate and share creative pieces, to develop essays and personal responses, and to form explanations and summaries.

Personal Writing:

Extended Reminiscence • Recall a phase or an important time of change in your life.

Personal Essay • Explore a subject of personal interest in a free-flowing essay.

Subject Writing:

Case Study • Develop an in-depth report about one person whose experiences typify the experiences of a larger group.

Historical Profile • Share your findings about an interesting aspect from our past.

Venture Report • Offer readers an in-depth look at a business or profession.

Personal Research Report • Present your research findings on a topic of personal interest.

Creative Writing:

Fictionalized Imitation • Imitate (or parody) the style or content of a story, movie, etc.

Genre Writing • Create a short story based on a specific genre.

Statement Through Poetry • Convey an important message in the form of a poem.

Playwriting • Write a one-act play complete with stage directions.

Reflective Writing:

Essay of Reflection • Reflect upon the importance of a time in your life, an experience, a decision, etc.

Essay of Speculation • Explore a subject, noting what effect it might have in the future.

Extended Literary Analysis • Develop an extensive literary analysis displaying a thorough understanding of an author and his or her work.

Position Paper • Present your position on a significant issue.

Academic Writing:

Problem/Solution Essay • Propose a solution(s) to a real problem.

Essay of Evaluation • Assess a policy, topic, class, etc., as to its value or worth.

***Impromptu Writing** • Develop clear, unified essays for different types of writing prompts.

***The Abstract** • Arrange the key words in a given selection into a shortened, readable version of the original.

* These extended units, as well as a sequence of letter-writing and on-the-job writing activities, can be found in the Practical Writing section of the SourceBook.

Writing Framework
Teacher's Notes

Extended Reminiscence

(pages 5-11)

Discussion:

Because students have often been asked to write about themselves, they should find the extended reminiscence to be an interesting and accessible assignment. This is not to say that the development of their work will be simple or easy. The very title, "extended reminiscence," assumes a certain level of maturity; the writer must look back at her or his life, recognize a distinctive period of time, recall details related to this period, and work with these recollections until they are shaped into a unified paper.

Thinking and Writing the Extended Reminiscence:

While the student models are very good examples of recalling and relating extended experiences, the professional model is clearly the result of a more complex and sophisticated level of thinking. As you will see, the Malcolm X piece is more than a moving memory of a difficult struggle in the life of the writer's family. Woven throughout is a quiet but strong critique of (1) the insensitivity of the welfare workers, (2) the insidious nature of prejudice, and (3) the price paid by a child who watches a parent trapped in a struggle for survival.

To help students move toward more complex levels of thinking in their reminiscence writing, have them apply the cubing technique to their subject. (Refer to "Writing process, Guidelines for shaping a subject" for an explanation.)

Framing Questions:

- What is there about this phase that makes it important for me?
- How does the phase fit into the big picture of my life?
- What would have been different if I hadn't lived through this group of related experiences?

Selecting Activity:

Provide students with a list of abstract qualities like *love, fear, security, disappointment,* etc. Then have them think, write freely, and/or discuss times in their lives when they experienced any or all of these feelings. Ideas for writing should emerge from this activity.

Real-World Writing Option:

Assignment: Write a related reminiscence about a time in your childhood when it was your goal to be a doctor, a nurse, a teacher, an actor or actress, etc.
Subject: Your choice
Purpose: To explore and share an important time in your life
Audience: Classmates
Form: Related reminiscence
Voice: Informal

Related Activities:

Writing Framework: Additional Model
"There Was a Time . . . ," pp. 39-40

Writing Workshops
"Focus Pocus," pp. 176-177
"Like a Train on Smooth Tracks," pp. 189-190
"Voice Choice," pp. 196-197

Writers INC References

Clincher sentence
Memory details
Metaphor, Writing
Quickguides, Reminiscence writing
Reminiscence, Writing
Writing, About an event

Personal Essay

(pages 13-19)

Discussion:

Students should think of the personal essay as essay writing in free form incorporating a number of different elements including recollection, evaluation, reflection, etc. The personal essay allows students to put the imprints of their personalities more directly into their expository writing. It is a form that allows them to display their distinctive writing voices. Students must obviously follow the principles basic to all narrative and reflective writing, but they should also be encouraged to add their own personal touches to their work. A personal essay without "voice" is like a computer without a keyboard—an essential element is missing.

Framing Questions:

- How do I personally feel about my subject? (Why do I want to write about this?)
- How should I approach my writing? What should it look like? How should I begin?
- What main point do I want to make in my writing?
- What can I do to make my writing truly sound like it comes from me?
- How do I want my readers to react to my ideas?

Selecting Activity:

Write open-ended sentences (like those that follow) on the board and ask students to complete them.

1. __________ always confused me because . . .
2. __________ always pleased me because . . .
3. __________ has changed my life because . . .

Then ask students to explore one or more of their statements in a free writing. An idea for a personal essay should emerge from this activity.

Real-World Writing Option:

Assignment: Write an essay presenting your personal view of some aspect of style.
Subject: You might write about a specific style of dress or way of carrying out an activity.
Purpose: To present your thoughts and feelings stemming from personal observation
Audience: Classmates
Form: Personal essay
Voice: Informal

Related Activities:

Writing Framework: Additional Models
The Autobiography of Malcolm X, pp. 10-11
"They're Driving Me Crazy," pp. 43-45
"My Brother, My Best Friend," pp. 108-109
"Adventures in the Real World," p. 115

Writing Workshops
"Talking Heads," p. 169
"Hooking Your Reader," pp. 180-181
"Let me repeat . . . ," p. 194
"Bridging the Gap," p. 207

Practical Writing
"Writing and Assessment," pp. 267-268
"Additional Prompts," pp. 281-284

Writers INC References

Chronological order
Outlining, Compositions
Personal Essay
Showing versus telling
Style, Writing with

Case Study

(pages 21-32)

Discussion:

In "Making a Case," students will investigate and share the experiences of one individual whose story speaks for the experiences of a larger group of people. One student might know someone who is elderly and totally dependent upon others for care. This one story could speak for many others in this ever-expanding segment of our population. Another student might know someone who has run away or someone who has recently immigrated to this country. Still another student might have an interest in a particular group of people (say Vietnam veterans or disaster survivors) and actively search for a representative of that group to investigate.

Students should draw upon all of their investigative experiences to collect information for their case studies. They will want to conduct interviews, make firsthand observations, refer to printed materials (articles, letters, journals, etc.), explore their personal thoughts and feelings, and so on. Point out that without a close and careful examination of their subjects, they will be hard pressed to produce effective case studies.

Framing Questions:

- Do I already know people who could serve as subjects for case studies? What particular groups do they represent?
- Conversely, which groups (types of individuals) would I be interested in investigating? Would I be able to find someone within one of these groups to investigate?
- How much information should or can I collect? How can I best prepare for interviews, find pertinent articles, and so on?
- How should I focus my thoughts for writing? Is it clear to me how or why this person's story speaks for similar individuals? Is there something in particular about this person that I want to emphasize?

Selecting Activity:

Have students as a class generate a list of possible groups to investigate in case studies. Challenge them to fill up the blackboard with ideas (*chronic dieters, bodybuilders, kindergarten teachers, vegetarians,* etc.). Afterward, ask students to note one or two of these ideas that they would personally like to investigate.

Real-World Writing Option:

Assignment: Write a case study based on an individual with a particular medical condition.
Subject: An asthma sufferer, a diabetic, a victim of a car accident, an AIDS patient, etc.
Purpose: To share one person's story so that it speaks for the experiences of others
Audience: Classmates and other concerned individuals
Form: Case study (in-depth narrative report)
Voice: Semiformal

Related Activities:

Writing Workshop
"Black Holes," pp. 240-241

Practical Writing
"In-Class Impromptu Writing: From Start to Finish," pp. 271-272

Writers INC References

Case Study
Journalism, writing
Observation
Research paper

Historical Profile

(pages 33-40)

Discussion:

In order to write well-organized, interesting historical profiles, students must immerse themselves in their topics. They must, in effect, transport themselves to another time and place and come to "feel" the people and events they are writing about—and then find a way to communicate that feeling to their readers. Students must know that effective historical profiles are both informative and entertaining, researched thoroughly and presented in a lively fashion.

Framing Questions:

- Where in my immediate world would I find possible subjects for a historical profile? Who could provide me with ideas?
- What do I already know about my subject? What questions about it would I hope to answer during my research?
- Do I have access to enough information to develop an informative and entertaining profile?
- What would be the best way to present the findings of my research? (A report? A story recalling my research efforts? An extended interview?)

Selecting Activity:

Challenge students to complete the following open-ended statements in a number of different ways:

1. One time, place, person, or event of the past that has greatly affected my life (by way of my ancestors) is . . . (the Civil War, Boston, Laura Ingalls Wilder, the invention of the telephone, the Great Depression).
2. I wonder about the first . . . (brain surgery, glass windows, elevators, zoos).
3. I wish I could go back in time to . . . (our house 50 years ago, the first winter at Plymouth Rock, the Battle of Gettysburg).

Real-World Writing Option:

Assignment: Write a profile of a business that was once important in your community.
Subject: A local business from the past
Purpose: To explore and show the historic impact of a business
Audience: Members of the community
Form: Newspaper profile
Voice: Formal or informal

Related Activities:

Writing Framework: Additional Model
"Angel Island Reveals Poignant History," pp. 56-57

Writing Workshops
"Real-World Writing," p. 195
"Agreement: Pronoun & Antecedent," p. 227
"Clear as Mud," pp. 229-230

Writers INC References

Evidence, using
Feature writing
Point of view
Profile
Writing, About an event

Venture Report

(pages 41-49)

Discussion:

Having students research and write venture reports gives them an opportunity to gather valuable information about particular professions and business opportunities. In the process of carrying out this framework activity, students will also gain valuable insights into the world of work in general.

It is important for students to search out firsthand information for their reports. In-person interviews with people involved in the field, job-site visits, firsthand experiences, and other types of direct contact are invaluable. Remind students that their most important task in writing a venture report is researching their subject thoroughly.

Framing Questions:

- What profession, field, or business am I genuinely interested in?
- Do I have access to information related to this particular venture?
- Who (or what) would be my best source of information?
- What specific things do I want to find out about my subject?
- How should I report my findings?

Special Note: Students may also write about personal experiences that lend themselves to venture reports. (See the student model.)

Opening Activity:

Invite a guidance counselor, college placement official, corporate personnel officer, and/or private employment headhunter to discuss the job markets of today and tomorrow. Also invite experts in the fields of health care, computer technology, electronics, etc., to share their insights into careers and the employment outlook in their particular fields.

Selecting Activities:

Have each student note interesting and/or unusual businesses listed in the yellow pages in the phone book. Or have them refer to the various career guides shelved in the guidance office or school library. Then again, you might encourage them to conduct a more creative subject search, perhaps surveying other students to see which professions or businesses they are most interested in learning about. They may also review the bulletin boards of business cards often found in the entrances to popular coffee shops and truck stops for writing ideas.

Real-World Writing Option:

Assignment: Interview someone who started her or his own business. It could be the neighbor who does child care in her home, or a professional lawn-care expert. Then write a venture report based on this interview and any additional research.

Subject: A small-business venture

Purpose: To investigate and report on a particular self-made business person

Audience: General public

Form: A report

Voice: Informal

Related Activities:

Writing Workshops

"Write Angles," pp. 178-179

"Comma Practice," p. 237

Writers INC References

Journalism, writing

Listening skills

Observation

Personal Research Report

(pages 51-59)

Discussion:

The personal research report gives students an opportunity to satisfy their own need to know about a subject of personal interest. They have had plenty of opportunities to develop reports and research papers on subjects related specifically to their course work. This activity gives them an opportunity to investigate a "real world" topic that is more closely in tune with their personal interests and needs. Most students will approach this assignment with a high degree of excitement and enthusiasm, and the results of their efforts will show it. Expect to receive honest and engaging final products from your students, detailing the stories of their investigative efforts.

Students must understand that printed material is only one of many sources of information for personal research reports, and often not the most important one. Other important sources of information include interviews, firsthand experiences, observations, and personal reflections. This is a significant departure from the traditional report where books and magazines are generally the sole sources of information.

Framing Questions:

- What have I always been curious about? What do I need to know right now? What would help me in the future?
- What do I already know about this subject?
- What do I want to find out?
- Who can I turn to first and second for advice and information?
- Where can I go for additional information? Is there some place I can visit? Can I get some firsthand experience?
- What would be the best way to present the findings of my research?

Selecting Activity:

Have students complete two or three "I always wanted to know how (or what) . . ." statements to share with the class. Use these statements to discuss possible subjects for research reports. Remind students that they should focus on subjects that they can actually research.

Real-World Writing Option:

Assignment: Help yourself overcome a fear, lay to rest a memory, convince yourself that you can do something, etc., through a careful investigation. Compile a report of this experience.
Subject: Your choice
Purpose: To satisfy a personal need and to compile the results in a report
Audience: Classmates/yourself
Form: Personal research report
Voice: Informal

Related Activities:

Writing Framework: Additional Models
"Overcrowded Classrooms: Do You Ever Feel Like a Teen Sardine?" pp. 148-149
"Transportation Alternatives: . . ." p. 150

Writing Workshops
"Six Faces," pp. 172-173
"Unsinkable!" p. 247

Practical Writing
"Planning an Open-Ended Impromptu Essay," pp. 273-274
"The Abstract," pp. 291-292

Writers INC References

Note-taking, In classroom
Personal Research
Research paper

Fictionalized Imitation

(pages 61-66)

Discussion:

Successful imitation demands more than a superficial familiarity with certain stylistic devices. Students should have a clear understanding of a writer's style or of a particular literary form. Imitating Hemingway, for example, consists of more than just writing short sentences. Students should approach this activity with some sense of playfulness and good humor. An imitation, by its very nature, almost always tips the scales more toward parody than toward a serious treatment of a subject.

Framing Questions:

- What is there about this writer's style that is unique? How is this writer different from other writers?
- How would I characterize this writer's material and general approach to writing? How does he or she look at the world?
- Should I try to imitate this writer's style in general, or should I focus my attention on one particular passage or form?
- How playful am I going to be in my writing?

Special Note: Generally, a student who feels an initial affinity for a writer has an impetus for the more intensive analysis necessary for effective imitation. We all tend to imitate and even parody those we admire or find interesting. The success of the students' fictionalized imitations will depend upon how carefully they engage in various higher-level thinking operations, especially analyzing, evaluating, and inventing. (You might want to discuss the differences between a serious imitation and parody, and, perhaps, the difference between parody and satire. See the handbook for definitions of parody and satire.)

Warm-up Exercise:

Provide students with samples of a simple literary form (like the fable) to analyze in terms of its form and structure. They should consider the following points in their analysis: *How are the characters introduced? What are these characters like? Is there any pattern to the development of the plot? How complicated are the sentences?* Discuss the results of their work, focusing on the basic elements that seem common to the samples. Then have students write original models (fables) using this information as a guide. This exercise can be used as a springboard into individual imitations of other forms of writing.

Real-World Writing Option:

Assignment: Imitate or parody an advertisement, and display your finished product in the classroom.
Subject: Your choice
Purpose: To imitate or parody an ad
Audience: Classmates
Form: Ad for magazine or newspaper
Voice: Appropriate for subject and form

Related Activities:

Writing Workshops
"What Makes 'Good' Good?" p. 219
"What I Like," p. 220

Writers INC References

Fictionalized Imitation
Satire
Style

Genre Writing

(pages 67-79)

Discussion:

"According to Form" asks students to develop an original story based on their understanding of a particular genre (*science fiction, science fantasy, mystery, urban fiction,* etc.). Those students who have read widely in one or more of the genre types will have no problem getting started on stories of their own. Others will have to learn as much as they can about the different genres through the work associated with this framework activity.

About the Different Genres: Provide students with a frame of reference for their work by discussing the basic features associated with some common genre types. (See "Typecasting" below for ideas.) During this discussion, encourage students to offer their favorite authors and titles (including movies) for the different genres as well as their insights into story lines, character types, settings, and conflicts common to each one. *Alternative Approach:* Science fiction, science fantasy, and mystery afficionados could be asked to provide minilessons or workshops on their "pet" genres. Or small groups of students could simply be asked to investigate particular story types for the rest of the class.

Special Note: Students don't have to be experts to attempt a genre story. All they really need is a basic understanding of the story type and a model or two for reference. The point is to experience the genre rather than master it.

Typecasting: Basic features of four common story types are listed here. Share this information with your students in an opening class discussion. (Provide as much information as you can for students interested in other genres.)

Science Fantasy: set in imaginary and/or unpredictable world, draws heavily on mythic elements, the fantastic is commonplace, frequently includes almost cartoon-like violence, logic is disrupted

Science Fiction: future-focused, exists in the realm of scientific possibilities, logical in its orientation, proceeds realistically within the context of the story line, may deal with social or moral issues (genetic engineering, etc.)

Mystery: focuses on who committed a crime (or how or why it was committed), revolves around the main character as crime solver, establishes the power of the mind, all important clues worked into the story line

Urban Fiction: urban setting or environment is crucial element, characters in conflict with environment, naturalistic in tone and outlook (man or woman vs. environment), starkly real

Real-World Writing Option:

Assignment: Write a school-related urban story using the model "Norma" as a guide.
Subject: Think of individuals, situations, and/or conflicts related to city and school life.
Purpose: To write a story reflecting the basic characteristics of urban fiction
Audience: Your classmates
Form: Short story
Voice: Appropriate for narrator and characters

Related Activities:

Writing Workshops
"One Form to Another," p. 206
"Concise . . . Naturally," p. 221

Practical Writing
"In Perspective," pp. 263-264

Writers INC References

Characterization
Genre Writing
Showing versus telling

Statement Through Poetry

(pages 81-87)

Discussion:

Students have had a great deal of practice developing thesis statements in paragraphs and essays. "More Than Pretty Words" gives them an opportunity to develop a strongly felt belief in poetic form.

It's important for students to consider the need for balance between what they want to say and the poetic manner in which they express themselves. They should remember that a strong statement does not automatically result in a strong poem. A poorly conceived poem can dilute the impact or importance of its message. An overstated message, conversely, can diminish a poem's impact by making the poem appear to be a by-product of the statement itself. A statement of belief should naturally evolve or build throughout the poem. The more indirection applied the better. The more readers have to read between the lines, the more effective the poetic expression becomes.

Framing Questions:

- What personal beliefs do I have that would lend themselves to poetic expression?
- What precisely is the nature of the statement or message I have chosen to develop?
- How can I deal with my subject poetically? That is, how can I convey my message in poetic form?
- What should my poem look like?

Warm-Up Exercises:

Have students dig out an old essay or paragraph and recast this writing (or a portion of it) into a poem. Have them start by circling the important words and phrases in the original writing. Then ask them to arrange and work with these ideas until they speak in some poetic fashion.

Beforehand, you might want to review the models provided in this activity so students can see how other writers have shaped their statements. Or you might refer to other poems you have covered during the year. Also discuss the variety of poetic forms available to students: prose poems, list poems, narrative poems, sonnets, lyrical poems, song lyrics, etc.

Selecting Activity:

If students have difficulty arriving at a subject to write about, try the following exercise. List general subject areas on the board: school, community, careers, environment, relationships, etc. Then ask each student to write statements of belief related to some or all of the topics you have listed. As a class, analyze a few of these statements to see if they could serve as starting points for poems. (You might then write a poem for one of these ideas as a class before students work on their own.)

Real-World Writing Option:

Assignment: Express an implicit statement about drugs, alcohol, crime, etc., in a poem.
Subject: Any story related to a serious social/personal problem
Purpose: To convey a specific belief through poetry
Audience: Classmates
Form: Free-verse poetry
Voice: Personal poetic voice

Related Activities:

Writing Workshops
"Metaphor Central," p. 193
"Cold Eye and Dirty Hands," p. 199

Writers INC References

Guidelines for writing, Poetry
Metaphor, Writing
Person, describing
Poetry

Playwriting

(pages 89-103)

Discussion:

The nineteenth-century Frenchmen Eugene Scribe and Victorien Sardou developed a form for play writing called the "well-made play." You might want to begin your discussion by examining the elements these men considered essential to playwriting:

Exposition (in the opening scene) gives the *who, what, when,* and *where* of the story. Characters may divulge this information through dialogue, or it may be revealed through stage directions.

Rising action is the problem the characters struggle with during the play. The conflicts people experience in life (and in plays) are closely related to *who* they are. Rising action develops through a series of events until the conflict reaches a breaking point or **climax.**

Climax occurs when the conflict breaks, and the action moves toward a **resolution.**

Denouement, or resolution, is the portion of the play where the conflict or problem is solved and important details are disclosed.

Explain to students that playwriting demands that they *get inside and know* their characters. The audience wants to know what motivates a character; they'll believe, and even consider heroic, a character they feel they understand, having watched that character struggle.

Elements of Playwriting:

There are four basic elements of playwriting that students should consider before they begin writing:

Dialogue: It is through the dialogue that audiences come to understand each character's identity, through not only what they say but how they say it. Dialogue can suggest subtexts, in which characters' surface statements carry deeper meaning. (See Mike in the model "When Time Dies.") Clues to voice or delivery (including a dialect if it fits) can be added to character description or stage directions.

Conflict: Be sure your conflict is believable and evolves from the core of your characters' identities.

Stage Directions: Stage directions indicate setting, entrances and exits, lighting, and use of props. They should also communicate what the writer envisions each character doing while on stage (including each character's action while other characters are speaking).

Forms: Encourage students to use the form that best fits the kind of story they are telling: *drama, farce, comedy, tragedy, melodrama,* or *mystery*. As they will discover, each form has its own special features, guidelines, and techniques that add to its impact.

Additional Reading: *Teaching Young Playwrights*, Gerald Chapman, Heinemann Educational Books

Related Activities:

Writing Workshops

"Smooth, Natural, and Concise," p. 222

"Complete and Mature," p. 233

Writers INC References

Dialogue, Writing

Playwriting

Essay of Reflection

(pages 105-115)

Discussion:

When writing an essay of reflection, students will be focusing on an important aspect of their past experience. But instead of simply trying to re-create this experience, they must work more closely with their subject, carefully examining it in order to form new understandings about its significance and importance.

A narrative piece of writing essentially says, "This is what happened." It is a form of reminiscing. A reflective piece of writing says, "This is what happened, *plus* these are some new thoughts I have formed about it (the experience)."

Students should think of reflecting as the process of examining, exploring, considering, and reconsidering ideas and experiences. To ensure that they understand what is meant by reflective thinking and writing, share with them sections in two or more of the model essays that seem especially reflective. Point out that certain sentence beginnings naturally signal reflective ideas (*Now I recognize, I suppose, I am amazed, It seems, Ever since,* etc.). Spend some time discussing how these ideas are formed, how they seem to follow the course of the writer's mind as he or she writes.

Warm-Up Exercise:

To give your students a feel for reflective writing, ask them to write freely for 10 to 15 minutes about their first year of high school. As they form their ideas, ask them to incorporate at least two or three reflective thoughts beginning with words like *Now I recognize* or *I suppose*.

Selecting Activity:

Have students explore the following scenario in an exploratory writing. *Suppose you are looking into a special mirror—one that reflects the real you on the outside and on the inside. Describe what you see.* Encourage students to look at themselves very carefully from a number of different perspectives. Afterward, ask them if there are any stories in their past experience that helped form some of their thoughts and feelings in their writing. These stories could serve as possible starting points for their essays.

Real-World Writing Option:

Assignment: Reflect upon a pivotal decision you have made.
Subject: A decision that changed a personal relationship, your understanding of something, or the way you act and react
Purpose: To gain new insight about a decision
Audience: Yourself, classmates, parents
Form: Reflective essay
Voice: Informal

Related Activities:

Writing Framework: Additional Models
"Swallowing Sorrow: Legacies of My Past," pp. 16-17

Writing Workshops
"How Do You Shape Up?" p. 171
"Hey, kiddo, let me tell you something . . . " p. 182
"Familiar First, New Next," p. 191

Practical Writing
"Basic Steps in the Impromptu-Writing Process," p. 266

Writers INC References

Event, guidelines for describing
Person, describing
Place, describing
Reflective details
Reflective writing

Essay of Speculation

(pages 117-124)

Discussion:

Students should regard the essay of speculation as a type of cause/effect writing in which the effects are not yet known. The effects will be the fruit of students' speculations—their reflections, projections, and educated guesses. *Reflections* involve deliberating, having a mental debate with yourself about a subject. *Projections* utilize current facts, trends, and information to predict the future. *Educated guesses* take into account as many variables as possible and consider what is already known to create logical theories about the future. On the one hand, speculation may be pure conjecture. On the other hand, speculation must maintain a firm grasp on present reality. The essay of speculation requires blending analysis and imagination. It's important for students to feel personal commitment to their topics.

Framing Questions:

- What issue concerns me most about the future?
- What do I already know about this subject? Can I imagine the long-term effects if things don't change, or if they do change?
- Is this subject worth examining? How is it significant? Am I willing to think seriously about this issue? Where can I find out more about it?

Special Note: Students should get specific. To create a manageable topic about a global issue like acid rain, students could ask a specific "what if . . . so what?" question. *What if* acid rain ended up destroying all freshwater fish habitats? *So what?* Students then make their forecasts: It would mean the end of sport fishing. It would reduce drastically a much-needed source of food. It would throw our ecosystem into a tailspin. It would . . .

Selecting Activity:

Suggest students explore the pitfalls of panaceas or easy solutions. Some wonderful-sounding speculations create problems. *If only* there was just one skin color, *if only* each man, woman, and child could be a millionaire, if only . . . Have students produce more "*if only* . . ." statements and discuss the problems they create.

Real-World Writing Option:

Assignment: You're a member of the class of '96—1896, that is. React to the changes you'd see if you had a chance to visit America today.

Subject: Limit your reactions and speculations to one area: work, school, entertainment, medicine, communication, etc.

Purpose: To broaden your idea of change by thinking of your present as the radical future

Audience: Classmates

Form: Informal essay

Voice: Familiar or informal

Related Activities:

Writing Workshops

"Using Parallel Structure," pp. 215-216

"More Bang for the Buck," p. 223

Practical Writing

"Planning an Open-Ended Impromptu Essay," pp. 273-274

"Planning a Response to a Scenario," p. 275

Writers INC References

Analyze

Cause and effect

Logic

Speculation, essay of

Extended Literary Analysis

(pages 125-135)

Discussion:

In this framework activity, students are asked to display an *extended* critical understanding of a literary subject. How students develop their work depends upon their particular literary interests and experiences. Some students may want to match their own interpretations of a favorite author's work (or a specific aspect of this person's work) with the viewpoints of one or two important critics. Others may want to compare the work of two different authors, relying exclusively on their own thoughts and feelings, or incorporating the insights of other critics as well. Still others may want to do something a bit more unconventional, perhaps analyze a film adaptation of a novel, and so on.

While the notes on this page and the student guidelines that follow address the extended *literary* analysis, students should be encouraged to develop analyses related to other artistic forms (art, music, video, etc.) if that makes more sense to them. One of the model analyses addresses the film *Fantasia*, while a second model analyzes the work of a famous blues guitarist Blind Willie Johnson.

Framing Questions:

- What authors (or literary texts) would serve as interesting and worthy starting points for my analysis?
- Do I already know something about the subject I have selected for analysis? And do I have the experience and ability to react critically and carefully to this work?
- What do other critics have to say about my subject? And to what extent should I incorporate their ideas into my analysis?
- What will be the most effective way to present my ideas? Should I work in a very conventional way by defending or supporting a basic thesis statement? Or should I try something a bit daring, perhaps presenting a *collage* of ideas and interpretations that explores more than defends a particular position.

A Word of Caution About Secondary Sources: Encourage (or demand!) that students rely first and foremost on their own thoughts and feelings in their analyses. References to secondary sources should be made only to enhance or embellish the students' own interpretations or to provide alternative points of view. An effective literary analysis is one in which the student writer is in complete control, speaking from a position of authority and understanding.

Real-World Writing Option:

Assignment: Develop an extended literary analysis for a specific audience other than your classmates.
Subject: An appropriate literary subject for your audience
Purpose: To share an extended under-standing of a literary subject with a specific audience
Audience: Your choice (a senior-citizens group, an individual from another country, etc.)
Form: Reflective essay (or semiformal letter)
Voice: Semiformal

Related Activities:

Writing Workshops
"R-R-R-R-Revising," p. 203
"When Complex Is Simpler . . . ," pp. 209-210
"Indefinite Pronoun Reference," p. 228

Practical Writing
"Unsent Letters," p. 277
"Literary License," p. 284

Writers INC References

Writing, About literature
Reflective writing
Research paper

Position Paper

(pages 137-143)

Discussion:

The purpose of a position paper is to have students take a positive and assertive stand on a significant issue of local, national, or global importance. Counterarguments should certainly be addressed, but the main thrust of the writer's efforts should be to assert her or his position. A position paper succeeds when it presents and supports a claim that readers find interesting and worthy of thoughtful consideration.

Special Note: A position paper is a special form of argumentative writing, and, thus, students could benefit from a review of the basic characteristics of building arguments. (Refer to "Thinking, Logically" in the handbook index for help.)

Framing Questions:

- What exactly is the position I wish to promote and support? How strongly do I feel about it?
- To what degree have I actually thought this position through?
- Is my position based primarily on emotions, or is it based on verifiable observations and ideas?
- How much additional support will be required to bolster what I already know? Do I have access to additional material?

Selecting Activity:

If students have trouble selecting a subject for their writing, have them complete the following exercise: Brainstorm for a list of important issues related to today's political, social, economic, cultural, environmental, and educational scenes. Try to fill up the board, listing ideas as fast as they are suggested. Then ask students to chart their attitudes or feelings toward each topic.

To do this, students should first list the topics on their own paper. Next to each topic they should put the letter *A, B, C,* or *D,* depending on how they react to each one. An **A** means students have strongly held beliefs about the topic, **B** means students are quite knowledgeable about the topic, **C** means students have little or no interest in the topic, and **D** means they have little or no knowledge about it. Topics marked with an *A* or a *B* certainly could be considered as possible subjects for writing.

Real-World Writing Option:

Assignment: Write a position paper on a business-related topic—affirmative action, minimum wage, maternity leave, etc.
Subject: Business-related issue
Purpose: To assert a position
Audience: Classmates, business community
Form: Reflective or argumentative essay
Voice: Semiformal

Related Activities:

Writing Framework: Additional Model
"The Environment Can Take Care of Itself," pp. 121-122

Writing Workshops
"Ready, Set, CHOOSE," pp. 174-175
"Hold Your Position," pp. 185-186
"Punctuating for Style," p. 244

Practical Writing
"Additional Prompts," pp. 281-284
"The Abstract," pp. 291-292

Writers INC References

Argumentation
Position paper
Reflective writing
Subject, choosing

Problem/Solution Essay

(pages 145-152)

Discussion:

Students should be reminded (and shown) that many magazine feature articles are problem/solution essays, as are most internal reports in industry and business. Both combine logical and creative thinking. Students should also be reminded that they must avoid the temptation to jump into creative problem solving before exploring the problem thoroughly. Good problem solvers know they have to understand the problem from the inside. For example, to suggest that racism is simply due to upbringing presents a superficial analysis. To suggest that racism is also caused by the stress of overcrowded conditions gets closer to knowing the problem from the inside.

Framing Questions:

- What problem do I want to write about?
- Can I state the problem clearly in a single sentence?
- Why do I see this as a problem?
- What might someone say who doesn't perceive this as a problem?
- What are the parts to this problem?
- Do I already know of solutions to this problem? What are they? If I don't have any significant solutions, how will I find them?

Special Note: Students often need help finding a logical procedure for exploring solutions. One possibility is to use a graphic organizer to map out a working analysis of the problem. (See the "map" on p. 147 in this framework activity.)

In-Process Activity:

Display the following outline on the board for students to use as a general planning guide when they are ready to develop their writing.

Planning Outline

Part I: What's the problem?
What may have caused it?
What are its parts?

Part II: What's the solution?
How can it be accomplished?
What are the steps?

Part III: Why will it work?

Real-World Writing Option:

Assignment: Analyze a serious communication problem you've experienced and explain a possible solution.
Subject: A communication problem with a parent, an employer, a friend, etc.
Purpose: To analyze a problem and plot a potential solution
Audience: Concerned individuals
Form: Problem/solution essay
Voice: Depends on the audience

Related Activities:

Writing Workshops
"Saving the Best for Last," p. 217
"Other Clarity Problems," p. 231

Practical Writing
"Getting Down to Basics: Establishing a Framework for Planning and Writing," pp. 269-270
"Instant Solutions," p. 276

Writers INC References

Essay, Problem/solution
Problem-solving method
Thinking, Logically
Writing Essays

Essay of Evaluation

(pages 153-161)

Discussion:

When writing essays of evaluation, students should think of themselves as roving critics, exploring and reviewing subjects that cover a wide range of areas, from personal incidents to casual observations, from important occasions to current trends, from memorable places to the latest gadgets or products. Impress upon your students that evaluating a subject generally means determining its value or worth.

Framing Questions:

- What thoughts, feelings, and attitudes does the subject call to mind?
- Should this subject be treated casually, or does it deserve more serious attention?
- Why is this experience important? What harm or good has it done?
- How has this person, place, idea, or event affected me or other people?
- What is the significance, usefulness, or ultimate value of the subject?
- How does the subject work? What are its main features?

Special Note: It's important to note that how students develop their essays can vary greatly. One student's efforts may result in a very measured end product, perhaps a matter-of-fact assessment of an old neighborhood or school. Another student's efforts may result in a more intense finished piece, perhaps an emotional assessment of a traumatic experience.

Selecting Activity:

If your students have trouble coming up with subjects, try this brainstorming activity. List the following phrases on the board: *something that needs improving, something that deserves support, something that's unfair, something that everyone should have to see or do,* etc. Then have students volunteer ideas that fit under each of these categories. A number of potential writing ideas should develop.

Real-World Writing Option:

Assignment: Evaluate a period of *change* in your life.
Subject: You may have moved; your neighborhood may have changed; you may have a new math teacher; you may have lost a friend or family member; and so on.
Purpose: To assess the significance of a change in your life
Audience: Your classmates (parents, guidance counselor)
Form: Personal essay
Voice: Informal

Related Activities:

Writing Framework: Additional Model
"Walking Tall," pp. 25-26

Writing Workshops
"Focus Pocus," pp. 176-177
"The Write Instincts," pp. 201-202

Practical Writing
"Unsent Letters," p. 277

Writers INC References

Evaluate
Event, guidelines for describing
Person, describing
Place, describing

Writing Workshop Planning Guide

The Sourcebook contains more than 60 writing workshops covering all phases of the writing process. The overview on the next two pages illustrates all of the different types of workshops included in the SourceBook. Also included in this section is a closer look at the design of the workshops plus suggestions for using the workshops in the classroom.

Overview of the Writing Workshops

All of the Writing Workshops are organized according to the following headings and subheadings.

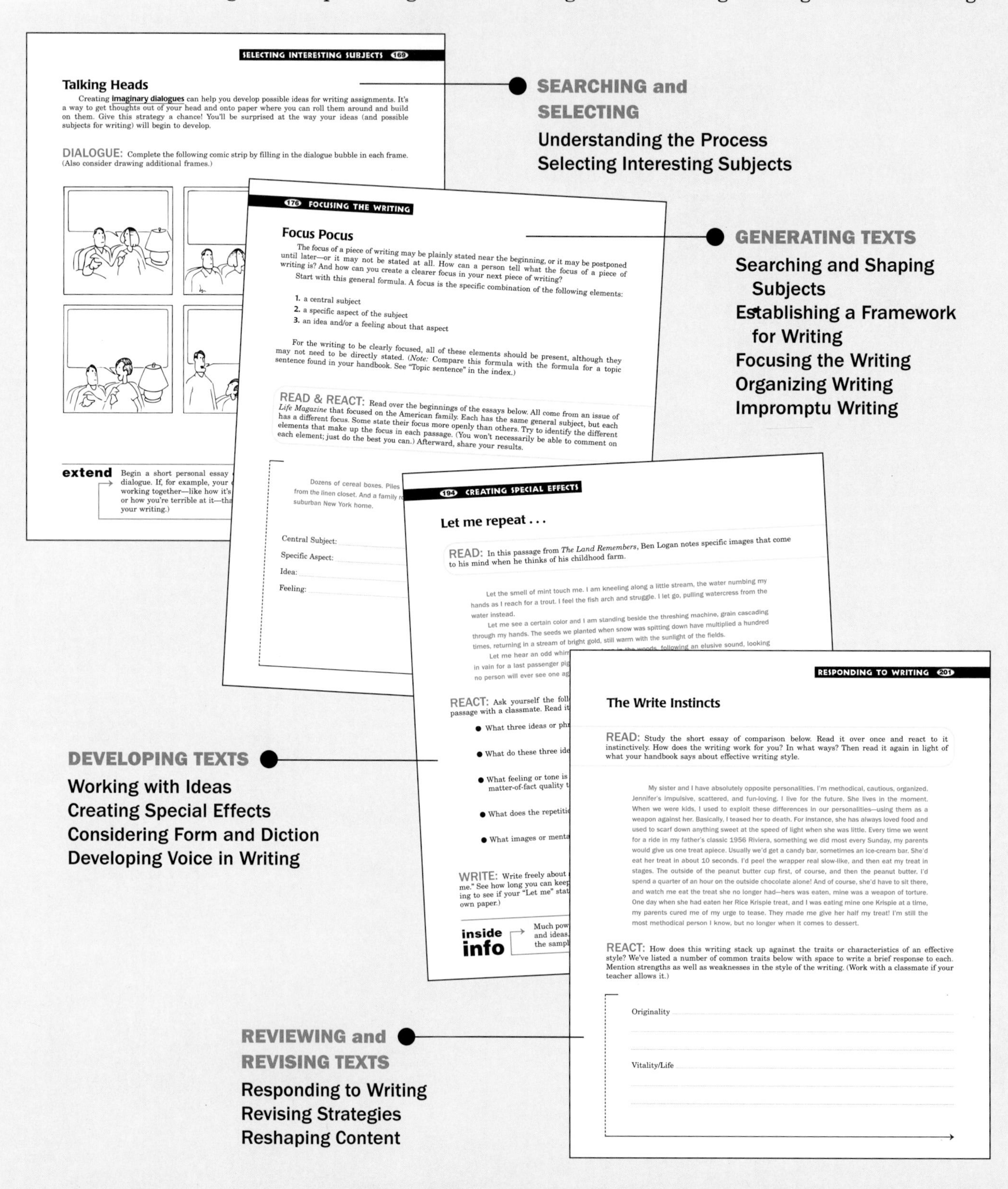

SEARCHING and SELECTING
- Understanding the Process
- Selecting Interesting Subjects

GENERATING TEXTS
- Searching and Shaping Subjects
- Establishing a Framework for Writing
- Focusing the Writing
- Organizing Writing
- Impromptu Writing

DEVELOPING TEXTS
- Working with Ideas
- Creating Special Effects
- Considering Form and Diction
- Developing Voice in Writing

REVIEWING and REVISING TEXTS
- Responding to Writing
- Revising Strategies
- Reshaping Content

REFINING: SENTENCE STRENGTHENING

Combining Sentences
Shaping Sentences

REFINING: IMPROVING STYLE

Traits of Effective Style
Ailments of Style

REFINING: EDITING

Editing Checklist
Editing for Clarity
Editing for Sentence Errors

REFINING: PROOFREADING

Proofreading Checklist
Proofreading Pretest
Proofreading for Punctuation
Proofreading for Usage
Proofreading Review

SHAPING SENTENCES 215

Using Parallel Structure

Parallel structure is the balanced or coordinated arrangement of sentence elements that are equal in importance; in other words, it is the arranging of similar ideas in a similar way. The use of parallel structure can add a sense of rhythm and emphasis to your writing style that makes it more appealing to your reader. (Refer to your handbook for more information on parallel structure.)

REVISE: To better understand parallel structure, look carefully at the sentences below. Each sentence contains two ideas or items that are equal in importance, but are not expressed in equal or parallel form. Those sentence parts that are not parallel and should be are underlined. Substitute a parallel expression in the place of one of those that is underlined. Revise each sentence as necessary so that the new expression fits in well and adds a sense of balance and rhythm to the overall sentence.

TRAITS OF EFFECTIVE STYLE 219

What Makes "Good" Good?

Everyone has his or her own individual tastes. While I really like Mexican food (earthy and healthy), you might like Irish food (homey and hearty) or French food (bon appétit!). I like purple; however, you may go for chartreuse. I really dig blues, but you may prefer heavy metal. With writing style, it's the same. Everyone has opinions about what makes for good writing.

REACT: What do you value in writing? What draws you to certain writers again and again? Is their writing fast paced, or highly descriptive, or a bit hard edged and sarcastic? And what do you strive for when you write? When are you most satisfied with your work? In the space provided below, list five things you like to see in writing (including your own). (You might, for example, enjoy writing that sounds friendly and unpretentious, like one person talking to another person.)

228 EDITING FOR CLARITY

Indefinite Pronoun Reference

A writer must be careful not to confuse the reader with pronoun references that are ambiguous. (*Ambiguous* means *indefinite or unclear*.) Indefinite pronoun reference results when it is not clear which word is being referred to by the pronoun in the sentence.

REACT: In each sentence, circle the pronoun below that is ambiguous or indefinite. Then rewrite each of the sentences so that the error in reference is corrected.

1. As he drove his car up to the service window, it made a strange rattling sound.
   As he drove up to the service window, his car made a strange rattling sound.
2. We moved the car out of the garage so we could wash it.

238 PROOFREADING FOR PUNCTUATION

Using Commas

INSERT: Insert commas where they are needed in the sentences below and circle each. After consulting your handbook, write the rule (or rules) for each comma you insert.

1. Although the brain requires 25 percent of all oxygen used by the body, it comprises only 2 percent of a person's total body weight.
   Use a comma after an introductory adverb clause.
2. Did you know John that a whale's heart beats only nine times a minute?
3. Hey please turn the music down! I'm trying to get some sleep!
4. If it would make you feel any better I'd be happy to come along and drive you home from the dentist's office.
5. "One-fourth of the 206 bones in the human body" explained Mr. Brown our biology teacher "are located in the feet."
6. Although it is a mind-boggling fact the body does indeed have 70 000 miles of blood vessels.

Workshop Implementation Guide

The writing workshops can be implemented in a number of different ways to meet the students' needs. As noted below, they can work hand in hand with the writing frameworks, serve as self-contained units for general instruction, or accommodate individuals who need enrichment work.

Integration into the Framework Writing Activities

Every effort should be made to integrate the writing workshops into the framework activities. (Working on various writing skills and strategies always makes more sense in context in the process of composing.) The "Teacher's Notes" for each framework activity cross-reference related writing workshops under "Related Activities."

Classroom Instruction

Specific writing workshops can be used as the starting point or focus of instruction for the entire class. For example, teachers who feel the entire class could benefit from work on a particular skill–perhaps writing focus or thesis statements–could implement an appropriate workshop to meet this need.

Mini-Units

Teachers may decide to implement *mini-units* of related workshops (two-four days) for classroom instruction. If, for example, students need help with their revising skills and strategies, a teacher could implement two or three appropriate workshops (selecting from those listed under "Revising Texts").

Small-Group Work

When members of a writing group share a particular concern (or need help with a particular problem) about their writing, teachers can direct them to an appropriate workshop for small-group work.

Individual Learning

The workshops can also be implemented on an individual basis (or in independent learning situations) to help specific students work on their basic writing skills.

Teacher/Student Conferences

When teachers and students meet one-on-one in a writing conference, teachers may use one of the workshops to illustrate a particular writing skill or strategy.

Practical Writing Planning Guide

Practical Writing covers three basic forms of writing including the letter of application and résumé, impromptu writing, and the abstract. The overview on the next two pages illustrates how the practical writing units work. Also included in this section are suggestions for using these units in the classroom.

Overview of Practical Writing

Each practical writing unit provides many different opportunities to learn about and practice a basic form of writing. As you can see on the next two pages, students work with each form from a number of different perspectives.

Writing the Letter of Application and Résumé

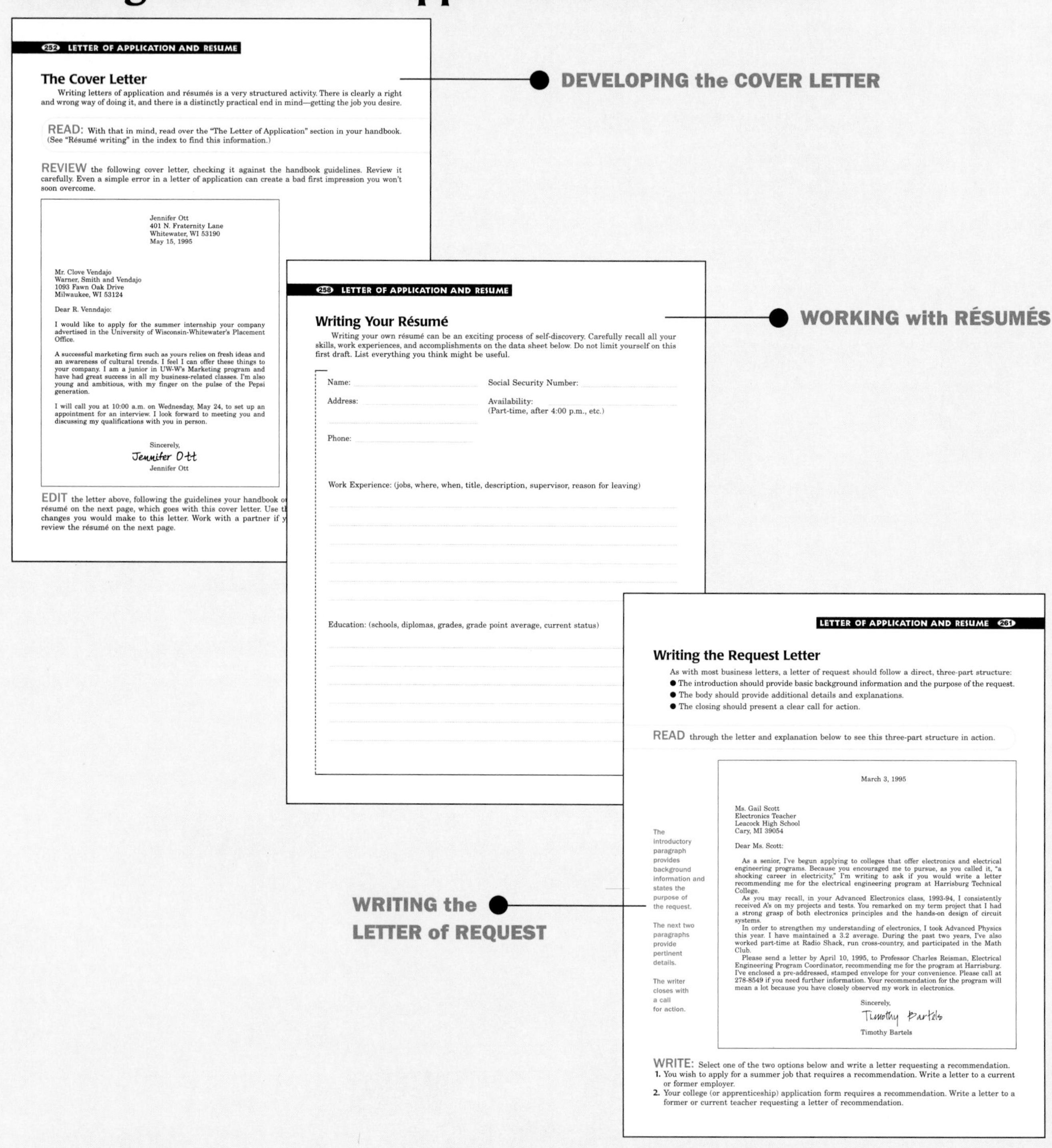

252 LETTER OF APPLICATION AND RESUME

The Cover Letter

Writing letters of application and résumés is a very structured activity. There is clearly a right and wrong way of doing it, and there is a distinctly practical end in mind—getting the job you desire.

READ: With that in mind, read over the "The Letter of Application" section in your handbook. (See "Résumé writing" in the index to find this information.)

REVIEW the following cover letter, checking it against the handbook guidelines. Review it carefully. Even a simple error in a letter of application can create a bad first impression you won't soon overcome.

Jennifer Ott
401 N. Fraternity Lane
Whitewater, WI 53190
May 15, 1995

Mr. Clove Vendajo
Warner, Smith and Vendajo
1093 Fawn Oak Drive
Milwaukee, WI 53124

Dear R. Venndajo:

I would like to apply for the summer internship your company advertised in the University of Wisconsin-Whitewater's Placement Office.

A successful marketing firm such as yours relies on fresh ideas and an awareness of cultural trends. I feel I can offer these things to your company. I am a junior in UW-W's Marketing program and have had great success in all my business-related classes. I'm also young and ambitious, with my finger on the pulse of the Pepsi generation.

I will call you at 10:00 a.m. on Wednesday, May 24, to set up an appointment for an interview. I look forward to meeting you and discussing my qualifications with you in person.

Sincerely,
Jennifer Ott
Jennifer Ott

EDIT the letter above, following the guidelines your handbook o
résumé on the next page, which goes with this cover letter. Use t
changes you would make to this letter. Work with a partner if y
review the résumé on the next page.

258 LETTER OF APPLICATION AND RESUME

Writing Your Résumé

Writing your own résumé can be an exciting process of self-discovery. Carefully recall all your skills, work experiences, and accomplishments on the data sheet below. Do not limit yourself on this first draft. List everything you think might be useful.

Name: ______ Social Security Number: ______

Address: ______ Availability: ______
(Part-time, after 4:00 p.m., etc.)

Phone: ______

Work Experience: (jobs, where, when, title, description, supervisor, reason for leaving)

Education: (schools, diplomas, grades, grade point average, current status)

LETTER OF APPLICATION AND RESUME 261

Writing the Request Letter

As with most business letters, a letter of request should follow a direct, three-part structure:

- The introduction should provide basic background information and the purpose of the request.
- The body should provide additional details and explanations.
- The closing should present a clear call for action.

READ through the letter and explanation below to see this three-part structure in action.

March 3, 1995

Ms. Gail Scott
Electronics Teacher
Leacock High School
Cary, MI 39054

Dear Ms. Scott:

As a senior, I've begun applying to colleges that offer electronics and electrical engineering programs. Because you encouraged me to pursue, as you called it, "a shocking career in electricity," I'm writing to ask if you would write a letter recommending me for the electrical engineering program at Harrisburg Technical College.

As you may recall, in your Advanced Electronics class, 1993-94, I consistently received A's on my projects and tests. You remarked on my term project that I had a strong grasp of both electronics principles and the hands-on design of circuit systems.

In order to strengthen my understanding of electronics, I took Advanced Physics this year. I have maintained a 3.2 average. During the past two years, I've also worked part-time at Radio Shack, run cross-country, and participated in the Math Club.

Please send a letter by April 10, 1995, to Professor Charles Reisman, Electrical Engineering Program Coordinator, recommending me for the program at Harrisburg. I've enclosed a pre-addressed, stamped envelope for your convenience. Please call at 278-8549 if you need further information. Your recommendation for the program will mean a lot because you have closely observed my work in electronics.

Sincerely,
Timothy Bartels
Timothy Bartels

The introductory paragraph provides background information and states the purpose of the request.

The next two paragraphs provide pertinent details.

The writer closes with a call for action.

WRITE: Select one of the two options below and write a letter requesting a recommendation.

1. You wish to apply for a summer job that requires a recommendation. Write a letter to a current or former employer.
2. Your college (or apprenticeship) application form requires a recommendation. Write a letter to a former or current teacher requesting a letter of recommendation.

Impromptu Writing

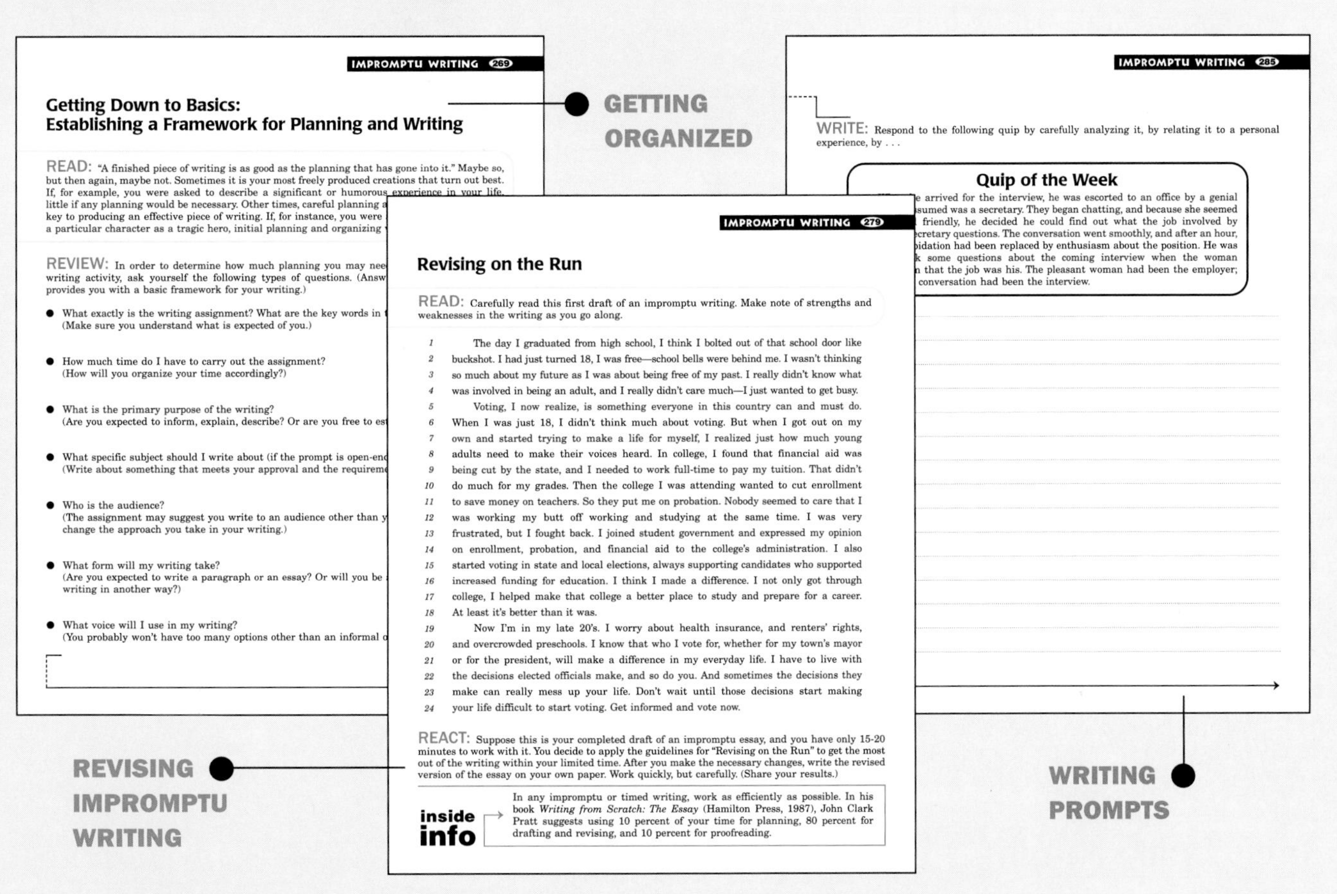

IMPROMPTU WRITING 269

Getting Down to Basics: Establishing a Framework for Planning and Writing

READ: "A finished piece of writing is as good as the planning that has gone into it." Maybe so, but then again, maybe not. Sometimes it is your most freely produced creations that turn out best. If, for example, you were asked to describe a significant or humorous experience in your life, little if any planning would be necessary. Other times, careful planning a key to producing an effective piece of writing. If, for instance, you were a particular character as a tragic hero, initial planning and organizing

REVIEW: In order to determine how much planning you may nee writing activity, ask yourself the following types of questions. (Answ provides you with a basic framework for your writing.)

- What exactly is the writing assignment? What are the key words in (Make sure you understand what is expected of you.)
- How much time do I have to carry out the assignment? (How will you organize your time accordingly?)
- What is the primary purpose of the writing? (Are you expected to inform, explain, describe? Or are you free to es
- What specific subject should I write about (if the prompt is open-end (Write about something that meets your approval and the requireme
- Who is the audience? (The assignment may suggest you write to an audience other than y change the approach you take in your writing.)
- What form will my writing take? (Are you expected to write a paragraph or an essay? Or will you be writing in another way?)
- What voice will I use in my writing? (You probably won't have too many options other than an informal o

IMPROMPTU WRITING 285

WRITE: Respond to the following quip by carefully analyzing it, by relating it to a personal experience, by . . .

Quip of the Week

e arrived for the interview, he was escorted to an office by a genial sumed was a secretary. They began chatting, and because she seemed friendly, he decided he could find out what the job involved by cretary questions. The conversation went smoothly, and after an hour, idation had been replaced by enthusiasm about the position. He was k some questions about the coming interview when the woman n that the job was his. The pleasant woman had been the employer; conversation had been the interview.

IMPROMPTU WRITING 279

Revising on the Run

READ: Carefully read this first draft of an impromptu writing. Make note of strengths and weaknesses in the writing as you go along.

1 The day I graduated from high school, I think I bolted out of that school door like
2 buckshot. I had just turned 18, I was free—school bells were behind me. I wasn't thinking
3 so much about my future as I was about being free of my past. I really didn't know what
4 was involved in being an adult, and I really didn't care much—I just wanted to get busy.
5 Voting, I now realize, is something everyone in this country can and must do.
6 When I was just 18, I didn't think much about voting. But when I got out on my
7 own and started trying to make a life for myself, I realized just how much young
8 adults need to make their voices heard. In college, I found that financial aid was
9 being cut by the state, and I needed to work full-time to pay my tuition. That didn't
10 do much for my grades. Then the college I was attending wanted to cut enrollment
11 to save money on teachers. So they put me on probation. Nobody seemed to care that I
12 was working my butt off working and studying at the same time. I was very
13 frustrated, but I fought back. I joined student government and expressed my opinion
14 on enrollment, probation, and financial aid to the college's administration. I also
15 started voting in state and local elections, always supporting candidates who supported
16 increased funding for education. I think I made a difference. I not only got through
17 college, I helped make that college a better place to study and prepare for a career.
18 At least it's better than it was.
19 Now I'm in my late 20's. I worry about health insurance, and renters' rights,
20 and overcrowded preschools. I know that who I vote for, whether for my town's mayor
21 or for the president, will make a difference in my everyday life. I have to live with
22 the decisions elected officials make, and so do you. And sometimes the decisions they
23 make can really mess up your life. Don't wait until those decisions start making
24 your life difficult to start voting. Get informed and vote now.

REACT: Suppose this is your completed draft of an impromptu essay, and you have only 15-20 minutes to work with it. You decide to apply the guidelines for "Revising on the Run" to get the most out of the writing within your limited time. After you make the necessary changes, write the revised version of the essay on your own paper. Work quickly, but carefully. (Share your results.)

inside info In any impromptu or timed writing, work as efficiently as possible. In his book *Writing from Scratch: The Essay* (Hamilton Press, 1987), John Clark Pratt suggests using 10 percent of your time for planning, 80 percent for drafting and revising, and 10 percent for proofreading.

Writing Summaries

WRITING the ABSTRACT

WRITING SUMMARIES 291

The Abstract

The abstract is a shortened form of a passage using the important words of the passage itself and working these words as simply as possible into sentences.

First, you underline the important words, as in the example below:

> This nation has recently developed a new national pastime: diet mania, or counting calories. Many of us do count them, but not everyone understands what it is we're counting. By definition, a calorie is a measure of heat: the amount of heat required to raise the temperature of one gram of water by one degree centigrade. At this very moment you are generating that same kind of heat; you are burning calories. You have been since you were born, and you will continue to every day of your life. Our bodies can be thought of as biochemical machines that burn the food we eat for fuel; the amount of burning that takes place is measured in calories. How much energy is produced by the burning of calories is determined by how active we are. Just sitting and resting, we expend about a calorie a minute. That means that just to stay alive, our body machines must burn 1,440 calories per day. The more active we are, the more calories we will burn up.

Then you write the abstract by joining the underlined words of the passage into sentences. Note that as few words as possible are added. The original passage contained 172 words; the abstract contains only 53 words, or fewer than one-third as many.

> This nation has developed a new pastime: counting calories. A calorie is a measure of the amount of heat you generate. Our bodies burn fuel (food) that is measured in calories. The energy we produce by burning calories is determined by our activity. Just to stay alive, we must burn 1,440 calories a day.

How to Use the Practical Writing Units

The practical writing units can be implemented in a number of ways to meet the students' needs. As noted below, they can serve as self-contained units for general instruction or accommodate individuals who need enrichment work.

Classroom Instruction

Each practical writing unit can serve as the focus of instruction for the entire class. Teachers simply have to decide at what point during the school year it would be most appropriate to implement the unit. (The activities within each practical writing unit are self-directed containing clearly identifiable introductions, instructions, and closing remarks.)

Mini-Units

Teachers may decide to implement the activities within each unit at different times throughout the school year. For example, three of the opening activities in "Writing Letters" may be implemented during one week, while the remaining activities may be implemented at other points throughout the school year.

Small-Group Work

When members of the class need help with a particular skill (finding a focus for writing, organizing information, etc.), teachers can have them work on activities in the appropriate units.

Individual Learning

The units can also be implemented on an individual basis (or in independent learning situations) to help specific students work on their basic writing skills.

Teacher/Student Conferences

When teachers and students meet one-on-one in a writing conference, teachers may use one or more of the activities in a particular unit to illustrate a writing skill or strategy.

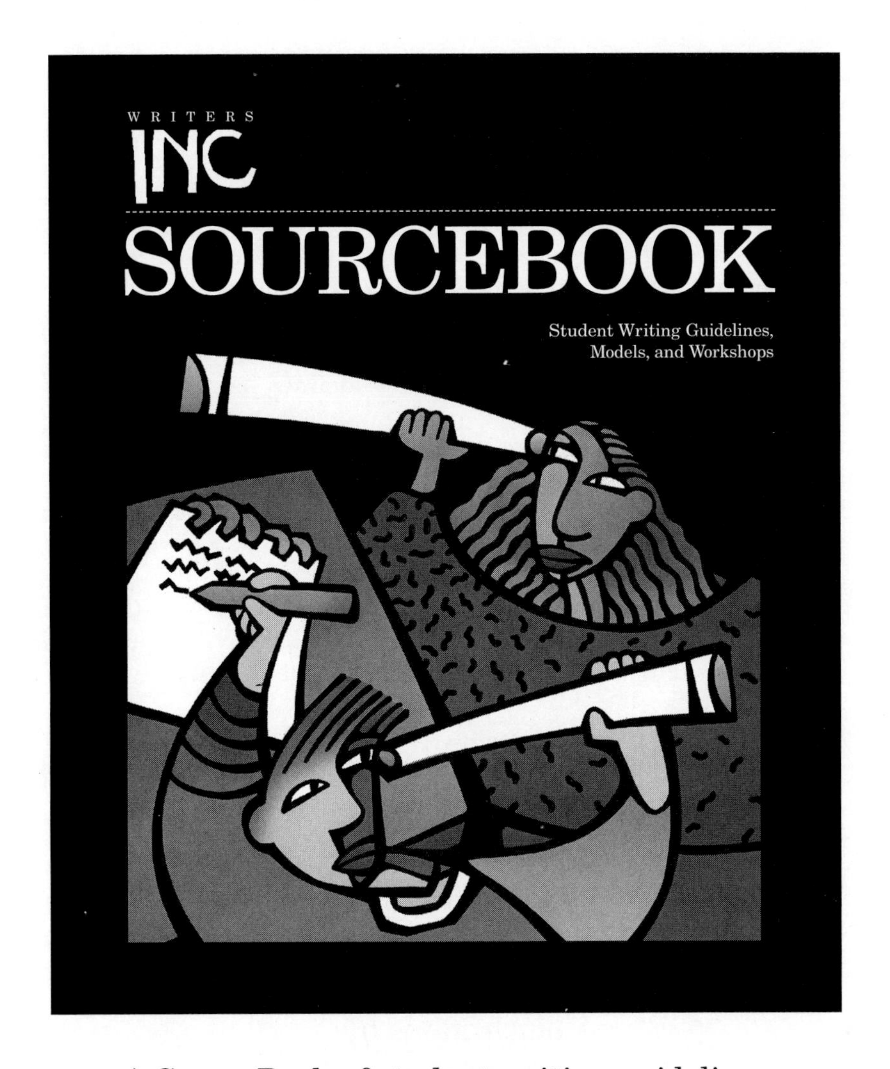

A SourceBook of student writing guidelines, models, and workshops to accompany

WRITE SOURCE

GREAT SOURCE EDUCATION GROUP

a Houghton Mifflin Company
Boston, Massachusetts

Before You Begin . . .

It is important for you to know a few things about your *Writers INC* SourceBook before you begin to use it.

First of all, your SourceBook contains a wonderful selection of narratives, stories, poems, plays, and essays written by students and professionals from across the country. You will not find a more interesting and diverse collection of writing under one cover anywhere. To go along with these models, we have included clear, step-by-step guidelines that show you how to develop your own writing. The models stimulate you to write; the guidelines help you to carry out your work.

Second, your SourceBook contains a collection of writing workshops covering all aspects of the writing process, as well as practical writing units covering basic forms of writing like paragraphs, traditional essays, and business letters. The skills and strategies that you practice here will lead to real improvement in your writing.

Third, your SourceBook is designed to be used with the *Writers INC* handbook. Whenever you see a reference like this ("Refer to . . .") in a SourceBook activity, you are being directed to the handbook for additional help. Together, these two books make quite a team.

Finally, take a few minutes to page through your SourceBook, section by section. Stop, look, and read as you go. Once you've completed your quick tour, you will be **ready to begin.**

Written and Compiled by

Patrick Sebranek and Dave Kemper
with Verne Meyer, Laura Bachman, Janis Hartley, and Randy VanderMey

Illustrations by

Kim DeMarco
Cover Illustration by Chris Krenzke

An Overview of the *Writers INC SourceBook*

The Writing Framework

The writing framework offers a variety of real-life writing experiences. Student and professional models are provided for each form of writing, as are step-by-step guidelines.

Writing Workshops

The writing workshops cover all phases of the writing process—from selecting interesting subjects to organizing writing, from advising in peer groups to editing for clarity.

Practical Writing

The practical writing section contains writing activities useful both in school and later on the job.

Part I The Writing Framework

Part II Writing Workshops

Developing Texts

198

Reviewing and Revising Texts

Part III Practical Writing

Part I

The Writing Framework

Grade 12 Activities and Outcomes

The activities in the grade 12 framework provide students with a wide variety of opportunities to re-create and connect past incidents, to describe other people and events, to generate and share creative pieces, to develop essays and personal responses, and to form explanations and summaries.

Personal Writing:

- **Extended Reminiscence** — Recall a phase or an important time of change in your life.
- **Personal Essay** — Explore a subject of personal interest in a free-flowing essay.

Subject Writing:

- **Case Study** — Develop an in-depth report about one person whose experiences typify the experiences of a larger group.
- **Historical Profile** — Share your findings about an interesting aspect from our past.
- **Venture Report** — Offer readers an in-depth look at a business or profession.
- **Personal Research Report** — Present your research findings on a topic of personal interest.

Creative Writing:

- **Fictionalized Imitation** — Imitate (or parody) the style or content of a story, movie, etc.
- **Genre Writing** — Create a short story based on a specific genre.
- **Statement Through Poetry** — Convey an important message in the form of a poem.
- **Playwriting** — Write a one-act play complete with stage directions.

Reflective Writing:

- **Essay of Reflection** — Reflect upon the importance of a time in your life, an experience, a decision, etc.
- **Essay of Speculation** — Explore a subject, noting what effect it might have in the future.
- **Extended Literary Analysis** — Develop an extensive literary analysis displaying a thorough understanding of an author and his or her work.
- **Position Paper** — Present your position on a significant issue.

Academic Writing:

- **Problem/Solution Essay** — Propose a solution(s) to a real problem.
- **Essay of Evaluation** — Assess a policy, topic, class, etc., as to its value or worth.
- ***Impromptu Writing** — Develop clear, unified essays for different types of writing prompts.
- ***The Abstract** — Arrange the key words in a given selection into a shortened, readable version of the original.

* These extended units, as well as a sequence of letter-writing and on-the-job writing activities, can be found in the Practical Writing section of the SourceBook.

Overview of the Framework Design

Each writing framework is designed to be efficient and user-friendly for both the teacher and student. Each student-guidelines page is presented in a clear, step-by-step fashion. All models contain an introduction and helpful margin notes.

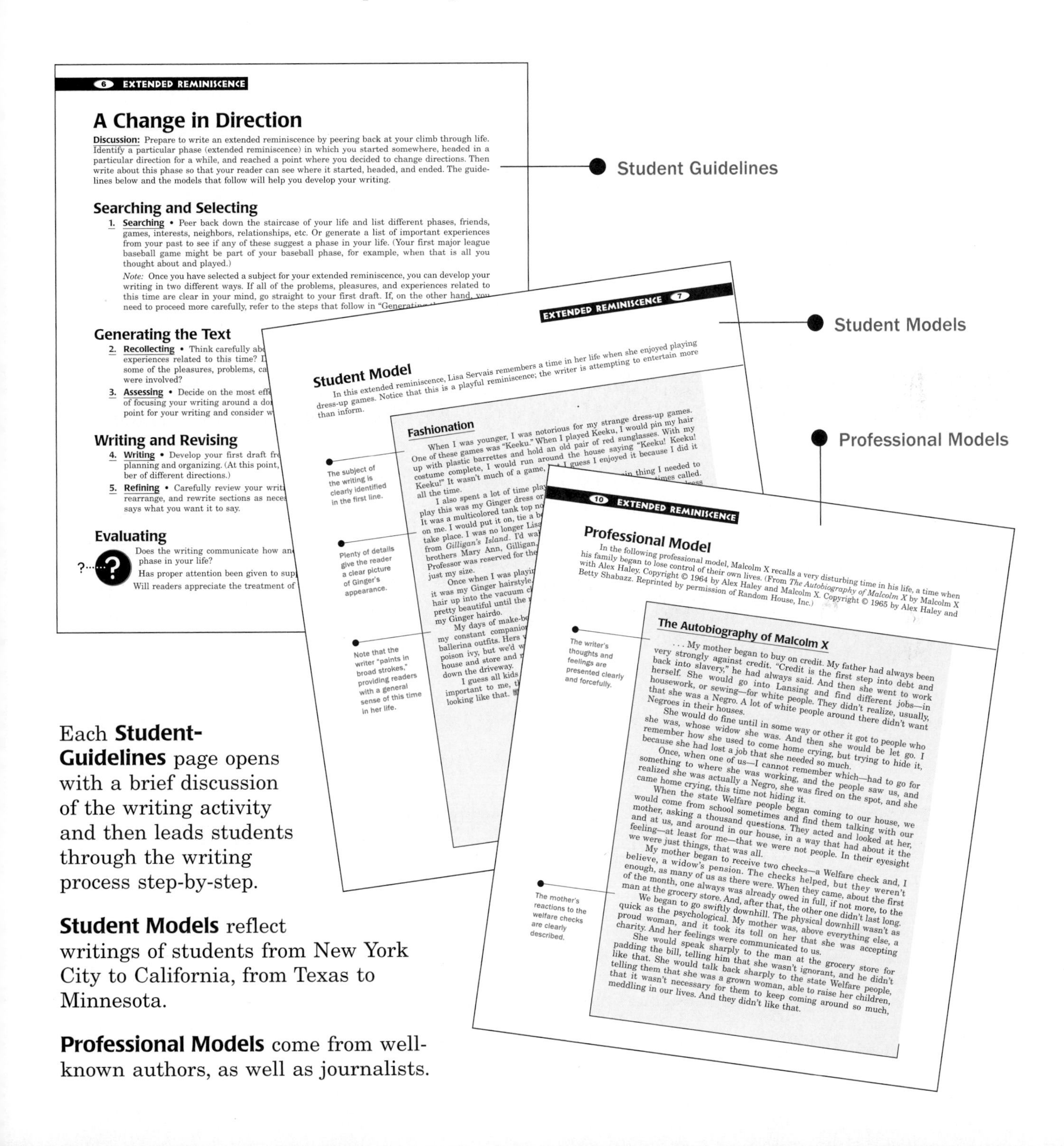

6 EXTENDED REMINISCENCE

A Change in Direction

Discussion: Prepare to write an extended reminiscence by peering back at your climb through life. Identify a particular phase (extended reminiscence) in which you started somewhere, headed in a particular direction for a while, and reached a point where you decided to change directions. Then write about this phase so that your reader can see where it started, headed, and ended. The guidelines below and the models that follow will help you develop your writing.

Searching and Selecting

1. **Searching** • Peer back down the staircase of your life and list different phases, friends, games, interests, neighbors, relationships, etc. Or generate a list of important experiences from your past to see if any of these suggest a phase in your life. (Your first major league baseball game might be part of your baseball phase, for example, when that is all you thought about and played.)

Note: Once you have selected a subject for your extended reminiscence, you can develop your writing in two different ways. If all of the problems, pleasures, and experiences related to this time are clear in your mind, go straight to your first draft. If, on the other hand, you need to proceed more carefully, refer to the steps that follow in "Generatin…

Generating the Text

2. **Recollecting** • Think carefully ab… experiences related to this time? I… some of the pleasures, problems, ca… were involved?
3. **Assessing** • Decide on the most eff… of focusing your writing around a do… point for your writing and consider w…

Writing and Revising

4. **Writing** • Develop your first draft fr… planning and organizing. (At this point, … ber of different directions.)
5. **Refining** • Carefully review your writ… rearrange, and rewrite sections as nece… says what you want it to say.

Evaluating

Does the writing communicate how an… phase in your life?
Has proper attention been given to sup…
Will readers appreciate the treatment of…

EXTENDED REMINISCENCE 7

Student Model

In this extended reminiscence, Lisa Servais remembers a time in her life when she enjoyed playing dress-up games. Notice that this is a playful reminiscence; the writer is attempting to entertain more than inform.

Fashionation

When I was younger, I was notorious for my strange dress-up games. One of these games was "Keeku." When I played Keeku, I would pin my hair up with plastic barrettes and hold an old pair of red sunglasses. With my costume complete, I would run around the house saying "Keeku! Keeku! Keeku!" It wasn't much of a game, … I guess I enjoyed it because I did it all the time. …

I also spent a lot of time pla… play this was my Ginger dress or… It was a multicolored tank top no… on me. I would put it on, tie a b… take place. I was no longer Lis… from *Gilligan's Island.* I'd wa… brothers Mary Ann, Gilligan, … Professor was reserved for the… just my size.

Once when I was playi… it was my Ginger hairstyle… hair up into the vacuum c… pretty beautiful until the … my Ginger hairdo.

My days of make-be… my constant companio… ballerina outfits. Hers … poison ivy, but we'd w… house and store and … down the driveway.

I guess all kids … important to me, t… looking like that.

The subject of the writing is clearly identified in the first line.

Plenty of details give the reader a clear picture of Ginger's appearance.

Note that the writer "paints in broad strokes," providing readers with a general sense of this time in her life.

10 EXTENDED REMINISCENCE

Professional Model

In the following professional model, Malcolm X recalls a very disturbing time in his life, a time when his family began to lose control of their own lives. (From *The Autobiography of Malcolm X* by Malcolm X with Alex Haley. Copyright © 1964 by Alex Haley and Malcolm X. Copyright © 1965 by Alex Haley and Betty Shabazz. Reprinted by permission of Random House, Inc.)

The Autobiography of Malcolm X

. . . My mother began to buy on credit. My father had always been very strongly against credit. "Credit is the first step into debt and back into slavery," he had always said. And then she went to work herself. She would go into Lansing and find different jobs—in housework, or sewing—for white people. They didn't realize, usually, that she was a Negro. A lot of white people around there didn't want Negroes in their houses.

She would do fine until in some way or other it got to people who she was, whose widow she was. And then she would be let go. I remember how she used to come home crying, but trying to hide it, because she had lost a job that she needed so much.

Once, when one of us—I cannot remember which—had to go for something to where she was working, and the people saw us, and realized she was actually a Negro, she was fired on the spot, and she came home crying, this time not hiding it.

When the state Welfare people began coming to our house, we would come from school sometimes and find them talking with our mother, asking a thousand questions. They acted and looked at her, and at us, and around in our house, in a way that had about it the feeling—at least for me—that we were not people. In their eyesight we were just things, that was all.

My mother began to receive two checks—a Welfare check and, I believe, a widow's pension. The checks helped, but they weren't enough, as many of us as there were. When they came, about the first of the month, one always was already owed in full, if not more, to the man at the grocery store. And, after that, the other one didn't last long.

We began to go swiftly downhill. The physical downhill wasn't as quick as the psychological. My mother was, above everything else, a proud woman, and it took its toll on her that she was accepting charity. And her feelings were communicated to us.

She would speak sharply to the man at the grocery store for padding the bill, telling him that she wasn't ignorant, and he didn't like that. She would talk back sharply to the state Welfare people, telling them that she was a grown woman, able to raise her children, that it wasn't necessary for them to keep coming around so much, meddling in our lives. And they didn't like that.

The writer's thoughts and feelings are presented clearly and forcefully.

The mother's reactions to the welfare checks are clearly described.

Each **Student-Guidelines** page opens with a brief discussion of the writing activity and then leads students through the writing process step-by-step.

Student Models reflect writings of students from New York City to California, from Texas to Minnesota.

Professional Models come from well-known authors, as well as journalists.

Personal Writing

"Once when I was playing 'Ginger,' I added something new to the game; it was my Ginger hairstyle. This delicate design was created by sucking my hair up into the vacuum cleaner hose until it stood on end." —*Lisa Servais*

Extended Reminiscence

In an extended reminiscence, a writer focuses on a specific phase, or extended period of time, from his or her past experience. The goal in this form of writing is to highlight certain aspects of the phase rather than recall all of the specific details.

A Change in Direction

Discussion: Prepare to write an extended reminiscence by peering back at your climb through life. Identify a particular phase (extended reminiscence) in which you started somewhere, headed in a particular direction for a while, and reached a point where you decided to change directions. Then write about this phase so that your reader can see where it started, headed, and ended. The guidelines below and the models that follow will help you develop your writing.

Searching and Selecting

1. **Searching** • Peer back down the staircase of your life and list different phases, friends, games, interests, neighbors, relationships, etc. Or generate a list of important experiences from your past to see if any of these suggest a phase in your life. (Your first major league baseball game might be part of your baseball phase, for example, when that is all you thought about and played.)

   Note: Once you have selected a subject for your extended reminiscence, you can develop your writing in two different ways. If all of the problems, pleasures, and experiences related to this time are clear in your mind, go straight to your first draft. If, on the other hand, you need to proceed more carefully, refer to the steps that follow in "Generating the Text."

Generating the Text

2. **Recollecting** • Think carefully about your subject. Can you remember a number of specific experiences related to this time? Discuss your initial ideas with a classmate. What were some of the pleasures, problems, causes, and costs of this time in your life? Which people were involved?

3. **Assessing** • Decide on the most effective way to write about your subject. Think in terms of focusing your writing around a dominant feeling or impression. Also establish a starting point for your writing and consider which facts and details are essential.

Writing and Revising

4. **Writing** • Develop your first draft freely, as thoughts occur to you, or according to your planning and organizing. (At this point, don't be afraid to let your writing take you in a number of different directions.)

5. **Refining** • Carefully review your writing. Have a classmate review it as well. Cut, add, rearrange, and rewrite sections as necessary. Continue working with your writing until it says what you want it to say.

Evaluating

Does the writing communicate how and why a set of experiences constitutes a distinct phase in your life?

Has proper attention been given to supporting ideas and details?

Will readers appreciate the treatment of this subject?

Student Model

In this extended reminiscence, Lisa Servais remembers a time in her life when she enjoyed playing dress-up games. Notice that this is a playful reminiscence; the writer is attempting to entertain more than inform.

The subject of the writing is clearly identified in the first line.

Plenty of details give the reader a clear picture of Ginger's appearance.

Note that the writer "paints in broad strokes," providing readers with a general sense of this time in her life.

Fashionation

When I was younger, I was notorious for my strange dress-up games. One of these games was "Keeku." When I played Keeku, I would pin my hair up with plastic barrettes and hold an old pair of red sunglasses. With my costume complete, I would run around the house saying "Keeku! Keeku! Keeku!" It wasn't much of a game, but I guess I enjoyed it because I did it all the time.

I also spent a lot of time playing "Ginger." The main thing I needed to play this was my Ginger dress or squiggly skirt as it was sometimes called. It was a multicolored tank top nobody wore anymore, and it was like a dress on me. I would put it on, tie a belt around it, and an amazing change would take place. I was no longer Lisa; instead, I was beautiful, glamorous Ginger from *Gilligan's Island*. I'd walk around the house calling my sisters and brothers Mary Ann, Gilligan, Skipper, or Mr. and Mrs. Howell. The title Professor was reserved for the St. Agnes statue in our living room, which was just my size.

Once when I was playing "Ginger," I added something new to the game; it was my Ginger hairstyle. This delicate design was created by sucking my hair up into the vacuum cleaner hose until it stood on end. I thought I was pretty beautiful until the neighbor boys began teasing me about it. I gave up my Ginger hairdo.

My days of make-believe sometimes included my sister Mary, who was my constant companion. We played long dresses or dressed up in our ballerina outfits. Hers was blue, and mine was pink. They itched worse than poison ivy, but we'd wear them for hours. We wore them when we played house and store and restaurant . . . and even when we rode our Big Wheels down the driveway.

I guess all kids go through a pretending stage. Why dressing up was so important to me, though, I don't know. Today I wouldn't be caught dead looking like that.

Student Model

In this extended reminiscence, Jessica Thompson recalls the phase in her life when she lived in Iowa in a small town called Lake Mills. As you read this model, note the ideas and details that suggest whether or not this was a positive phase in her life. (Reprinted from the April 1992 edition of *High School Writer* with permission.)

Growing Up in Town

"We are shaped and fashioned by what we love."
— Johann Wolfgang von Goethe

In the first few sentences, the author identifies a specific time in her life.

It was a somewhat prejudiced little town, but I didn't know that at the time. How could a child growing up in a small, all-white, all-Christian, midwestern town know about prejudice? All I know is that I loved growing up in Lake Mills, Iowa. The town was only one square mile in size and 2,200 people in population. We had one school; it held grades K-12, and 902 students. There was one swimming pool, always in bad need of repair; two grocery stores (we always went to Jerry's Foodland) and one doctor's office, where my mother worked. My father ran some businesses on Main Street, selling appliances and outdoor equipment, and also repairing them. We had a small video rental store at one time.

She provides many details related to this time.

We lived in a big, white, two-story house on Lake Street. It was old and creaky, but I liked it. It had a large lawn with several towering oak trees, a swing set, and a sandbox. There were no fences to mark your property in Lake Mills; you could walk right through the middle of a block without getting barricaded in anywhere. While growing up there, my friends and I took advantage of this, playing tag and hide-and-seek throughout the neighborhood.

Oak Tree Park was a block from my house. It got its name because of the couple dozen oaks growing there. I remember when one of the trees fell during a tornado, crushing one of the shelter houses. Railroad tracks separated my house from the park. Sometimes when we were playing, a train would go by and we'd try to count the cars; there were usually more than 100. The man in the caboose would sometimes throw gum to us out of his window. The park and the school yard ran into each other, but the teachers kept a close watch on us during recess. Everyone knew everyone in Lake Mills, and everyone's business. There was never a problem of making friends for me. I knew practically everyone in my class since birth. We went to preschool together; we would play together when our mothers had coffee.

In the winter, you practically never saw the sun. I guess it was probably depressing for the adults, but all that my friends and I saw was the four to five feet of packed white snow. (And occasional no-school snow days.) We'd make snowmen and have snowball fights, dig holes in drifts for forts, and slide down the ice-covered streets. It's

The writer highlights what it was like to be a child in Lake Mills during winter and summer.

strange, but I never remember being cold. At school, the yard workers would pile up all the snow from the blacktop into a huge "snow mountain." Then, during recess, we would slide down it. Sometimes we were allowed to go into the park to ice-skate on the frozen tennis courts. I must have gone through two or three pairs of snow boots every year.

In the summer, my friends and I would play *The Dukes of Hazzard* on our bicycles. We'd play in the mud and climb trees and go swimming. I don't remember ever being bored in the summer. There was a big whistle in the park that would sound off at noon and again at 6:00 p.m. every day; those were our signals to go home to eat. After we had shoveled down our fried chicken and watermelon, we'd go out to play again until the streetlights came on. That was sort of everyone's curfew.

Every Fourth of July week, the whole town would celebrate with the "July Jubilee." There were sidewalk sales, dances, picnics, rides, games, food. That was usually the best part of summer vacation.

From a distance, the author reflects upon this time in her childhood.

School was a lot harder in Iowa than in Arizona, where I now live. I found it very strange to come to a new school having its halls outside. In Iowa, everything is inside. There were some portables, but they ended up being used for storage.

I learned good morals, values, and beliefs in Lake Mills that I possibly would not have being brought up in the city. I made some good friends that I miss a lot, and I miss my relatives; but I'm glad my family moved here to the city. My friends in Lake Mills do not have the opportunities that I have now; different things are expected of them. I used to think Lake Mills was huge. Now, when I go back to visit, I can't believe how small it is. I guess to see something for what it really is, sometimes you have to step away and look at it from a distance. They say you're shaped and fashioned by what you love; I loved growing up in a small town.

Professional Model

In the following professional model, Malcolm X recalls a very disturbing time in his life, a time when his family began to lose control of their own lives. (From *The Autobiography of Malcolm X* by Malcolm X with Alex Haley. Copyright © 1964 by Alex Haley and Malcolm X. Copyright © 1965 by Alex Haley and Betty Shabazz. Reprinted by permission of Random House, Inc.)

The Autobiography of Malcolm X

The writer's thoughts and feelings are presented clearly and forcefully.

. . . My mother began to buy on credit. My father had always been very strongly against credit. "Credit is the first step into debt and back into slavery," he had always said. And then she went to work herself. She would go into Lansing and find different jobs—in housework, or sewing—for white people. They didn't realize, usually, that she was a Negro. A lot of white people around there didn't want Negroes in their houses.

She would do fine until in some way or other it got to people who she was, whose widow she was. And then she would be let go. I remember how she used to come home crying, but trying to hide it, because she had lost a job that she needed so much.

Once, when one of us—I cannot remember which—had to go for something to where she was working, and the people saw us, and realized she was actually a Negro, she was fired on the spot, and she came home crying, this time not hiding it.

When the state Welfare people began coming to our house, we would come from school sometimes and find them talking with our mother, asking a thousand questions. They acted and looked at her, and at us, and around in our house, in a way that had about it the feeling—at least for me—that we were not people. In their eyesight we were just things, that was all.

My mother began to receive two checks—a Welfare check and, I believe, a widow's pension. The checks helped, but they weren't enough, as many of us as there were. When they came, about the first of the month, one always was already owed in full, if not more, to the man at the grocery store. And, after that, the other one didn't last long.

The mother's reactions to the welfare checks are clearly described.

We began to go swiftly downhill. The physical downhill wasn't as quick as the psychological. My mother was, above everything else, a proud woman, and it took its toll on her that she was accepting charity. And her feelings were communicated to us.

She would speak sharply to the man at the grocery store for padding the bill, telling him that she wasn't ignorant, and he didn't like that. She would talk back sharply to the state Welfare people, telling them that she was a grown woman, able to raise her children, that it wasn't necessary for them to keep coming around so much, meddling in our lives. And they didn't like that.

Time and experience helped the writer better understand his mother's actions.

But the monthly Welfare check was their pass. They acted as if they owned us, as if we were their private property. As much as my mother would have liked to, she couldn't keep them out. She would get particularly incensed when they began insisting upon drawing us older children aside, one at a time, out on the porch or somewhere, and asking us questions, or telling us things—against our mother and against each other.

We couldn't understand why, if the state was willing to give us packages of meat, sacks of potatoes and fruit, and cans of all kinds of things, our mother obviously hated to accept. We really couldn't understand. What I later understood was that my mother was making a desperate effort to preserve her pride—and ours . . .

Pride was just about all we had to preserve . . .

"You may think that because your car looks like trash nobody is going to steal it, but you're wrong. Many people will a steal a car for any reason."
—from "Confessions of a Teenage Car Thief"

Personal Essay

The personal essay is largely based on the writer's past experience, but it does much more than share details related to a certain time and place. A writer develops a definite viewpoint in a personal essay and fully expects a number of different reactions to this viewpoint from the readers.

The Way I See It . . .

Discussion: Write an essay about a subject you find personally interesting or important. A review of the models following these guidelines will give you some idea of the wide range of subjects that are developed in personal essays. Your goal should be to produce an essay that is based on personal experiences, thoughts, and feelings, that informs and/or entertains, and that gets your readers thinking. Refer to the guidelines below and the models that follow for help with your writing.

Searching and Selecting

1. **Reviewing** • Review your journal entries for ideas, or list ideas that come to mind as you review the model essays. (Anything that is part of your life—and you care about—has the potential to be an effective writing idea.)
2. **Searching** • Still stuck? Check your wallet or purse for ideas. What about the ticket stub or receipt stuck in the corner? What about a picture, your driver's license, a membership card? Also think about any concerns, observations, and questions you would like to explore.

Generating the Text

3. **Collecting** • Free-write about your subject (for at least 10 minutes) letting your ideas take you where they will. One of the following open-ended sentences could serve as a starting point for your writing:
    - (*The subject*) makes me remember . . .
    - (*The subject*) causes me to . . .
    - (*The subject*) concerns me because . . .
4. **Assessing** • Examine your free writing carefully to help you get a feel for your subject. Look for parts of the writing that you like and want to explore further. Also look for any emerging main idea or feeling that could serve as the focus for your essay. Continue gathering and focusing your ideas until you feel ready to write a first draft.

    (The eventual shape of your essay really depends on your subject. Your writing may turn out to be a rather free-flowing exploration of ideas, or it may evolve into a tightly structured essay.)

Writing and Revising

5. **Writing** • Write your first draft freely, allowing your own personality to come through in your writing. Don't strain for a voice or try to make your essay sound too formal. Write what you are thinking and feeling.
6. **Revising** • Review, revise, and refine your writing. (As you work with your essay, try to maintain its original freshness of thought.)

Evaluating

Is there a personal attachment between the writer and the writing?

Does the writing move smoothly from one point to the next?

Will readers appreciate the treatment of the subject?

Student Model

The student writer of "Confessions of a Teenage Car Thief" uses his own experience to discuss the methods and motivations of young car thieves. (Reprinted from *YO! (Youth Outlook)*, the Journal of [San Francisco] Bay Area Teen Life [Spring 1992], published by the Center for Integration and Improvement of Journalism at San Francisco State University and Pacific News Service.)

Confessions of a Teenage Car Thief

Editor's note: The 16-year-old writer of this essay has been arrested four times for auto theft for joyriding. Convicted once after pleading guilty to a misdemeanor, he is now studying auto repair.

The essay's style is very matter-of-fact, contrasting with the shocking criminal activity of the young writer.

You may think that because your car looks like trash nobody is going to steal it, but you're wrong. Many people will steal a car for any reason.

I was 13 when I stole my first car, and it wasn't very easy. The car was a piece of junk—dirty and all crashed up—but it was the kind of car everyone was telling me to steal: a 1986 Honda Accord DX. The first time was hard, but after that I got to where I could steal a car in under a minute. Some of the other thieves were doing it in 15 to 30 seconds.

When I started stealing cars, I did it just for fun, but after a while it got boring. I started doing it for money, but as soon as I got the money, I would go out and spend it. Before I knew it, the money was gone. So then I'd go out to steal another car—I just kept on doing the same thing over and over. Sometimes I stole a car for the dumbest reasons. "I'm bored with nothing to do"—that's how I was thinking at 13 and 14.

A couple of years ago, it seemed like kids were stealing cars just for fun—to drive around, show off, or learn to drive. These days most car thieves only break into cars for items of value, or if they need parts for their own car. So if your car looks good, the thieves will notice, and they'll think you've got some good stuff inside.

Personal experience leads into objective statements about auto theft and the experiences of one car thief in particular.

Even if your car doesn't look good, it's still at risk. Some people need money, so they steal your car to sell it and the buyer strips the car totally naked. Some car owners might get into an accident and look for a car that's the same as theirs to replace the parts that got wrecked. Or someone from the younger generation might steal your ugly car just for fun and driving lessons.

Typical cars Asian kids like me steal are Hondas and Toyotas, and cops will suspect that an Asian kid driving a Honda is a car thief. But statistics show that a Chevy Camaro is the number one stolen car in the Bay Area.

I know one guy who's got a family business in auto theft—his dad steals cars with him. They take the car home, and the mother helps them strip it. They aren't poor either. They drive a 1989 BMW 325i and a Toyota MR2, and they own a condo in the Sunset. But this kid has been in trouble with the law on six counts of auto theft, and after his sixth arrest he got six months at Log Cabin, a camp for juvenile offenders.

A strong sense of irony is evident in the concluding paragraph.

You might think that just because I'm a car thief I can avoid getting my car broken into, but I can't. My car got broken into in broad daylight, even though it had nothing worth taking. And lots of my friends have had their cars broken into for stereo equipment. Right afterwards they'd go out thieving to get their lost parts back.

Student Model

San Marcos High School student Lili Yee won first place in the University of California at Santa Barbara's Creative Studies Essay Contest (1991) with the essay "Swallowing Sorrow: Legacies of My Past," from which the following excerpt is taken. In her essay, Ms. Yee writes about the legacy of hope and sorrow that she carries as a first-generation Chinese-American. In addition, the essay establishes a comparison between Ms. Yee's life and the life of the Chinese-American daughter in Amy Tan's novel *The Joy Luck Club*.

Swallowing Sorrow: Legacies of My Past

The opening quotation stirs the reader's curiosity.

"In America, I will have a daughter just like me. But over there nobody will say her worth is measured by the loudness of her husband's belch. Over there nobody will look down on her because I will make her speak only perfect American English. And over there she will always be too full to swallow any sorrow!" Thus begin the legacies of four Chinese immigrant women and their four American-born daughters. *The Joy Luck Club* by Amy Tan kindles many memories and stories of China and Hong Kong that my relatives still tell me, of a childhood long gone, of the hardships of being poor, of the excitement, confusion, and fear of leaving home forever for America. My mother still tells me of her youth . . .

I grew up in a cold, grey stone house as a child in Hong Kong; everyone called it "The Stone House." Five families lived here, each sharing an individual room . . . A seven-by-eight-foot room housed seven of us. We slept on hard, wooden, three-tiered beds, staring at the bleak stone walls, dreaming of the future . . .

Unbeknownst to them, the future meant coming to America, the land of opportunity. For my mother, it was the experience of a lifetime. She was the first member of her family to immigrate to America. To her, America was an entirely different world where inhabitants spoke in a language she did not know.

During her first few months in Santa Barbara, my mother stayed home and watched television all day while my father worked at a hotel. She remembered watching *Gilligan's Island* and *The Flintstones* without any idea what the characters were saying. The television was, in many ways, her English teacher. Now, my mother occasionally tells me about those few months of living in Santa Barbara and the trauma of leaving her loved ones . . .

The shift from the mother's story to Ms. Yee's story signals the beginning of the heart of the essay.

Now it is time to tell my own story. I am a first-generation Chinese born in America just like the four daughters in *The Joy Luck Club*. I was raised by my aunt and grandparents, who arrived four years later in 1973, while both my parents worked. I looked like those cute, chubby, little, round-faced Chinese girls in travel magazines and films wearing pretty dresses and Chinese outfits. I spoke only Chinese then, but once I went to kindergarten I underwent a dramatic change. Gradually, I became the "daughter who grew up speaking only English and swallowing more Coca-Cola than sorrow." My relatives would speak to me in Chinese, and I would respond in English. Whenever I tried to talk in Chinese, especially to my grandparents, my American accent interfered, so they laughed at me. I never learned how to read and write in my native language, but I loved hearing stories about "The Stone House" and the hill on which the house was situated. I still remember the time when . . .

The italicized sections signal a departure from the basic development of the essay.

My mother, uncle, grandfather, and I took a trip to Hong Kong during Christmas of 1987. They took me around the city, and I was fascinated by the tall buildings, busy streets, and atmosphere of Hong Kong. Then my mother took me to another part of the city and showed her "Stone House" to me. I stood there right in the dim light of the porch. The building was dilapidated. Faded wintergreen paint was peeling off the cold stone walls in curly strips. Cracked, red wooden shutters hung on rusty hinges. The house was one of many bunched together on a side of a hill. Corrugated metal sheets placed on the rooftops between each house kept out the rain and strong sunlight. This was where my mother grew up . . .

Like Jing-Mei Woo, one of the daughters in *The Joy Luck Club*, I entered mainland China and became Chinese during my trip to Hong Kong. I met relatives that I never knew existed. I communicated with them as much as my American-accented Chinese could permit, and they tried to respond in their limited Chinese-accented English. It was wonderful how we could communicate with such limited means. We laughed and smiled at each other. They would correct my Chinese, and I would correct their English. We had a grand time together.

The essay ends on a reflective note as the writer comes to terms with her personal legacy.

Before my journey, I thought that I was "always too full to swallow sorrow." I grew up in a different culture and time, and I did not fully appreciate what my mother and all my relatives went through in order to get where they are now. I consider myself to be different from them, a "Coca-Cola-swallowing American," but looking into the browned faces and holding the calloused hands of my great-grandmother and my multitude of cousins, aunts, and uncles, never before did I realize how important my roots were to me. If it were not for them, I would not be where I am now. As I think back, I understand their suffering, their pain, their happiness. I realize how lucky I am to be an American, for what I am is what they dream of being: to be in America, a dream that probably will never be fulfilled. I recognize the sorrow that is ever present in my native homeland, a sorrow that I'll never forget and that will always be a part of my life. ▣

Professional Model

This personal essay by T. J. Gilding contains a little bit of everything: action, conflict, drama, reflection, and real feelings. As you will see, the writer's ideas are presented in the form of an internal dialogue that relives a most important cross-country meet. (This essay won second place in a 1993 writing contest sponsored by the *Milwaukee Journal*. It is reprinted with permission of the author.)

Passing on a Hill

The next red flag at the far end of the golf course signaled a hard right turn ahead. Reaching for a burst of energy, I lengthened my stride and positioned myself just enough ahead of the runner, a half step behind me, to safely make the turn around the bend. The conference cross-country meet was the last meet of the year, and the last race of my high-school career.

Looking out at the field ahead, I thought, "Seven runners to pass, with two miles to go. This race was my last and my only chance."

The essay begins right in the middle of the action, with two miles to go in the race.

Running was always my "ticket out." It was what I needed to do—to sort out my life, to build strong thoughts and strong words. Also, it was a way of building a record of wins, and winning a college athletic scholarship. I needed that, now, more than ever.

But my purposeful thoughts kept giving way to disturbing thoughts at the very time I needed to concentrate most. I couldn't get them out of my head—thoughts of my dad's words and my mom's speech. And the more I tried, like trying too hard to get to sleep, the harder it was to push them out. I knew I needed to concentrate on this race. Yet the thoughts kept screaming back and the infernal, internal dialogue in my head continued.

Angry at myself, with clenched fists, I knew what I had to do. I burst ahead of a runner, feeling no sympathy . . . but my thoughts again turned back to the scene of my father sitting down in the den with me. His words echoed in my head, "I know you blame me for what is happening, but you don't know the whole story. And I don't expect you to understand, perhaps someday you will, but you need to know I'm sorry and . . ." His voice trailed off. I knew he loved me—his eyes that were directed to the floor, his shoulders that were hunched over, his hand that touched his cheek, not his words, had told me that. But I still did not understand.

What whole story? All I had known and had heard was the yelling and the accusations. And I knew what Mom had told me that next morning about Dad's "official" leaving. And I knew she—all of us—from then on, would have it tough.

Disturbing thoughts about the writer's family surface again and again throughout the essay.

I felt cheated as I angrily passed another runner who couldn't keep up because of a side cramp. I knew the feeling of running in pain. But I had my own pains to think about, and I took advantage of this break.

I paced ahead, my mind springing back into the race. I deserved this win. Every morning for two years, up before dawn, out on the back roads, running to win. I tried to keep focused on the race, but it was hard.

"It's not fair." (Think about the race.) "They owe me." (Put it out of your mind.) "I can't do this myself." (Think, think, think.) Inner conflict was striding, pacing right along with me, keeping up with my every step, every heartbeat.

I thought back to Mom's announcement telling me my parents' marriage was over, their business split, and the money all tied up—unattainable. I would be on my own to earn my way through college. All that money needed for college. Where would I get it? Mom couldn't have helped if she had wanted to. Dad was gone, out of the picture. Even the two jobs I had lined up wouldn't do it.

"Honey, I'm really sorry. But I . . ." And her voice had trailed off as the tears came. Yeah? Well, I was sorry myself! Sorry I had been suddenly forced to fend for myself. I had seen the pain my mother was going through. I felt compassion for her, but . . . Okay, okay, it was all going to be fine. She would be fine; I would be fine, if I just focused on this race. I had to build it back.

The pace of the writer's thoughts reflect the breathless pace of the race.

Thoughts were racing in and out of my mind; there was a gaining of physical and mental momentum. Water from my eyes streamed down my cheeks. I had to keep it going—the rhythm of mind and body moving forward. The footsteps and breathing at my back was the runner I just passed! Passed? I hadn't even realized it.

Remembering a strategy Coach had taught me, psyching out the other runner, I tried to look stronger, more confident, showing that there was no way I could be beaten. I passed another runner without competition. And digging my toes deep into the grass on the hill, I passed yet another runner as I reached the top.

Passing on a hill I knew was something Coach had told me not to do. He would be mad about that, I thought as I remembered his last words to me, "And don't you ever pass on a hill." I grinned, and I ran.

Two ahead now, and less than a half mile to the finish. I was in this race. I had to be. I had practiced too hard before and after school when I could have been making money like many of my friends. I always said my running came first and meant it. Sure, I saved my money, but I had known my parents would be there for me. And then, slam! Now I needed to win this race, not for the glory, but for the money. A victory here meant a great chance at a state scholarship. Coach said a list of first-place finishers from around the state, especially in a major conference such as ours, was an immediate "send" to all state university athletic scholarship review boards.

Drama and intensity build as the finish line draws nearer.

It was all mixed together: the past, the present, the future. All coming together as I passed the next runner and squared down on the final jersey still ahead. It was all coming to me at once—the finish line two hundred yards away, Mom's surprise announcement, Coach's words of a must win, and my dad's sad expression as he asked for my understanding.

My thoughts cleared. It was my race. I was on my own, to fend for myself. My fate was in my hands—actually my feet. Yeah, a pun. Funny. I had to reach back, do what was needed. I had to realize the future, pass the last runner, run straight ahead—toward that line, toward that goal. It was mine!

Subject Writing

"Erica is no different than any other teenager. She wants to run to her next-hour class if she is late or be able to dance the night away. And she's tired of crutches and wheelchairs. Everything she has been through has not soured her personality or dimmed her determination, however." —*Heather Bachman*

Case Study

In a case study, the story of one individual's experiences speaks for the experiences of a larger group of people (disaster victims, recent immigrants, etc). The effectiveness of a case study depends upon the writer's ability to conduct interviews, make firsthand observations, and gather timely information from print materials.

Making a Case

Discussion: Develop a case study based on your careful and thorough investigation of one individual whose experiences typify a particular group of people (runaways, displaced farmers, recovering heart patients, musical groupies, etc.). Gather information for your study through interviews, observations, articles, letters, journals, and so on. Your finished work should be developed as a narrative report detailing the story of your subject's experiences. Keep personal comments and conclusions to a minimum. Instead, let your story speak for itself. Refer to the models that follow and the guidelines below to help you develop your writing.

Searching and Selecting

1. **Selecting** • Think of individuals you know whose experiences in a particular area speak for the experiences of others. (You may know a farmer who has recently lost his land, or you may know a runaway.) Also think about general groups of people that you would like to know more about. (Perhaps you're curious about a new immigrant population or foster children or first-year teachers.)

   Special Note: If the starting point for your work is a group, your challenge, obviously, will be to find a worthy *and* accessible candidate for your investigation.

Generating the Text

2. **Collecting** • Plan for and carry out your interviews, observations, readings, and so on. (The lifeblood of an effective case study is information, so gather a good supply of facts, remarks, anecdotes, and observations.)
3. **Focusing** • Carefully review all of the information you have collected. Make sure you understand how or why your subject's experiences speak for similar individuals. Also determine what it is about this person that you would like to emphasize in your writing—a specific turning point, a particular experience, an extended period of time, etc. And make some initial decisions about the structure of your writing. (What are you going to say first, second, third, and so on?)

Writing and Revising

4. **Writing** • Develop your first draft freely and naturally, working in ideas according to any planning you have done. (You may want to experiment or play with the sequence of events in your subject's story. The writer of "Health Care?" begins by describing how her subject passed away, drawing the reader's attention into the rest of the study.)
5. **Revising** • As you review your first draft, ask yourself two important questions: Have I addressed my subject's story in enough detail? Have I presented the details in an effective manner? Revise and refine accordingly.

Evaluating

Does this study read like a narrative report, effectively detailing an individual's story?
Is it clear how the subject speaks for, or represents, a larger group?
Will readers appreciate the treatment of this subject?

Student Model

In this model, student writer Rohan A. Dewar shares the story of one streetwise young man who eventually makes some smart choices. Dewar's case study typifies the experience of many young people who have turned their lives around. (This article first appeared in *New Youth Connections: The Magazine Written By and For New York Youth*, May 1992. It is reprinted with permission.)

In the first few paragraphs, the writer introduces his subject and offers some background information about him.

Notice how effectively the writer incorporates many of his subject's direct comments into the text.

A Street Kid Goes Straight

As a kid growing up in the Bronx, Troy Morrell, 23, was quiet, kept to himself, and never went outside much. He was a teacher's pet and a mama's boy, always getting picked on but never wanting to fight.

Troy lived a model life in the Bronx for 13 years. But then he moved to Brooklyn, changed schools, and started hanging out with the wrong crowd.

Troy rarely went to school and constantly disobeyed his mother. He got involved with a gang, started blowing up cars with "cocktails" (homemade firebombs), and began forging other people's signatures to cash checks.

At 15, Troy was arrested for injuring a couple with a firebomb and imprisoned in Spofford Juvenile Detention Center. He spent five months there before being released. But going to Spofford didn't help. Troy says it only made him worse.

When he got out, the neighborhood youths gave him the street name "Psycho." "I had that name," Troy said, "so I had to live up to it."

He went on a rampage. He threw TVs from roofs, wounding people below, hit people with hammers, burned people's eyes with paint remover, and carried a large butcher knife.

HE FELT ASHAMED

That was eight years ago. As Troy grew older, he started developing a conscience. He remembered his days in the Bronx and realized how much he'd changed. He started feeling ashamed and vowed to better himself.

He transferred to Lafayette High School where a guidance counselor named June Feder pushed him to do better. She scheduled Troy's classes in order to ensure that he didn't cut. She'd schedule his gym classes for the beginning and end of the day and put the classes and teachers Troy liked best in between.

Feder also introduced Troy to Operation Success, a program that encourages kids to come to school by rewarding them for good grades. Participants go on trips, have contests, and belong to a co-op program where students go to school one week and work the next. She also helped him get his first job at a toy store.

With Dr. Feder standing by him, Troy became more active in school. "She really turned my life around," he said. "She was always on my back." Troy won awards for art and play writing and the President's Award for achievement and improvement in school. "But the best thing I got," said Troy, "was my diploma."

WORKING WITH KIDS

Now, at 23, Troy has a 3-year-old daughter he helps support. He is the head counselor at a Manhattan after-school program for young children.

The essay emphasizes the importance of an individual's *power to change* the circumstances of his life.

He watches over and interacts with them. "I would've never thought it would be my career," Troy confided.

But he enjoys his job. "It's cool working there," he said. "You keep the kids entertained and it brings out the kid in you . . . you almost believe they're your own."

While some people may think that working with children is a woman's job, Troy doesn't. He feels that he can do a great job with the children because he understands and can relate to them.

"All these kids are from the neighborhood," he said. "They're going through what I went through. I'm an inner-city kid just like they're inner-city kids."

Troy has another job at a supermarket where he works in the evening to better support his daughter. He works long hours but he can handle it. "At the beginning it was [hard]," said Troy. "But when you get used to a certain pace, it's no problem."

As Troy wanders through his old neighborhood, he sees that things have changed. Asked the whereabouts of his old gang, he said, "Some are down South. Some are married. Some are in jail. I walk around now and I hardly see anyone I know."

In his teen years, Troy Morrell seemed like a lost cause—a boy who would never grow up to see manhood. All it took for him to realize his true potential was a little inner strength and a helping hand from someone who cared.

By using his life experiences, Troy is touching the lives of kids like himself and making sure they too live up to their potential.

Student Model

In this model case study, Heather Bachman shares the story of a freshman girl in her high school who has had to live with a rare, painful bone disease. This person's story speaks forcefully for all young people with disabilities who struggle to fit in, who want desperately to be like their peers.

Walking Tall

Erica Lovell acts like any freshman in high school. She's bubbly, energetic, and one of the sweetest people I know. She's in Honors Art Club and loves golfing. I was somewhat surprised the first time I saw her walking down the hall with what appeared to be a limp. But I didn't really think anything of it until recently when Erica entered the hospital for major surgery.

Background information about the subject's disease is provided.

I discovered that Erica has *leggs perthees*, a disease that is rare among boys and almost unheard of among girls. Leggs perthees causes the portion of the femur that fits into the hip socket to deteriorate and grow into a rigid oblong shape. In Erica's case, this portion of bone grew to double its normal size and caused intense pain in her hip and left knee. And due to her condition, her left leg stopped growing, making her legs noticeably uneven. "I tried to make up the difference by walking on my tippy toes," Erica says. Although the cause is unknown, doctors know how to correct the unevenness caused by leggs perthees once the bones have stopped growing.

At one time Erica had to wear awkward braces on her legs. Around her waist was a belt from which two metal bars went down the sides of her legs. Plastic, velcro-secured cuffs around her calves were attached to the end of the bars. Finally, a rigid bar connected the two cuffs. This forced her to walk stiffly, cowboy style. She remembers, "My classmates would tease me and call me names." Their comments hurt, especially those made by her friends.

In July 1990, the pain became unbearable and doctors had to operate. Erica spent six and a half hours on the operating table while the doctors reduced friction between the hip bones and added pins and screws for support. Her recovery time included five weeks in a body cast, two weeks in bed, a month in a wheelchair, and a month on crutches. Erica started junior high on crutches. She had another operation in December 1990 to remove the pins and screws. The two surgeries relieved a lot of the pain, somewhat improved her bad hip, but did nothing to change her uneven legs.

Erica lost some friends during her years in junior high. "People would ask me what was wrong, and then they would stop being my friends." She couldn't participate in gym, sports, or dances. And the pain persisted, especially in her knee.

Finally on February 11, 1993, the doctors felt that Erica was ready for corrective surgery. The three-and-a-half-hour operation involved taking out a 1.25-inch section of her longer right femur and securing the bones together with plates and screws.

Direct quotations are used effectively throughout the case study.

As Erica says, "I can't wait to try out my legs," but she faces a long recovery period. The femur takes the longest to heal of all the bones in the body. She must be in bed for four weeks (which means missing school), in a wheelchair for two to three weeks, on crutches for two to three weeks, and finally, by May of 1993, she hopes to be walking again. She is not supposed to move or bend her legs for the first month after surgery. Then physical therapy will begin for her leg and will entail a lot of weight lifting, leg risers, and careful bending of the knee. Some of the exercises will be done with a therapist while others will be done at home.

Throughout the essay, the writer describes how leggs perthees has affected the subject's life.

Erica's list of "can't do's" has been rather lengthy: no soccer, no track, no cheerleading, no gym, no fast dancing, no twisting . . . basically anything involving heavy impact to the legs and joints has been out of the question. Erica roller-skates, ice-skates, walks, bikes, and lifts weights to stay in shape. She will still have to refrain from more strenuous activities in the future, because the pin that remains in her hip could detach from the bone and even possibly puncture her skin.

"Leggs perthees is like cancer in how it affects a family," Erica says. "It is very hard on my parents. My mother had to quit her job at one point to take care of me while I was in a body cast and confined to bed." It was hard on other family members too. "My sister was jealous of all the attention I got from my parents." Fortunately her family has very good insurance to help them cover the high costs of hospitals, doctors, and physical therapy.

Soon Erica will be able to wear something other than shoes with lifts. She can't wait to wear high heels. Golfing will be much easier since she won't have to compensate for her shorter leg while swinging. And tripping should no longer be the problem it was. "I once fell in a crosswalk in front of a line of cars right when the light turned green," she remembers.

The case study ends on a positive note, with Erica looking toward the future.

In her early twenties, Erica hopes to have a complete hip replacement. That would finally put an end to the pain and probably enable her to participate in more strenuous activities. Erica eagerly anticipates that surgery.

Erica is no different than any other teenager. She wants to run to her next-hour class if she is late or be able to dance the night away. And she's tired of crutches and wheelchairs. Everything she has been through has not soured her personality or dimmed her determination, however. Erica is, as always, upbeat and positive, someone who richly deserves our respect and our support. ■

Professional Model

Laura Bachman gathered the information for this case study from someone who was well acquainted with a dying man—someone who was at this man's side through his final, painful hours. Once you read this case study, you will see that it speaks eloquently for the experiences of all elderly men and women who have lost control of their own lives because of infirmity. (This essay was used at an in-service for resident physicians at Lutheran Hospital, La Crosse, Wis.)

Health Care?

The elderly gentleman being monitored in the cardiac intensive care unit lies buried in wires and electrical pads. When the monitor suddenly sounds an alarm and shows a straight line, his nurse, who happens to be out of the room at the time, as well as two or three others, comes rushing in. However, they make no attempt to revive him.

Lester and Esther DeBow celebrated their 60th wedding anniversary several years ago. In his later years, Lester kept active maintaining various gardens. He also made the rounds of his neighborhood taking the widows shopping, running errands, and doing odd jobs. Lester had been a master plumber and could often put those old skills to use fixing leaky faucets, clogged drains and even more serious problems. He took everything in stride with his indomitable sense of humor.

Background information not only places the case study in its larger context, but also brings the individual to life.

Three years ago, Lester's sense of humor served him well as he faced losing his right leg due to a blockage that cut off his circulation. He was insistent and, in fact, convinced the doctors not to take his leg above the knee. And unlike many amputees, he eagerly did everything necessary to speed the fitting of an artificial leg. He couldn't hide his amusement when he discovered the initial leg was simply a piece of pipe fitted with a shoe.

Having to use a cane didn't slow Lester down one bit. Although it was his right leg, he quickly learned to drive again. His widow friends never felt neglected. Though Lester and Esther never had children, they were constantly driving to communities across Wisconsin and Minnesota visiting their many friends and relatives.

Then Lester fell and cracked a hip, an injury requiring hospitalization. His nurses had to be on guard because he kept sliding out of bed, slipping on his leg, and sneaking off to the bathroom unassisted. Thinking they could solve the problem, the nurses took the artificial leg away. However, that didn't stop Lester, who simply used a chair for support and kept scooting around.

One of his favorite phrases, in or out of the hospital, was "It's a great life, if you don't weaken." At first, that naturally seemed to mean staying physically active; but on the fateful day when his bodily strength gave out, "not weakening" clearly referred to something different—his mind and spirit.

At age 86, with a failing heart that had been weakening him for a month or so, Lester was admitted to St. Mary's Hospital in the small community of Sparta (Wisconsin), on Thursday afternoon, March 17. The following afternoon he was moved to Lutheran Hospital in La Crosse.

From his bed in the cardiac intensive care unit, Lester said, "The doctor told me I'm going to die tonight." Later, still with a touch of humor, he said,

"I'm not going to die tonight . . . maybe tomorrow, or maybe I'll wait a few days. . . ."

Meanwhile, the doctor continued serious efforts to monitor and control Lester's blood pressure. To do so required lowering the head of the hospital bed periodically. Earlier in the afternoon, Lester had been sitting up on the edge of his bed, despite having some trouble getting enough oxygen. His mind remained perfectly clear, and he just wanted to sit up and talk.

Instead, he spent the evening tossing in pain created by a catheter. Because any medication could interfere with his already weakened heart, pain killers were withheld. Eventually the catheter was removed—too late to significantly reduce the pain it had already caused. (In the end, the catheter may not even have been effective with the bed slanted head down.)

The "buried" image in the introduction is reinforced by each added medical procedure.

Occasionally Lester's bed would be raised to a level position, but never elevated as he so fervently desired. Due to Lester's difficulty breathing, the doctor ordered an oxygen mask. Now conversation, already labored, became almost impossible. The best he could do throughout the night was mumble, "If I could only sit up for five minutes, five minutes, that's all I ask." Lester was not delirious. He was not crazy. He wasn't saying, just let me sit up and I'll be fine; I'll get out of here. No. He simply wanted to sit on the edge of the bed one last time.

And the nurse would respond each time, patiently, but firmly, "Your blood pressure couldn't take it."

At one point Lester admitted, "If this is what it's going to be like, then I just wish it would end."

Not only was Lester monitored constantly by the heart machine he was wired to, but he also had to contend with an automatic blood-pressure cuff on his arm, which pumped up and took his blood pressure every few minutes. This device required that the arm remain at a very exact angle. Otherwise a beeper went off, and then Lester had to be realigned. After numerous beeper alarms and painful realignments, Lester's arm was taped to a board to keep it properly positioned.

In the very early hours of the morning, efforts to reach the doctor succeeded, and permission was granted to give Lester some pain medication. This special medicine would have to be administered by syringe very slowly into the IV, in timed dosages. Too big a dose, or a dosage given too quickly, would be fatal.

Lester never got free of the blood-pressure cuff, never got his bed raised, never got to shed his oxygen mask, never got to sit on the edge of the bed and talk to his wife one last time. Because, less than 15 minutes after the final IV medication injection, he died.

The writer concludes by connecting the subject of this study to a larger group.

The nurse felt bad, but he was only following orders. All night, Lester endured being manipulated, maneuvered, and monitored. Painful, inconvenient, and even degrading efforts to control his blood pressure during his last hours were admittedly futile. Despite all the obvious concern expressed for Lester, this gentle man, who lived so long and so well, was forced to die, almost in self-defense. How many others spend their final hours subjected to procedures intended to prolong life (for a matter of hours), only to be robbed of their final peace and dignity?

Professional Model

In the following model (an excerpt from an in-depth report), professional writer Gary Smith shares the story of a gifted high-school athlete named Jonathan Takes Enemy. As you read this model, notice how Takes Enemy's story speaks for the plight of other Native American athletes in Montana. (The following article is reprinted courtesy of *Sports Illustrated* from the February 18, 1991, issue. Copyright © 1991, Time, Inc. "Shadow of a Nation" by Gary Smith. All rights reserved.)

A dramatic, almost poetic introduction draws readers into this study.

Shadow of a Nation

. . . Young Indian boys formed trails behind him, wearing big buttons with his picture on their little chests. They ran onto the court and formed a corridor for him and his teammates to trot through during pregame introductions, they touched his hands and arms, they pretended to *be* him. The coaches had to lock the gym doors to start practice. Girls lifted their pens to the bathroom walls: "I was with Jonathan Takes Enemy last night," they wrote. "I'm going to have Jonathan Takes Enemy's baby." He was a junior in high school. Already he was the father of two. Already he drank too much. Already his sister Sharolyn was dead of cirrhosis. Sometimes he walked alone in the night, shaking and sobbing. He was the newest hero of the tribe that loved basketball too much.

Takes Enemy felt the bus wheels rolling beneath him. The sun arced through the Montana sky. The circle was the symbol of never-ending life to the Crows—they saw it revealed in the shape and movement of the sun and moon, in the path of the eagle, in the contours of their tepees and the whorl of their dances. As long as the people kept faith with the circle, they believed, their tribe would endure. Jonathan settled back in his seat. Sometimes it seemed as if his life were handcuffed to a wheel, fated to take him up . . . and over . . . and down . . .

The experience of another legendary Crow player puts Takes Enemy's own situation into perspective.

Somewhere behind him on the highway, his first cousin would soon be getting off his job on the reservation's road crew and joining the exodus to the ball game in Billings—*the* legendary Crow player, some people said; the best player, *period*, in Montana high school history, said others; the one who ignited his tribe's passion for high school basketball back in the 1950s and seemed to start this dark cycle of great players arising and vanishing: Larry Pretty Weasel. The one whose drinking helped drive him out of Rocky Mountain College in Billings and back to the reservation in 1958, just a few days before the NAIA's weekly bulletin arrived proclaiming him the best field-goal percentage shooter in the country.

Horns honked in the caravan behind Takes Enemy, passengers waved. In the long-ago days before white men had brought their horses or guns or cars or liquor, his people had chased buffalo in this same direction, across these same valleys, stampeding them over cliffs near the land where Billings would one day arise. This same creature whose skull the Crows would mount on a pole and make the centerpiece of their religious Sun Dance . . . they would drive over the edge of the cliff and then scramble down to devour.

The bus ascended another hill. Takes Enemy looked back at his people one more time.

. . . He knew the danger he was wooing. The night he learned he had made the varsity, a rare honor for a freshman, he and a few friends went out in a pickup truck to drink beer. A tribal police car pulled up to the truck. Alcohol was banned on the reservation, but Crow policemen sometimes looked the other way. "Go home," this cop ordered the teenagers, but the kid at the wheel panicked, jammed the accelerator and roared away. Suddenly, Takes Enemy, a boy who was afraid even on a sled, found himself hurtling down a curving country road at 100 mph, four police cars with flashing lights and howling sirens just behind him. One came screaming up beside the truck, trying to slip by and box the teenagers in. Instead of letting it pass, Jonathan's friend lurched into the other lane to cut the car off. The pickup truck skidded off the road, toppled onto its roof and into a ditch. Takes Enemy limped out, somehow with just a badly bruised hip.

Learning about the subject's past helps readers better understand where he is headed.

He vowed not to drink again. He remembered how uneasy he had been as a child, awakening on the mattress between his parents' beds to see the silhouette of his father stagger into the room. Even in an alcoholic haze his father was a gentle man, but still, that silhouette was not Dad—it was a *stranger*. Then, too, there was what alcohol had done to his cousin the legend, Pretty Weasel. So many fans thronged gymnasiums to watch Pretty Weasel play for Hardin High that his team had to crawl through windows to get to its locker room. He could shoot jump shots with either hand, fake so deftly that he put defenders on their pants and, at five-ten, outjump players half a foot taller. It was almost, an opponent would muse years later, "as if you were playing against a kind of enchanted person." Pretty Weasel's younger brother Lamonte got drunk and died in a car accident. Then Pretty Weasel partied his way out of a four-year college scholarship and onto a reservation road crew.

But Jonathan couldn't keep his vow. He felt as if he were locked up in a tiny room inside his body, and it was only when he was playing basketball or drinking that he could break out of it. The first time he was drunk had been in seventh grade at Crow Fair, the week-long celebration every August when the field on the edge of his town became the tepee capital of the world. Hundreds of tepees were erected, and Indians from far away came to dance and drink and sing with his people deep into the night. Jonathan slipped the bootlegger four dollars for a half pint of whiskey, poured it down—and out poured the talking, laughing Jonathan he had always yearned to be. His mother came and found him at the fair at 3 A.M. Dorothy, a sweet, passive woman dedicated to the Pentecostal Church, began yelling that he would end up just like his father . . . but that was all. In many homes across the reservation . . . that was all.

A feeling of entrapment underlies the entire essay—"the danger he was wooing," "his daydream of escaping snuffed out," etc.

His sophomore year he moved in with his girlfriend and her parents, to help her bring up their baby daughter. Four months after his girlfriend delivered, she had news for him. She was pregnant again. His whole life seemed hopeless, his daydream of escaping snuffed out. Was it his fault? No matter how hard Jonathan thought about it, he could never be sure. So many things had happened to his people that *were* beyond their control, it had become almost impossible to identify those that were *not*. He watched three brothers go to college and quickly drop out. He watched all three of them take turns with the bottle.

There were no movie theaters or bowling alleys or malls on the reservation. When it became too dark to see the rim on the courts behind the elementary school, Jonathan and his friends would drive up and down the main street of Crow Agency—from JR's Smokehouse to the irrigation supply yard and back again—seeing the same people, the same mange-eaten dogs and rust-eaten cars, until the monotony numbed them. Then someone would say, "Let's go drinking." It was a ritual that had become a display of solidarity and shared values among his tribe, so much so that to say no was to mark oneself as an alien. None of the teenagers had enough money to buy liquor, but all of them had Indian wealth—relatives. Uncles and aunts, cousins and grandparents are as close to most Crows as parents and siblings are to a white child; a boy can walk into five or six houses without knocking, open the refrigerator without asking, eat without cleaning up the crumbs. Jonathan and his friends would each ask a relative or two for a buck, and all of the sharing and family closeness in which the Crows pride themselves would boomerang. Each kid would come up with three or four dollars to pitch into the pot, and off they'd go to the liquor stores that waited for them half a hiccup past the reservation borders. It wouldn't take long to see someone they knew who was of drinking age—the boys were related by blood or clan, it seemed, to *everyone*. They whisked their beer or whiskey back onto the reservation, where the statutes against juveniles drinking were less severe, and began gulping it as if they were racing to see who could sledgehammer reality quickest, who could forget his life first.

The writer obviously did a lot of interviewing and observing in order to present so many facts and details.

Jonathan's absences from school mounted. That was how he responded to trouble. He disappeared. His parents wanted him to get an education, but to make the house quiet for two hours each night and insist that he study, to pull him out of his bed when the school bus was rolling up the road—no, they couldn't quite do that. Each of them had dropped out after the ninth grade, but there was more to it than that. Almost every Crow parent had a close relative who had been forcibly taken from his home by white government agents in the early 1900s and sent off to a faraway boarding school, where his hair was shorn, his Indian clothes and name were taken away, and he was beaten for speaking his own language. How many Indians could chase an education without feeling an old pang in their bones?

On intelligence alone, Takes Enemy had made the honor roll in junior high, but now he fell behind in class and was too ashamed to ask the white teachers for help. He lost his eligibility for the first half-dozen games of both his sophomore and junior seasons, regained it after each Christmas and started dropping in 25 or 30 points with a dozen assists a game, leading his teammates flying up and down the floor. His coaches called it Blur Ball. His people called it Indian Ball. And his brothers, three of whom had also been stars at Hardin High, would whip the crowd to wildness, reaching back into imaginary quivers on their backs, loading their make-believe bows, and zinging invisible arrows at the other teams; vibrating their hands over their mouths to make the high, shrill *wooo-wooo* battle cry that once froze frontiersmen's hearts; shouting themselves hoarse, making Takes Enemy feel as if he could simply lift up his legs and let his people's ecstasy wash him up and down the hardwood.

He scored 49 points in a state tournament game his senior year and was named the tournament's MVP. The outside walls of his house literally vanished, swathed in posters of congratulation from his fans. "A great major college prospect," said then BYU coach Ladell Andersen.

As this case study steadily builds in suspense, so does the reader's interest in Jonathan Takes Enemy's special problem.

The stress and confusion experienced by the subject is captured in a series of "why" questions.

Do it, teachers urged him. Do it so *they* could once more believe in what they were doing, do it so *all* the Crow children whose eyes were on him could see how it was done. "Just *one*," they kept saying to him. "If just one great basketball player from here could make the break and succeed, it could change *everything*. College recruiters would start coming here, other kids would follow your example. You can be the one, Jonathan. You can be the breakthrough."

. . . Takes Enemy's head spun. There were just too many mixed signals, too many invisible arrows from the audience whizzing by. Like most Crows, he'd been brought up not to make autonomous decisions but to take his cues from his immediate family, his extended family, his clan and his tribe. If *they* hadn't decided whether to assimilate into the white man's world or to recoil from it, how could he? And then, his two little children—he couldn't just walk away from them. The small living room he grew up in, with its sixty-five photographs of family members on the wall—a warm, happy place that the people in those pictures would flow into with no invitation, sit around sipping coffee and exchanging the sly puns and double entendres that his people excelled at, talking until there was nothing left to talk about and then talking some more—he couldn't just leave that behind. "Why?" he remembers wondering. "Why do I have to do it the white man's way to be a success in this world?" Why did all the human wealth he had gathered in his life, all the close friends and relatives, count for nothing when he crossed the reservation borders; why did material wealth seem to be the only gauge? And then his eyes and whys would turn the other way: "Why am I so important to my people? Why do *I* have to carry the hopes of the Crows?" All he had really wanted to do, ever since taking apart a stereo in the tenth grade and staring in wonder at all the whatchamacallits inside, was to go to a vocational school and learn electronics. But no, the herd was rolling, the people were waving and shouting him on, his legs were pulling him closer and closer to the ledge. He drank to close his eyes to it. One night at a school dance an administrator found out he was drunk. The next day he was ordered to take a chemical-dependency class. . . .

Postscript: *The report goes on to describe Jonathan Takes Enemy's life once out of high school. After a few difficult and aimless years on the reservation, Takes Enemy and his wife moved to Billings (Montana) and entered college. When this article was first published, he was the leading scorer on his college's basketball team.*

"In those days, lake passenger shipping was a very common practice. I remember that you could set your watch by the Christopher Columbus, which was a whaleback passenger vessel that ran between Chicago and Milwaukee." —Leonard Palmer

Historical Profile

A historical profile explores a specific person, place, time, or event from the past. The writer's challenge is to present a report that is historically accurate, thorough, and engaging.

Another time and place . . .

Discussion: Write a profile or feature article presenting information you have gathered about a particular person, place, time, or event from the past. Your writing can be based on interviews, library research, and/or personal experiences or reminiscences. The important thing to remember is that a historical profile or feature must somehow re-create (bring to life) a person, a place, or an event of an earlier time. Refer to the guidelines below to help you develop your writing; also refer to the model articles that follow.

Searching and Selecting

1. **Choosing** • Think of people you know who could share interesting stories about the past (neighbors, parents, grandparents, senior citizens). Think of older buildings or places in your community that you could investigate. Think of events from the past that have always interested you, or think about the history behind certain objects.
2. **Limiting** • Talk to any of your teachers about possible subjects and possible approaches. Review old newspapers in the library; talk to someone from the local historical society; dig out your family tree or photo album.

Generating the Text

3. **Preparing** • Determine how you are going to gather information related to your subject. Prepare for interviews. Develop a working bibliography of books, magazines, and newspapers that contain information related to your subject. Then begin gathering information.
4. **Collecting** • Collect as much information as possible. Tape interviews if at all possible. (Also take general notes as the interview progresses.) Note page numbers for all quoted or summarized information you gather from texts.
5. **Assessing** • Carefully review your notes to help you identify a main idea, a story line, or a dominant impression that can serve as the focus of your writing. Also decide how you want to present your information—as a basic report of information or as something a bit more imaginative. (Review the model articles for ideas.)

Writing and Revising

6. **Writing** • Write your first draft freely, working in facts and details according to your planning. As you write your rough draft, jot down any questions about your subject and writing that come to mind.
7. **Refining** • Read your essay out loud to check for gaps in thought, organizational problems, awkward expressions, missing transitions, and so on. Revise and refine accordingly.

Evaluating

Does the writing work? Does it re-create a sense of what it was like during this time period?

Does the writing display a sufficient amount of research?

Are sources of information cited properly?

Will readers appreciate the treatment of the subject?

Student Model

Some people avoid cemeteries, while others, like student writer John Nichols, seem irresistibly drawn to them. As he researched the old gravestone epitaphs in a local cemetery, he made many discoveries about the pioneers who settled in his hometown.

And When I Die . . .

At the outset, the writer explains his personal interest in cemeteries.

I've always had a feeling for cemeteries. It's hard to explain any further than that, except to say history never seems quite as real as it does when I walk between rows of old gravestones.

I know there's a cemetery in Concord, Massachusetts, where Ralph Waldo Emerson, Louisa May Alcott, and Henry David Thoreau are buried within a few feet of each other. The story behind that burying ground is pretty obvious, and no doubt quite romantic. When I first began looking into the prospects of doing an article on the Union Grove Cemetery, I was afraid I wouldn't find anything too interesting. My fears were unfounded.

I soon found that within a mile of my home was the grave of a Revolutionary War veteran and one of a man who may very well have been Abraham Lincoln's bodyguard on the night he was shot. I also found the graves of less famous but equally interesting people, many of whose gravestones are as beautiful as the artwork you might find in a museum.

Then, in the cemetery's older section, I found the graves of the Cadwell family. The Cadwells were early Union Grove area settlers. If you were to view their graves on Memorial Day (when the American Legion places flags by the graves of veterans), you'd quickly get the impression that the Cadwells believed strongly in supporting America's military efforts. Phineas Cadwell, the oldest member of the family to emigrate from New York to Wisconsin in 1850, fought in the Revolutionary War.

Phineas, who the family Bible claimed was "enticed" into the army at age 18, served under Washington and rose to the rank of corporal. By the time he reached Wisconsin, he was totally blind and seldom ventured from the family home. Still, he kept an interest in the affairs of his nation, especially the slavery situation. The inscription on his tombstone reads: "Oh my country, how sure I loved thee. In my youth I fought for, sought, and saw thy prosperity. Free all thy sons. May thy Freedom be universal and perpetual. I leave thee."

A real sense of local history emerges with the details about the Cadwell family.

Phineas' son, Ebenezer, served in the War of 1812. He was a captain in the New York Militia for four months in 1814, during the closing days of the war. Like so many veterans of the War of 1812, he received no real compensation for his service until the late 1840's when he was awarded 40 acres of land near Union Grove (in what now is the town of Paris). Ebenezer brought his father, mother, wife, and children to live on that land.

The writer expands the coverage of his report by including stories about some of the other settlers in the community.

A thought about cemeteries as "living" history concludes this article.

Two other Cadwells, also buried in the cemetery, carried on the family tradition of service to their country. Both Erastmus and Walter fought in the Civil War. Erastmus was Union Grove's first blacksmith. He entered the Union Army in 1864 after meeting Abraham Lincoln in Racine. It seemed Erastmus was so impressed with Lincoln, he immediately joined Company A of the 22nd Wisconsin Infantry. Erastmus died in Tennessee near the end of the war, and his body was brought back to Wisconsin for burial.

Thirty-three other Civil War veterans are buried in the cemetery. Fordyce Lincoln, veteran of the Blackhawk War, and Earl McCormick, who served in the Spanish-American War, were also laid to rest there, as was Harley Osborne, who fought in World War II as a member of the Canadian army.

More than just soldiers' graves make up the Union Grove Cemetery, though. It provides a strong tie with Union Grove's past. While John Dunnam, the village's first settler, was not buried there, many other pioneers were. Among them was Gideon Morey, the town's first store owner and postmaster. The graves of the village's presidents and local officials, its shop owners, blacksmiths, and printers are there—all with unique and wonderful names—from Miles Hulett, the only Racine County sheriff from Union Grove, to Menzo Bixby, the first Union Grove boy to die on foreign shores.

It is in its cemetery that much of Union Grove remains alive. Beneath its grounds lies our past, and on its stones, our history, as telling as any book or article.

Student Model

In this excerpt from a much longer historical profile, Ann Cerne skillfully balances historical fact with the real-life experiences of her grandmother. You will note that the writer brings history to life in a unique and personal way.

Strangers at the Door

From six continents, seven seas, and several archipelagoes,
From points of land moved to wind and water
Out of where they used to be to where they are,
The people of the earth marched and travelled
To gather on a great plain.
—Carl Sandburg, "The People Yes"

Over 20 million men, women, and children flocked to America in search of freedom and opportunity between 1855 and 1934. Their story is one of poverty and harshness . . . and this personal tale is no exception. Grandma Martin came from a little town in Yugoslavia, and, by scraping and saving, she secured enough money to book passage on a steamship to New York. In this excerpt from an interview with her, Grandma Martin graphically outlined her past—the frightening trip across the Atlantic, the humiliating experiences on Ellis Island with the officials, and the uphill struggle to make it in the new world.

What follows is a tale of deep personal value—it provides a link between myself and the old country. In compiling this story, my grandmother and I truly gathered at a crossroad—together we captured a memory dating over fifty years.

However, this tale is also one of universal appeal. Several of my classmates, as well as members of our community, can trace their beginnings in America to immigrants similar to Grandma Martin. Her saga marks one of the most dramatic events in our nation's history—the knocking of "Strangers at the Door."

After establishing a context for this profile, the writer steps back and lets her grandmother speak.

I comm heer in ninten tventy von. I left home Janary saven an' I vent to Slatina. I den seet on train an' I ride to Italy—Trst [Trieste]. Ve vas dere for von veek, my brodder Frank an' me. Ve comm dere too soon an' ve vait eight day for sheep Vilson [Wilson]. Ve have notink to do, just vait for meal to meal.

Boat finally comm—ve vas on boat tventy von day. Dere vas a lot of pipple. Oh, dere vas a lot of pipple, datsa right! But I 'member von time it vas soo foggy you can't see close to von person. Da boat gave seegnal—our boat vas commink an' de odder boat vas commink da same vay. Dey vere goink to heet! Everybody vas frightened—an' ve vas preparink to jump in de vater. But den jinglink, da bells ver jinglink, dey say everthink is all right. My modder heer dis in Europ—dey say de Vilson sheep vas drowned: but it not true—ve vas okay.

. . . There was money in immigration—even at thirty dollars a head the steamship companies cleared a handsome profit. To drum up business, companies would distribute lavish posters describing the wonders of the New World—"The land of milk and honey." (Greenleaf 134)

Dere vas long table on boat vher ve eat. Food not really so goot. I never saw before ting like dat macaroni—look like beeg vorm. . . .

Boat vas poor—sheep vas shakink bek an' fort. Girl fromm Lika keep on sayink dat she is goink to die. I must hold her over leetle ditch in boat so she can trow up. Dere vas leetle ditch on boat just to get sick in.

The immigrants were grouped below deck in the steerage compartment. Every lunge of the ship was felt ten times worse down in steerage than in any other part of the boat. Bunks were wedged in with people sleeping shoulder to shoulder, preventing them from being spilled onto the floor. The air was foul and stifling—the tiny portholes did not provide adequate circulation. Old food, seasickness, and unwashed humanity contributed to the nauseating stench. (Novotny 7)

The writer meticulously transcribes her grandmother's grammar and rich Yugoslavian accent.

Dere vasn't much doink—ve just sat 'round an' talk, vent on boat an' look at vater. Looked at feesh jumpink in da vater.

Oh, dat vas soo lonk! I tought dat ve never comm no more.

I forget land an' I think only of vater. I tought dat ve vould never leave it.

Den ve comm to Ellis Island. But dis boy on sheep had typhus, so dey kep us for two veek—de whole sheep. Dey kep us in beeg houses. De vurst pot vas ven ve go trough de cleanink. Ve must tek off de close, de shoos, de stockinks. Ve ver naked—sterilizink, you know. Everthink goes trough machine. Dey ver women all together, men in odder room. Den dey tek a leetle mop an' vent over you body. Can you imagine? Dat vas HELL! Dey do dis tree time in our two veeks. I say if I know dis, I vould have never gone in America.

Each transcription is complemented by related factual information.

. . . Once accepted, the immigrants quickly dispersed, heading for industrial centers such as New York, Chicago, and Pittsburgh. Two immediate problems cropped up: where to sleep and how to find a job as quickly as possible. If the newcomer had relatives or friends already settled, the solutions were easy: he would be taken home, boarded in a small corner of a tiny tenement room, and introduced to a boss or foreman the next morning. (Novotny 76)

I get to de Milvaukee an' I live vit my brodder George in a boardink house. At furst I vas sick—I vas so sick dat everbody tink dat I vas goink to die. I vas seasick fromm comink over. Den I get vell. . . .

Dis neighbor lady vork in a laundry an' she ask me if I vant to vork. An' I say yeh, anyplace just for vork. So I vork in laundry pressink heavy coats. I got tventy-five cents an hour—ve vorked hard, too!

. . . Grandma Martin worked hard all her life and achieved the Great American Dream that seems to have disappeared in our society today. A penniless farm girl when she arrived, she is now the proud owner of an eight-unit apartment building in Milwaukee. Out of nothing, she created something—quite an accomplishment for an 80-year-old woman who can barely speak the English language. . . . ▣

Professional Model

Commercial fishing was once a major industry on the Great Lakes. In the following excerpts from "There Was a Time . . . ," writer Leonard Palmer shares the story of 79-year-old Jack Myers who grew up on Simmons Island (WI), where his father ran a large commercial fishing operation. ("There Was a Time . . ." is an oral history interview with Jack Myers, compiled by Leonard Palmer. Reprinted by permission of the Kenosha County [WI] Historical Society.)

There Was a Time . . .

Letting Jack Myers tell the story (first person) adds personality to the account.

There was no real industry on the Island other than fishing. My father was, I guess, one of the largest commercial fishermen on the Great Lakes. They fished two boats out of here—the *William Engel*, which was a 78-foot steam tug; and the tug *Sport*, which was a 55-foot tug. My grandfather had skippered the *Sport* over in Michigan, and it was the first metal boat built on the Great Lakes. She was built out of iron. My father fished both of those rigs out of here—he had as many as 27 men working for him, and they were fishing, at one point, ten gangs of nets, ten boxes to a gang. It seems to me, back in those days, that a box of nets was worth a hundred dollars. They were all linen—linen nets.

Because of the ice situation that developed up in Door County, some of the Washington Island fishermen were attracted to Kenosha. The first of those were the Engelson brothers—there were Bill and Martin Engelson, they came down here with the tug *Buick* and they fished out of Kenosha. Then came the Ellefsons . . . I can't remember the name of their tug. And then there was Al Shellswig, who came down with the tug *Palmer*. Then my father had a young guy come down here and work for him by the name of Ray McDonald. Ray came down and fished for my father, and he introduced hook fishing. They'd always been net fishermen at that time, and Ray got my father into fishing hooks. They would alternate between hook fishing and net fishing. They were "set" hooks, and I remember one of the worst jobs I saw them do, [was] when they were clearing hooks because once they reeled all these in, these hooks would become all tangled in the box. They'd take the fish off, and then they had to clear these [hooks] again, so they were ready to set, and there was a little rack in each box, and they had to do this with the hooks (here Jack makes a rolling motion with both hands, as if twirling a line).

The writer adds an occasional parenthetical explanation to clarify the story.

They set the hooks with small chubs. All they caught was lake trout. Perch were never fished commercially then. It was always trout. We used to smoke chubs—my father had a smokehouse on the Island. We had a lot of customers, a lot of the butchers and so on, who sold them in their stores. My brother used to deliver smoked fish to some of these stores.

. . . The fishermen went out except during closed season. This was always a point of interest, because my father always said that it was too bad the fish couldn't read, because they'd have closed season in Wisconsin, but have open season in Illinois, Michigan, and Indiana. And the seasons varied—and very often, if the weather was fair, Michigan boats would come clear across the lake to fish in Wisconsin waters, because it was open season here. Then, as soon as the season closed here, the Wisconsin boats would go down maybe into Illinois. Now, they license only so many boats that fish chubs. I think they have only, maybe, 40 licenses for the whole lake. At one time, they had as many as 15 tugs out of this harbor alone.

Very often, when we had an east wind, in the dead of winter, heavy ice would move in and we'd sit here (his home on the Island) at night, and watch the lights of the boats coming in as they got caught in the ice. Frequently, they'd have to wait for the tug *Sport*—something about the configuration of her hull—she could back through almost anything, and she would back through the ice and make a trail for these vessels to follow in. I can remember my father, they'd leave here at four in the morning and they wouldn't return until nine at night, in the winter. A normal day, they'd maybe be back at five.

. . . I can remember my father would pull out of the lake . . . they would stop fishing if they couldn't get a thousand pounds in a lift. And it was nothing for them to catch two, three, four thousand pounds of fish in a catch. All lake trout. Occasionally a lawyer. A lawyer is in the eel family, a scale-less fish. That was one of the few fish I would eat. It was a very firm-fleshed fish with pink meat. That I would like, because it wouldn't taste as fishy. Trout, to me, was very fat. The biggest trout that I remember my father catching was 44 pounds. But my brother reminds me that he remembers a trout that went 50 pounds.

A tragic event anchors this article in a specific period of history.

. . . Directly across from us was the Hill Steamship Company. They had the *Charles McVay*, the *City of Marquette*—those were two big steamers they had. And then, post-World War I, they bought three wooden mine-sweepers—they were really seagoing tugs—and renamed them the *Sheboygan*, the *Kenosha*, and the *Waukegan*. I also remember the *Wisconsin*. As a matter of fact, our house was headquarters for the press when the *Wisconsin* went down (October 29, 1929). I think we had probably the only telephone on the Island at that time. Our telephone number was 876. The *Chicago Tribune* was here, the *Milwaukee Journal*, and so [on] and so forth, and they were calling their papers getting the reports on the *Wisconsin*. I'll always remember that night, because I was in high school at the time and I was in the Sea Scouts. We were called out of school, the Sea Scouts were, to patrol the beach looking for bodies or anything that washed up from the *Wisconsin*.

The depth of detail provided in this article indicates that Mr. Myers speaks from experience.

In those days, lake passenger shipping was a very common practice. I remember that you could set your watch by the *Christopher Columbus*, which was a whaleback passenger vessel that ran between Chicago and Milwaukee. She would pass here going north at noon and going south back to Chicago at six o'clock. Twelve and six, she would pass the Kenosha light[house], way off shore, of course. There are no big old steamers left. There used to be the *North America*, the *South America*, the *Alabama*, the *Virginia*, the *Nevada*. . . .

I can remember that my brother used to row across the harbor to go to work at the Simmons plant when he was home from the university in the summers. Then he would row back home for lunch and then back again for work in the afternoon. It wasn't like it is now. It was a different time then.

"In 1990 . . . [Lori Beebe] started Beebe's Babies; some days now she auditions more than 150 of them, ranging in age from two weeks to ten years. 'Personality is everything; looks are nothing,' she says." —*Cindy Pearlman*

Venture Report

Many contemporary magazines present articles on different occupations, professions, or businesses. These are venture reports—in-depth investigations into different aspects of the world of work. The information in venture reports is based almost exclusively on interviews, job-site visits, and other types of direct contact.

Nothing Ventured . . . Nothing Gained

Discussion: Do you consider yourself an entrepreneur? No? Well, consider this: Every time you start a new job or plan an extended project or plot the ultimate money-making scheme, you're doing entrepreneurial thinking. In this activity, you are going to put some of that thinking to work. First, select a venture (business, profession, project, team, etc.) that interests you. Thoroughly investigate your subject and write an in-depth report based on your findings. Photographs, illustrations, and interview quotations will add impact to your final product. (You might even consider turning your report into a video documentary.)

Searching and Selecting

1. **Selecting** • Think of occupations, professions, businesses, or organizations that you find interesting or intriguing. (Focus on ventures that are accessible and practical to investigate.)
2. **Exploring** • Think about people who might be able to help you conduct your subject search and places you might visit for ideas. Also review magazines such as *Entrepreneur*, *Omni*, and *Working Woman* for potential subjects.

Generating the Text

3. **Noting** • Determine what you already know about your subject and what you would like to find out or explore. (Are there 5 to 10 key questions about the venture you would like to answer during your investigation?)
4. **Investigating** • Read about your subject, conduct in-person interviews, and gather firsthand experiences. (Don't forget that you can write or call for information as well.)
5. **Assessing** • How will you present your findings? Will you highlight information received during one or more of your interviews? Will you focus more of your attention on your firsthand experiences and observations? Or will you tie in information from a variety of resources? After determining a focus for your report, plan and organize your work accordingly.

Writing and Revising

6. **Writing** • Develop your first draft, working in facts and details according to your planning and organizing. (Include as many important details as possible.)
7. **Revising** • Review, revise, and refine your writing. Make sure that at least one or two classmates review your work as well. Any questions your classmates raise should be addressed during revising.

Evaluating

Does the profile offer an in-depth look at a specific venture?

Has proper attention been given to detail, organization, and clarity?

Will readers learn something from reading this report?

Student Model

Learning to drive a car can be a disheartening (and expensive) venture, as writer Chris Kanarick discovered. A conversational tone makes this report enjoyable as well as informative. (Reprinted with permission from *New Youth Connections: The Magazine Written By and For New York Youth*, January/February 1993.)

They're Driving Me Crazy

The writer introduces the reasons for undertaking his venture—freedom and independence.

Ever since I was little, I wanted to drive. I thought it would be so cool not having to ask anyone for a ride to the mall, or anyplace else for that matter.

Needless to say, I was quite happy when it came time to start driver education. I signed up to take it at a high school near where I live. Soon I would no longer have to thumb a ride to work with my stepfather at six o'clock on a Saturday morning. No longer would I have to greet my dates by saying, " . . .and this is my mom." I was 16 years old, and it was time to break the chains that bound me to Mommy . . . and her car.

When I went to sign up for driver's ed, I was shocked to discover that it cost $275. Driver's ed is not mandatory here in New York; but if you don't take it, you have to wait until you're 18 to get your license. If you do take it, you can get your license a year earlier. It was a lot of money, but $275 was not too high a price to pay for my freedom, right?

The first class was pretty boring. We filled our registration forms and were given our textbooks. Every Monday we met, and the teacher drew diagrams that tried to show the right way to park and turn. We learned about alcohol and driving and about different kinds of insurance policies.

NO ACTION FLICKS

Details of the driver's-ed experience add humor and interest to the report.

Overall, I already knew most of it, like not to drink and drive. They didn't even show those really cool movies like *Blood on the Highway*, the ones where you see cars ramming into people and each other, really gory stuff. Actually, the only film I remember seeing is *Mr. Smith's System of Space-Cushion Driving*. I think I fell asleep.

My first time behind the wheel I think I handled the car pretty well. I didn't hit anything, always a good sign. My major problem was turning. The hardest part was steering the car on the highway and rolling the window up at the same time. (Solution: power windows.)

The driving part was cool, though. We would always make fun of each other and crack jokes. I remember one time when my friend was driving, our teacher, Mr. Spock (we called him that because he had funny ears and showed no emotion), told her to make a left turn, and she quickly responded by turning on the windshield wipers. From then on, every time he wanted her to turn, we would tell her to turn on the wipers.

NOT ENOUGH HANDS-ON EXPERIENCE

We drove on Wednesday afternoon from 4:30 to 6:00. Now, that's one and a half hours for four people. That means each of us got about 20 minutes to drive. When the course ended, I still had no confidence behind the wheel, and I didn't feel ready to take the road test yet.

The writer holds the reader's interest by incorporating specific details and personal thoughts throughout the report.

So I went to the Department of Motor Vehicles (DMV) to take my permit test. With a learner's permit [and if you're 17], you're allowed to practice—but only if you are accompanied by a licensed driver or, if you are 16, with a licensed driving instructor in one of those cars with a brake pedal on the passenger's side. Since I was only 16, in order to practice with Mom or Dad, we would have had to go to Long Island where it was legal.

I decided to go to a private driving school called Scott's. When I first heard the name, I imagined Scotty from Star Trek sitting beside me yelling, "Coptin, ya con't push it any foster than thot!" Instead, all I got was a very nice woman's voice saying, "That'll be $200 for five hour-long lessons."

But at least after that I felt confident behind the wheel. I felt like I could drive. I couldn't parallel park to save my life, but hey, not even Scott can work miracles.

A GOOD INSTRUCTOR IS HARD TO COME BY

Since I'd already passed driver's ed, I didn't have to take a written exam to get my license. I scheduled the road test, and on the morning of the big day, Nick from Scott's Driving School came to pick me up (for an extra $45). You have to use your own car for the road test, and since my parents work, this was the best way. I got in the car and handed him the papers I had with me, and he asked for the rest. Whoops.

I went back inside the house, and my mother and I searched hopelessly for the papers. I went back out and told Nick that I couldn't find them, so he said we would go to the test site. I would probably be permitted to take the test, but they wouldn't give me the results on the spot, like they usually do.

This report is developed in story form, detailing the writer's experiences with driver's education as they unfolded.

Out of the three instructors I had at Scott's Driving School, I think Nick was the best. He taught me how to parallel park using a different technique than anyone else had. Instead of lining up right next to the car you want to park behind and turning the wheel as you back up, he said to line your mirror up with the center of the other car and turn the wheel all the way to the right; then start backing up and straightening out when you're in the right position.

After I took the test, I had the feeling that I had passed. I waited for almost a week after that test to find out that the guy failed me because he said that when I started to make a broken U-turn

The report concludes by summarizing the writer's current situation: he's the owner of a car, but without a license to drive it.

(otherwise known as a K- or three-point turn) away from the curb, I had the car in reverse. So I had to schedule the test all over again.

The next time, John from Scott's picked me up (for $78 this time because it wasn't part of my original package deal) to take me to the test site. First we had a little practice lesson in which I screwed everything up, and John was no help at all.

STRIKE TWO

We got to the site and this time I had all the papers with me, so I could find out I failed on the spot. That's right, this time they failed me for parking. The driving inspector was a lot nicer, but apparently, if you touch the curb, it's automatic failure. Which, if you ask me, is totally unfair because if you can handle a car, and can drive well and safely, then parking should not count so much. Of course, that's only my opinion.

When you fail the road test twice on the same permit, you lose the permit, and it has to be renewed.

So here's the present situation: I am 17 years old, I have a car that I bought from my stepsister, the car is registered with license plates and the whole bit, I am paying $1,400 a year for insurance, I know how to drive, but I don't have my license yet.

The other night, I wanted to go out to the movies with my friends, but my friend's car had just broken down. So I let him drive my car. I put gas in the car, and I haven't even driven it yet.

To tell the truth, it's really starting to get to me. Now, I have to renew my learner's permit for $10 and take the road test all over again for a third time. The whole thing just doesn't seem worth it. I tell you, it's making me car-azy.

Professional Model

In this report, writer Cindy Pearlman captures the novelty and humor of Lori Beebe's business, Beebe's Babies—a company that casts babies in television advertising. (This report originally appeared in *Chicago* magazine, January 1993. It is reprinted with permission.)

The writer's humorous approach captures an important aspect of this venture: Beebe's ability to take things in stride.

Direct quotations bring interest and humor to the report, allowing the reader to learn about the business and about the entrepreneur who runs it.

Infant Gratification

In Lori Beebe's business, success is measured in an odd way. "If I haven't been peed on once, something is wrong," she says. So it goes when you're a baby wrangler—someone who casts and directs babies in television commercials. Beebe does just that, with spots running this month for Clorox, Tyko, Osco, and Playskool. Hers is not a job for most grownups: In fact, it's full of life's little ironies. Consider that in the Clorox spot Beebe, 33, had to show a group of nine-month-old babies how to get messy. "I do whatever it takes to bring out the performer in the child," she says.

For a recent Huggies commercial, Beebe cast 25 babies, including The Biter. "He couldn't wait to sink his teeth into the other babies," she says. Sometimes she loses control—or her charges do. She was doing a diaper commercial with six naked babies. "One started peeing and suddenly they were all peeing. It was like someone flipped a switch."

When Beebe got into the business, she was a Naperville mom bored with staying home. She took her then nine-month-old son to a cattle call for a Service Merchandise ad. "On the set I was telling him what to do and finally a casting director came over and asked me if I wanted to work on her next baby job."

In 1990, she started Beebe's Babies; some days now she auditions more than 150 of them, ranging in age from two weeks to ten years. "Personality is everything; looks are nothing," she says.

Considering that she comes home with black-and-blue knees and Froot Loops in her hair, you'd think the last thing she'd want to see was kids. "I never get tired of them. I love coming home to my four boys," she says. And at least they don't bite. "They're a kick," she says, "and I don't mean that literally."

Professional Model

Writer David Thome based the following venture report on interviews with his subject, the owner of a limousine business. The result is a personal, interesting, and informative account of one young woman's "ride" to success. (This article originally appeared in *Business Connections*, October 1992. It is reprinted with permission.)

The report immediately introduces the entrepreneur and her venture.

Profile: Lambie's Limousines

Many entrepreneurs continue working for someone else until a new venture gets established. But, though Shiela Lambie cut back from three jobs to one while getting Lambie's Luxury Limousines off and rolling, her new business didn't shift into full gear until she made it a full-time priority.

. . . "I get my entrepreneurial drive from my mother," Lambie says. "She's the person who pushed me into how I do things. She always told me that there's nothing you can't do if you put your heart into it, and that whatever you do, do it to the best of your ability."

. . . The day after graduating from high school, Lambie went to work in the business department of the Kenosha Public Library, where she did general secretarial work and some bookkeeping. She says she liked the job, but she wasn't sure where she wanted her career path to lead. So, she took classes at Gateway Technical Institute (now Gateway Technical College) to fill the core requirements for a degree.

She never received a degree, but instead took a job in the service department of Vigansky's TV and Appliance, where she did secretarial work and served as a dispatcher.

She stayed with Vigansky's for four years, working up to manager of the parts department.

Background information establishes the starting point for the venture.

"I left after the birth of my first child, thinking I'd never work again," she says. "I had this idea of being a wonderful, perfect mother who stayed home all the time. Within two weeks, I was back at Vigansky's."

The store had already filled Lambie's old position, but the owners needed someone to sell microwave ovens—a new, unfamiliar item at the time. After taking cooking courses offered by a few major manufacturers, Lambie gave cooking demonstrations at the store. About the same time, she started teaching cooking classes at Gateway and worked independently as a home decorator.

She kept on working all three jobs to support herself and her two children after a divorce in the early '80s. A few years later she became engaged to Al Lambie, an over-the-road trucker who was growing tired of making the long hauls. Vigansky's, hurt by the recession and the closing of Kenosha's AMC plant, began to cut back Lambie's hours. At the same time Lambie's sister, Sherri, and her husband, John, bought a limousine so they could make extra money chauffeuring wedding parties on weekends, but with John's job as a sheriff's deputy, the couple found it increasingly difficult to continue moonlighting.

Lambie recognized an opportunity in this confluence of events. "It was incredibly good timing," Lambie says. "Sherri and John wanted to get rid of the limo, and Al and I thought a limo service could be a good business if you did things a certain way."

Shiela and Al bought a house and used the equity to buy the limo for $9,000. At first, they too limited the limo service to weekends, while Al kept his job and Shiela quit Vigansky's to open a kiosk for Total Furniture in the Kenosha Factory Outlet Centre. They soon found that with the cost of gas, repairs, insurance, phone calls, advertising and hiring an answering service, the limousine service did little to enhance their income.

Direct quotations add authenticity, insight, and human interest to the report.

"In fact, we were losing money," Lambie says. "I was taking my entire paycheck and putting it into the limo business. We weren't getting the results we wanted, so we decided we had to make a commitment."

Lambie quit her job in 1985 to devote her energies to the limo service. Business doubled the first month and tripled again in the second.

At first, most of Lambie's business came from weddings. "Our biggest competition was funeral homes," she recalls. "Of course, they all had black cars, so rather than go head-to-head with them, I had only white cars."

To expand her business, Lambie placed ads in the Yellow Pages and *Happenings* magazine. She did some prospecting. And, by approaching businesses about driving executives and clients to and from airports, she hit upon a rich vein that had been largely untapped in this locality.

The growth of the venture is described step-by-step.

By 1989, Lambie's had moved into a former boat builder's shop. . . . The company grew to 11 cars that year—still mostly white. Clientele included steady corporate customers, as well as one-time patrons who wanted to ride to the prom in style.

. . . Today, transporting corporate executives and guests has supplanted weddings, dances, and funerals as Lambie's bread and butter. And she's not shy about telling people that taking a limo can be as good for one's business as it is for one's ego.

"Often, we're driving people who are on their way to important business conferences, and they can relax or get a lot of work done if they take a limo," she says. "And on the way home, they can take care of their expense accounts and finish any other paperwork in the car, so that when they get home, they can watch TV or play with their kids."

The way of the future is offering more service, and more services, she asserts.

. . . Lambie sums up the importance of service with this story: "One of our drivers took a man to Chicago for a morning meeting. He was supposed to return at 11 a.m., but the meeting kept getting delayed. The chauffeur went out and got the man some lunch so it was waiting for him when he finally got back into the car at 2 p.m. The guy was overjoyed. He said, 'You don't know how many lunches I miss because of meetings that get delayed.' Little things make a difference. We like to spoil our clients."

Spoiling clients, of course, begins with the car. Since none of the major automakers builds limos anymore, all new limos have to be custom-built by cutting stock models in half and extending them in the middle. Add posh interiors, compact disc juke boxes, cellular phones, color TVs, and wet bars, and the price can run up to well over $60,000.

The report ends with the subject's business philosophy: a statement that summarizes her entrepreneurial spirit.

. . . Lambie said that in spite of the rising cost of cars, insurance, repairs, and gas, she expects her business to grow over the next few years. She should know: Lambie's has already grown from $5,000 in sales in 1985 to nearly $500,000 in 1991.

She has two simple secrets for success: work hard, and keep in touch.

"You work three times as hard when you work for yourself as you do working for someone else," she says. "An employee can punch a clock and go home. When you work for yourself you can't do that. The business becomes part of your life. . . ."

" 'You can imagine how these people felt,' says Shaw. 'They had nothing when they got here. They were just full of hope.' The immigrants could not speak the American language, they did not know American customs, but they knew they wanted to be American." —*Sylvia Chan*

Personal Research Report

A personal research report presents the story of a writer's investigation into a subject of personal interest. A research report may discuss a writer's experience with a certain new technology, describe a writer's attempt to learn about a particular place, share the story of a writer's investigation into a current fad, and so on.

"I was just wondering . . ."

Discussion: Investigate a subject of personal interest and compile a report based on your discoveries. Your subject may be related to a profession, a place, a lifestyle, an upcoming purchase (the best computer for the money), a quirky curiosity (how do you tear down a building?), and so on. Base your investigation as much as possible on interviews, firsthand experiences, and observations. Then share the results of your work in one of two ways—as a personalized story recalling the details of your research as it unfolded or as a more traditional, objective report. Refer to the guidelines below and the models that follow to help you develop your work.

Searching and Selecting

1. **Searching** • To begin your subject search, think of the different categories listed in the opening discussion (professions, places, etc.). What career would you like to would pursue? Is there a particular place or building that you would like to explore?
2. **Reviewing** • If you are still not sure what to write about, review the local newspaper or the yellow pages for ideas, or brainstorm for subjects with your classmates. (Try to select a subject that stems from a genuine interest and is within your abilities to research.)

Generating the Text

3. **Planning** • Determine what you already know about your subject, what you hope to find out, and how you plan on conducting your research. Remember: Your first and primary source of information should be people.
4. **Exploring** • Make contacts. Conduct interviews and record observations. Also refer to magazines and books that have been recommended to you.
5. **Assessing** • Decide how you are going to compile the results of your research. A personalized account of your work should address four basic areas: *what I already knew, what I hoped to find out, what happened as I conducted my investigation*, and *what I learned*. If you are going to compile a more traditional report, decide on a focus for your work and plan accordingly.

Writing and Revising

6. **Writing** • Develop your first draft according to your planning and organizing.
7. **Revising** • Carefully review, revise, and refine your writing. Make sure that your writing accurately reflects the results of your investigation, and double-check to make sure that you quote your sources correctly.

Evaluating

Is the report informative, entertaining, and based on sincere investigative efforts?
Has proper attention been given to accuracy and detail?
Will readers appreciate the treatment of this subject?

Student Model

Memorable childhood experiences often influence a person's decision to investigate a particular profession or occupation. In the following research report, the lingering memory of his grandmother's funeral motivates writer Ben Meyer to investigate the mortuary business. Notice that this model is compiled as a *personalized* story recalling the details of an interview and a visit.

The Dead Business

"You're going to tour a what?"

"A funeral home."

My friends were shocked. They giggled as they described scenes from *Night of the Living Dead* and *The Shining*.

Their ghoulish stories didn't frighten me; I was scared of something else.

When I was ten years old, my grandmother died. When my family arrived at the funeral home to view the body, I noticed the funeral director standing in the corner looking like a too-eager-to-please salesman who'd made a deal he didn't deserve . . . a sort of twentieth-century grim reaper in a business suit. The guy's plastic, thin-lipped smile seemed unnatural—almost glib—in the presence of a death that unnaturally stopped my grandmother's beating heart midway through the doxology that cold January night in Calvary Christian Reformed Church. Death shattered her relationship with me. No more cookies, no more coloring books, no more Rook games, no more laughing, no more.

I chose to investigate a funeral home to cure myself of the grim-reaper syndrome. But I was still scared. I drove to the VanderPloeg Furniture Store/Funeral Home with visions of the thin-lipped smile I had seen when I was ten.

When I walked inside, I half expected to meet a well-dressed ghoul standing by his cash register, sharpening his sickle. Suddenly, a man from behind his desk hopped out of his chair.

"Hi!"

I looked at the tall, smiling man, paused a moment, and glanced back at the door. His skinny partner had stepped in front of the exit while scribbling on tags that dangled from Lazy Boy rockers. I realized this interview was something painful I had to do . . . like getting a tetanus shot.

Howard Biernink led me into a jungle of furniture until he found a soft, purple couch. We sat down, and he narrated the tale of the furniture store/funeral home.

In 1892, a pioneer community established the town of Sioux Center, Iowa. Winter storms and disease pummeled the tiny community, and soon someone was needed to bury the dead. A funeral director wasn't available; a furniture craftsman was. He was the only

This essay grabs the reader's attention by beginning with a question—and a rather shocking answer.

The writer's account of first entering the funeral home reflects his negative feelings toward morticians.

The interview with Mr. Biernink and the tour of the embalming room provide the writer with all he needs to know for his report.

Honest expressions like "I was baffled" and specific details like "Howard pulled out another bottle . . ." add a personal touch to the report.

person who had the tools, the hardwood, and the knowledge to make coffins. As a result, VanderPloeg Furniture Store/Funeral Home was born.

Today, a funeral home director must complete two years of college and one year of embalming school to become a qualified embalmer. After he or she graduates, the person must perform as an apprentice for one year. Every subsequent year the embalmer must pass a state exam in order to retain certification for his work.

"But why a funeral home director?" I was baffled. Why would anyone want to embalm dead bodies for a living?

"Because it's a family business." Howard smiled as if he expected my question. "VanderPloegs and Bierninks have run this place for generations. Today it's difficult to start a funeral home because there are so many of them with long histories and good reputations."

After he buried the rest of my questions, Howard asked if I wanted to see the embalming room.

"Ok," I said, still a little scared.

He led me through doors, hallways, staircases, and a well-lighted display room containing several coffins. Finally, we entered a small, cold room that contained a row of cupboards, a large ceramic table, and a small machine that resembled a bottled water cooler.

"We like to keep the room cold when we're not using it."

"What is all this stuff?"

Howard described the process of embalming.

The purpose of embalming a corpse is to extend the period for viewing the body. Embalming consists of draining the body fluids and replacing them with embalming fluid.

Howard opened a cupboard and pulled out a bottle of fluid.

"Here . . . smell."

"It sorta smells like Pepto-Bismal."

After he embalms the body, Howard applies makeup so the body appears "more natural." His cosmetics consist of powders and tints sold by the local Avon lady.

"But sometimes we also have to use this." Howard pulled out another bottle from the cupboard.

"Tissue builder?" I asked, squinting at the label.

"It's sort of like silicon implants. We inject it into the cheeks if they're sunk in, like the cheeks of a cancer victim."

When the body is ready for burial, the funeral director must show a price list to the family of the deceased. The Funeral Rule, adopted in 1984 by the Federal Trade Commission, requires that a price list be shown to the family before they see caskets, cement boxes, and vaults. The purpose of the Funeral Rule is to prevent unethical funeral directors from manipulating the customer with comments like, "But that's a pauper's casket, you wouldn't want to bury your mother in that. Bury her in this beauty over here." Unfortunately, only a third of the country's 22,000 funeral homes abide by the Funeral Rule.

"After I show them where the casket is, I step away from the customers and let them talk among themselves," said Howard. "It's unethical to bother the family at this difficult time."

When they bury the body, Howard and his partner place the casket in either a cement box or a vault. A cement box is a container that is neither sealed or waterproofed; a vault is both sealed and waterproofed.

"Years ago, cemeteries began to sink and cave in on spots. That's why state authorities demanded containers. It makes the cemetery look nicer."

After the tour I asked Howard, "What impact has this job made on your life?"

He smiled, glanced at the ceiling and said, "It's very fulfilling. My partner and I try to comfort families during a very upsetting and emotional time, and it strengthens our bond with them."

The writer closes by explaining what he has learned from his investigation.

As I walked back to my car, I thought about Howard's comment. He was right. His job isn't to remind me of broken relationships; he helps create new ones. He comforts families and encourages them to move on in their lives.

I started up my car and decided I wasn't afraid of the grim reaper anymore. I'm still scared of death. I'm still scared of the pain of losing someone I love. But am I scared of the grim reaper? No. The grim reaper has been replaced by the compassionate funeral director. He is as necessary in a community as the man in the local supermarket, providing food and services to the community.

Student Model

It is the history of an "incredible place" that prompts this detailed research report by Sylvia Chan. Notice that this report is more objective than the other models. (Reprinted from *East Bay Teen Voices* [July 19, 1991], which is published by the Center for Integration and Improvement of Journalism at San Francisco State University.)

Angel Island Reveals Poignant History

On this day of the eclipse, the sun continues to beat down on Angel Island.

People in this state park on the 11th of July are asking others if they have seen the overlapping of the moon and sun. Many say no, they did not see it, they did not even notice it. Not surprising though, because most likely, their attentions have been focused on the incredible history of this place.

The writer puts Angel Island in historical perspective by providing background information about this setting.

Between 1910 and 1940, Angel Island served as an immigration station for the West Coast. Immigrants had to pass through this station to either obtain entrance to the United States or be sentenced to deportation back to where they had come from. Ninety-five percent of these immigrants were Chinese, while the other five percent were Japanese mail-order brides, Europeans, and Africans.

Due to the Chinese Exclusion Law of 1882, it was very difficult for a Chinese person to obtain citizenship in the U.S. The immigrant had to have a relation that was a citizen, or arrive in the U.S. as a student. It was also much easier for wealthy families to obtain citizenship. Many were honest about their backgrounds, but many Chinese obtained false papers claiming they were somebody else. All had to endure a grueling interrogation process to test the truth of their stories. The film *Carved in Silence* by filmmaker Felicia Lowe gives examples of the questions asked by the Angel Island administration. "How many windows do you have in your house?" "Do you have a dog?" "How many feet apart is your house from your neighbors?" The same interrogation questions could be asked of the same person repeatedly for confirmation purposes.

A good deal of the important information for this report is gained through an interview with a park official.

Since the questioning was exhaustive and extremely detailed, a series of questioning sessions would usually have to be conducted for each immigrant. According to park docent John Shaw, the shortest stay at the island was three days, while the longest was 22 months.

Sometimes when immigrants arrived on the island, they would have such a stench on their persons and belongings from the boat that officials would fumigate them. If the immigrants were sick, they were sent to the quarantine station. Otherwise, they were sent to the interrogation room in the Administration Building or to the living quarters.

"You can imagine how these people felt," says Shaw. "They had nothing when they got here. They were just full of hope." The immigrants could not speak the American language, they did not know American customs, but they knew they wanted to be American. The stories of "gum san," or "Gold Mountain," meaning California, were those of a beautiful, prosperous land, one where all people could succeed and make a better life for themselves.

The green foliage of Angel Island fits the image of the Gold Mountain. The air is clean, the trees rustle gently in the wind, and the view of the San

Francisco Bay is magnificent. But most likely, the detainees at the immigration camp never got a chance to see these things without the glare of a guard nearby. Shaw explains that guards followed the immigrants everywhere they went. No one was ever left alone.

Ms. Chan's close observations help readers see Angel Island in their mind's eye.

In seeing how cramped the living quarters were, one sees that these people could never be alone on their stay here. One hundred women were crammed into a room the size of a large classroom. . . . There was less than half a foot of space between the three-tiered steel bunk-bed structures. The beds themselves were about two feet wide. Sometimes a mother and her child would have to share one of these beds. Families were always separated, not even allowed to speak to each other. The rooms were dirty and loud, says Shaw. Many resorted to carving poetry on the wooden walls to vent frustrations about their situation. One of the poems, supposedly written by a woman, speaks of leaving the station:

From now on I am departing from this building
All of my fellow villagers are rejoicing with me
Don't say that everything within is Western styled
Even if it is built of jade, it has turned into a cage
Detained in this wooden house for several tens of days
It is all because of the Mexican exclusion law which implicates me
It's a pity heroes have no way of exercising their prowess
I can only await the word so that I can sway Zu's whip.

Note how smoothly the writer is able to incorporate the comments of the interviewee, her own observations, and other facts and details gained through reading.

Though poetry on the walls could expose one's soul, it was much easier for the Chinese to expose their souls than their bodies. The toilets and bathing facilities in the living quarters were completely open, with no doors or covers of any sort. "The Chinese are very modest; they don't like to expose their bodies," says Shaw. In entering the washroom called the "New Women's Toilets" (because there was an older bathroom facility, hence the word "new"), one can almost feel the embarrassment of the women at the station. Also felt by many is the presence of spirits in this room. Undocumented reports by witnesses on the island tell a story that explains this presence.

At times, the U.S. government would sentence immigrants to be deported because they could not pass the interrogations or could not prove their rights to American citizenship. For the immigrant, returning to China was an admittance of failure. Their families had sent them to the United States to become a success. The only time they could return to China was when they had succeeded in the U.S., not before. Success was defined as making enough money to support the rest of the family. Rather than return, some chose to commit suicide. The sounds of their self-inflicted deaths were muddled by the running water of the showers.

Ms. Chan closes her report on an emotional note.

The air in the washroom does hang heavy, and if not with spirits, then with memories. The toilets lie rusting, the tiled walls are covered with mildew, the sinks are dry with brown dust, and the smell of age lingers in the air. Many have forgotten about this little immigration station in the San Francisco Bay. But among the wooden walls of a building on this island, immigrants once lived. And carved on a part of the wall in the men's living quarters is this poem:

There are tens of thousands of poems on these walls
They are all cries of suffering and sadness
The day I am rid of this prison and become successful
I must remember that this chapter once existed.

Professional Model

Curiosity plays an important role in personal research. In the following model, columnist Jan Brunvand investigates the origin of an urban legend—and, while the exact source is never identified, the writer discovers some interesting information along the way. (Reprinted from *Curses! Broiled Again!* by Jan Harold Brunvand, with the permission of W. W. Norton & Company, Inc. Copyright © 1989 by Jan Harold Brunvand.)

The reason for the writer's investigation is immediately identified.

"The Body on the Car"

The question is: Was Ann Landers taken in by a horrifying urban legend? Many of her readers—at least, those who are also *my* readers—seem to think she was, and they wrote to ask my opinion.

People from coast to coast, plus a few from abroad, sent me Ann's column dated September 24, 1986. In it, a reader relates a tragic story of drunken driving.

It seems that a woman's husband came home from work at 2:00 A.M., cockeyed drunk. He managed to get up for work in time, though, and began pulling his car out of the garage, into the driveway. His wife realized that he had forgotten to take his lunch and began running out to give it to him. She got "as far as the porch and fainted." The husband got out of the car to see what was the matter. There, embedded in the grill of his car, was the lifeless body of an eight-year-old girl.

The letter was signed, "Still Horrified in Portland."

Ann Landers replied, "What a grisly story! Bone-chilling, to say the least. I hope it makes an impact on drivers who chance 'a few' and don't think it will make any difference."

I also hope it has an impact, but not because I think it's true. Until someone can offer conclusive proof that this cautionary tale really happened, I'll have to say that that's just what it is: a mini-morality play that got started up and gained currency because it demonstrates our rising concern with the dangers of drunken driving.

The writer analyzes a letter to Ann Landers and then contacts MADD to get their feelings about the authenticity of the letter.

There are a number of questionable elements here. For one thing, there are no corroborating details of time or place. The letter writer simply begins, "I would like to tell you about another woman who had a nervous breakdown because of the same problem"—i.e., her husband's drunken driving, discussed in a previous Ann Landers column.

I called Mothers Against Drunk Driving (MADD) in Houston, Texas, which keeps track of alcohol-related accidents. They told me that they assumed the story to be true—but even they could provide no further details.

Yet, in April 1987—seven months after the Ann Landers column—I received a letter from a Covina, California, reader who had heard a variation of "The Body on the Car" told at a Students Against Drunk Driving (SADD) presentation. In this version, the wife goes out for the morning newspaper and discovers the "embedded" body, while her husband, still passed out from the night before, is lying on the living-room couch. Either other versions of the story had been circulating, or the one in the Ann Landers column was acquiring variations from repetitions.

Another letter sent in the spring of '87 reported "The Body on the Car"

Most of the evidence and information for this report are provided by individuals who read Mr. Brunvand's newspaper column.

told in Carbondale, Illinois. One slight variation here: she was a seven-year-old girl.

The notion implied in all versions that a young child was out on the streets at 2:00 A.M. seems farfetched. We're asked to believe that the girl became integrated with the car's grillwork (like the VW Bug in the preceding legend) instead of being hurled through the air, which is what normally happens in a head-on collision with a pedestrian. We're also supposed to accept the idea that the driver was so drunk, he didn't notice that he'd just hit a young child—nor did anyone else on the road—as he drove around town with her riding on his car like a hood ornament. Yet, this semiconscious man was still alert enough to park his car in the garage without incident.

The fainting woman is another familiar touch of urban-legend fantasy, as is the unlikely detail that the driver was up bright and early for work the day after his adventurous night.

One reader sending me the clip added the footnote, "Please, Ann, tell us it's just a story." Several others sent me copies of their own letters to Ann Landers, tipping her off that it smelled like a legend to them. But as far as I know, there has been no disclaimer for this one in any subsequent Ann Landers column.

I suppose I cannot blame Ann; she really wasn't the first to spread the story. A reader wrote to me some weeks before the Ann Landers column (letter dated August 27, 1986) that she had heard it told in Santa Monica, California. At this time, it was attributed to the traditional "friend of a friend" and had the variation of the man himself making the discovery. He goes to a party, where he gets drunk. His host and hostess try to make him stay over, but he insists on driving home. In the morning, he returns to his car and sees "draped across the hood . . . a dead body."

The day after most of the above discussion appeared in my column (in late March 1987), Professor Malcolm K. Shuman of the Museum of Geoscience at Louisiana State University in Baton Rouge wrote. He remembers reading a story very similar to the legend while browsing through the comic-book collection of a younger cousin some thirty years ago ("ca. 1953, give or take a couple of years").

As Professor Shuman recalls the horror-comic episode, a man driving on a highway (fast, but not under the influence) is well aware that he has struck a pedestrian but decides to ignore the accident and drive on. But in the next town, an angry crowd stops him when they see the dead pedestrian caught between bumper and grill. So the hit-and-run element of the story seems to have existed much earlier than the 1980s, although the ultimate source of all details in "The Body on the Car" is still obscure.

The writer closes by explaining what he has learned from this mini-investigation.

Considering all these references to "The Body on the Car"—yes, folks, I do believe that Ann Landers fell for a legend, although her motives were only the best. After all, the reason so many grisly urban legends like this one continue to circulate is that they teach us worthwhile lessons in highly dramatic ways. The warning contained in "The Body on the Car" story should certainly be heeded, but that does not mean that the incident is true.

Moral(s): Don't drink and drive. But don't believe all the scare stories you hear, either.

Creative Writing

"The struggle upwards is a battle against strength, against the constant thudding of the heart, against the burns and scratches of the rope that suddenly lashes out to unseat the unwanted guest. The girls could only wander past, closing their eyes to the glimpses of what the next hour held in store . . ."

—Elizabeth Balin

Fictionalized Imitation

Writers may imitate their favorite authors out of respect and admiration for their unique styles. The purpose of such exercises is to learn about or experiment with new writing techniques. Other imitations may be intentionally critical in a comical or exaggerated way. This type of imitation is called *parody*.

Don't Hesitate . . . Imitate!

Discussion: Write a fictionalized imitation (or parody) based on specific features related to a particular writer or literary form. The success of your writing depends upon your familiarity with the writer or form you choose to imitate. The actual subject or situation for your writing can be as serious or as playful as you want to make it. Refer to the guidelines below and the models on the following pages to help you develop your work.

Searching and Selecting

1. **Selecting** • Choose a writer (*Jack London*, *Ernest Hemingway*, *Emily Dickinson*, *Dr. Seuss*) or a literary form (*myth*, *mystery story*, *parable*) to imitate.
2. **Reviewing** • If you have trouble coming up with a subject, review your class notes for writers or forms you have studied. Ask your teacher for recommendations. Talk to classmates. (Or, if all else fails, imitate one of the models we have provided.)

Generating the Text

3. **Noting** • Study the specific features the author uses to get his or her writing to look and sound the way it does. Study sentence length, word choice, unique expressions, tone, rhythm, punctuation, etc. (It's easier to focus your attention on one particular passage and try to imitate that.) Or study the specific parts of a particular form.
4. **Planning** • Select a specific subject (situation) to use as a starting point for your own work, and then make some preliminary decisions about your writing. How are you going to start? What specific elements are you going to imitate? Is the writing going to basically follow a passage you have studied, and so on? (If you can't think of a subject or situation for your writing, try reworking one of your old papers into a fictionalized imitation.)

Writing and Revising

5. **Writing** • Write your first draft, imitating your author (or chosen form) to the best of your ability. Don't expect to zip through your writing. This type of writing has to be approached carefully and selectively.
6. **Revising** • Carefully read and review your writing. Have a classmate read it as well. Then revise and refine until your imitation works as well as you can make it work.

Evaluating

Is it clear that this writing is an imitation of another writer or a literary form?

Does the writing form a meaningful whole so that it is easy to follow?

Will the writing hold the interest and attention of the reader?

Help File: In a summary paragraph, indicate which elements in your writing are most easily identified with the writer or literary form you have imitated.

Student Model

Student writer Kristin Ammon used Geoffrey Chaucer's *Canterbury Tales* as the model for the following imitation. Her writing presents an unsavory character in much the same way as the old master would have done it.

The poem mimics Chaucer's use of rhymed couplets.

The writer presents details suggesting that the lawyer is, at best, self-serving.

THE CROOKED LAWYER

There's a posh office, right down the long hall,
Where all his diplomas hang on the wall.
His hair is slicked back, he greets you with, "Hi!"
In a pressed suit and conservative tie.
You tell him the facts, so he'll understand;
He says, "Thanks. That will be a cool five grand."
His price is high and his answers are short —
He's a millionaire before he's in court.
He works in, and I'm sure you've guessed by now,
The law office of Dewey, Cheetum, and Howe.

Student Model

Student writer Helen Stickney chose to imitate the moral fable in this parody. The writer follows the rules for writing a fable but obviously has had a great deal of fun bending and stretching this form in the process. (This model first appeared in the December/January 1991 issue of *Merlyn's Pen: The National Magazine of Student Writing*. It is reprinted with permission.)

This model begins in typical fable fashion: "Once upon a time . . ."

The wordplay and use of contemporary expressions add humor to the fable.

Like all fables, this model ends with a moral—in this case, a clever reshaping of a familiar moral.

A Word to the Wise

Once upon a time a hen had three chicks. They were fine little girls, so she decided to make them baseball pros. The first thing she had to do was teach them to catch a ball.

The hen took her eldest daughter, and they began tossing the ball to each other. They had not been playing for long when the rooster, the chick's dad, came along. He looked at his daughter's feeble efforts to catch the ball and burst out laughing.

"My grandmother can catch better than you! You're a wimp!" the rooster called, and the chick was so upset that she ran into the woods and was never seen again.

There was nothing for the hen to do but teach her middle child to catch the ball. They hadn't been playing long when the rooster came back. Again, he made fun of his daughter's lack of skill, calling her a clumsy cluck, and she burst out crying. She cried until she floated away in a river of tears and was lost.

Now the hen was fuming, but there was nothing for her to do but teach her youngest daughter to catch.

Sure enough, before long, the rooster wandered over to their game. He saw how badly his daughter was doing. But when he opened his beak to let the insults fly, the hen, seeing her chance, threw the ball at him. The ball lodged in the rooster's throat and killed him on impact.

Mother Hen resumed her game with her daughter and, in a few years, turned her into the best chicken baseball player in the world.

The moral: Don't hound your chickens before they catch.

Student Model

In this fictionalized imitation the student writer, Elizabeth Balin, successfully captures both the style and tone used by Charles Dickens in *A Tale of Two Cities*. The model demonstrates not only a firm grasp of various technical elements of Dickens' writing, but also a feel for his treatment of subject matter. (Note: Ms. Balin's model results from an assignment in which she was asked to imitate a 20-line passage from *A Tale of Two Cities*.)

. . . It Was the Worst of Classes

Thus it had come to pass, that Gym Class was the triumphant perfection of inconvenience. The shivering group of girls, with much dread and consternation, filed singly through the hollow corridor, over the waxed and weary floor (polished into submission so many decades before beneath the well-calloused and competent hands of its guardian), and through the gaping set of doors, solidly wooden like all else, following in the footsteps of the hordes of anxious youths of last year, yesterday, tomorrow that had and would burst through those aging floodgates. And when the last captive had passed through the gateway, the door would creep closed, ever so slowly, sending its ominous shriek to echo through the room and into the very souls of its victims until it would shudder with the noise. The girls, blinking away the malevolent fluorescent bulbs, breathing in the pungent fragrances of exertion, stumbled forward through the thick and impersonal dusty haze, towards the solitary figure that waited expectantly at the front. With each step deeper came more terrifying visions. In one corner, the vicious glare of metal, the cruel pull-up bar, its icy smoothness marred only by the bruises of some previous victim's grip, the scars of sweat and agony in the hopeless struggle for a few more seconds of glory before the strain became too much, and her body fluttered, then trembled, then shook violently until the tragic release let her fall back down to reality and humility. The victory would always be short lived and then quickly forgotten. From the ceiling leers the most frightening device of them all, the serpentine rope that sleeps silently until it feels the weight of its prey who, like the panic-stricken feline clutching violently to its tree branch to escape the jaws of the enemy below, scrambles from the shelter of the ground to appease the demanding bellows of the instructor's whistle. The struggle upwards is a battle against strength, against the constant thudding of the heart, against the burns and scratches of the rope that suddenly lashes out to unseat the unwanted guest. The girls could only wander past, closing their eyes to the glimpses of what the next hour held in store, but never quite shutting out the urgent cries and scents of exhaustion that emanated from the chamber. But the journey was finished, the waiting was over, and with a deep sigh of resignation, each girl stood to face the indifferent teacher and his glittering whistle to hear what tortures the day would bring and, as always, to persevere. ▣

The opening lines immediately incorporate many of Dickens' stylistic techniques: lengthy sentences, parenthetical additions, personification, etc.

The writer mimics Dickens' use of extensive, detailed description to help establish the emotional tone in this model.

Professional Model

Ernest Hemingway, the famous "Papa" of American literary style, has had a profound impact on writers all over the world. The Hemingway style, so deceptively simple on the surface, stubbornly resists mastery. The author of this piece, a high-school English teacher, admits his inability to imitate the master, escaping instead to the safer refuge of parody. The writer bases his parody on the scene at the end of *For Whom the Bell Tolls* where the hero is waiting for and thinking about his imminent death.

Short sentences and repetition of key words and phrases, characteristic of the Hemingway style, are exaggerated.

The hero's concern regarding the test on Faulkner points to the dramatic differences in style between the two writers.

The English Test

The test would come soon. It would be a difficult test and he did not want to think about the difficulty. He truly did not wish to think at all. He truly did not want to think about the test and its difficulty. English tests were bad at all times and this one he knew would be very bad. Don't think about the bad, he told himself. The worst part, of course, is the waiting. Yes, the waiting is always bad. Don't think about the bad, he told himself. Bad waiting for a bad test. No, it certainly would not be a good test at all. It would be very bad.

If you have to think, he thought, you could think of something pleasant. You do not have to think about the test. You can think of many other things that are pleasant and not think about the test at all. Better not to think about the test then. Better to just let it come. It will come, of course. Of a certainty it will come. Think of something pleasant. Do not think of the test coming or its degree of difficulty. It will be of a high degree of difficulty. Of that there is a certainty. Of many things there is no certainty. But of the difficulty of this test, there is a very great level of certainty.

The test will be on Mr. William Faulkner, he of the extensive sentences. Do not think of Mr. Faulkner and his very long sentences. The sentences have been written. You cannot unwrite Mr. Faulkner's sentences. The sentences will come on the test. You will have to read Mr. Faulkner's sentences. There will be a great many sentences. The sentences will be very, very long. There will be many adjectives. Certainly there will be adjectives. Of the adjectives you may be certain. Definitely it is the time now to stop the thinking. ▣

"I was transfixed by her face that torpedoed the room with brilliance. She pirouetted problem after problem on the blackboard. We all thought genius. Norma is a mathematical genius." —Sonia Sanchez

Genre Writing

Writers are naturally influenced by the different types of stories they enjoy reading. For example, if they like to read science fiction or mysteries, it would follow that they may also like to write stories of this type. Popular genres, or story types, include science fiction, science fantasy, mystery, urban fiction, and contemporary drama.

According to Form

Discussion: Write an original short story based on your understanding of a particular genre (science fiction, science fantasy, mystery, urban fiction, contemporary drama, horror, etc.). If you happen to be well-read in a certain genre (perhaps you love mystery stories), you'll want to develop a story of that type—not only because it is interesting to you, but also because you understand how such a story is put together. The guidelines below and the models that follow will be especially helpful if you first need to develop an interest in and an understanding of a particular genre.

Searching and Selecting

1. **Searching** • Read the models that follow for examples of three different genres: *science fiction*, *mystery*, and *urban fiction*. Also read additional examples of these or other genre types. (Ask your classmates and teacher for recommended titles.)
2. **Selecting** • After reading in and among the different genres, decide which type of story you would like to write. Then select a story of this type to serve as a basic reference model for your own work.

Generating the Text

3. **Analyzing** • Carefully examine your selected story, paying special attention to the basic working parts—the setting, the development of the characters, the shaping of the story line, and so on. Also make sure you understand why or how this story reflects the characteristics of a particular genre type. (Use the prepared "Story Analysis Sheet" as your guide when you examine your story.)
4. **Focusing** • Make some preliminary decisions about your own story (at least how and where you plan to start), using your story analysis and general understanding of the genre as your guide. (The point is not to imitate your model story, but to learn from it.)

   Remember: In most stories, there are *people* in a particular *setting* doing some *activity*, and a *conflict* occurs. The story develops around this conflict.

Writing and Revising

5. **Writing** • Develop your first draft according to any planning you may have done, but don't fight your story if it begins to take on a life of its own. You may end up with a far more interesting story than you first envisioned.
6. **Revising** • Review your first draft a number of times, first to get an overall sense of the characters and story line as they develop, and second to look more carefully at specific parts. Ask at least one classmate to read and react to your work as well. Revise and refine accordingly.

Evaluating

?...

Does the story reflect a basic understanding of a particular genre?

Does the story exhibit the qualities of effective fiction writing: interesting and/or believable characters, an engaging story line, effective use of dialogue, etc.?

Will readers appreciate the treatment of this story?

Activity Sheet

Story Analysis Sheet

Use this activity sheet as a guide when you closely examine a particular story type in preparation for your own writing. (Use your own paper if you need more room for your responses.)

1. In what ways does this story reflect the characteristics of a particular genre? Draw upon information gained during class discussions and from your own research and understanding of this story type.

2. How is the main character introduced in this story? (Where is this person, and what is he or she doing?)

3. How would you describe the main character in terms of his or her actions and words? (Do you consider this person to be believable in the context of the story? Explain.)

4. How does the opening scene lead to the events that follow in the story?

5. How is suspense built into the story? (That is, how does the author keep the readers interested and involved in the action?)

6. Are there any surprises in the story (positive or negative)? Explain.

Student Model

In the following science fiction story, writer Gann Bierner creates a whole new world of possibilities set in the distant future. What basic notion does he ask the reader to accept? Can you discover the writer's guiding theme? What social or moral issue seems to be the focus here? (This story first appeared in the February/March 1991 issue of *Merlyn's Pen: The National Magazine of Student Writing*. It is reprinted with permission.)

The Leap

Stars flashed by the ship as it accelerated through the airless void of space.

In streaks of red, blue, green, and violet, Sesom Rom saw them outlined against the inky blackness as he stared, mesmerized, through his half-meter-thick cabin window. He had not realized before his voyage that stars could have any color besides the dull yellow of his own planet's sun. He had an uneasy feeling that he would discover much more before the dimension jump even took place.

He glanced at the upraised symbols simulating his position and making dull clicks with each movement. They showed that the time had come to join the others in the control room. Reluctantly, he turned away from the celestial fireflies. With a faint grating of metal upon metal, the door slid into the floor and he left his quarters.

He did not have to walk far to reach his destination. His prominent position as chief engineer gave him many privileges, including quarters in close proximity to the bridge. As he entered, he immediately sensed that something terrible had happened. Silence coated the room like a layer of tar; not even the breathing of the eleven Gehad made any sound. Nor could any movement be detected.

The writer sets the story in motion by identifying the main character and his basic conflict (the destruction of the planet Areth).

A tragedy of the highest order must have taken place, for nothing else could have moved a Gehad to silence for longer than a few seconds.

Sesom dared to break the stillness. "What happened?" he asked, his voice low and harsh and his hands slippery with perspiration.

The communications officer, K'cen, answered haltingly, "The sun . . . we knew it would . . . but not so soon."

Sesom felt as if a great weight had settled upon his heart, making him feel weak. "It didn't. It couldn't have . . . not so early!"

"It did," Captain E'veins said without removing his eyes from a discolored spot on the floor. "The sun has gone to a red giant fifty years ahead of schedule. It engulfed our planet Areth. It never stood a chance."

Sesom sank to his seat in despair; the mission had failed before it had even begun. They were to find a livable planet in their neighboring dimension to which the Gehad could gradually ferry their population and escape their aging sun. But the scientists had made a drastic error, or fate had intervened. Either way, the result was the same. They had reacted much too late and, as a result, they were now the last of their race.

Sesom's mouth had become dry, and he had trouble speaking around the taste of despair. "And without a home, we are doomed as well," he stated simply.

The scientific possibility of leaping into another dimension adds suspense and interest to the story.

Sesom's thoughts, addressed in a realistic manner, build tension into the story.

The gray fog of hopelessness hung over the entire ship.

The twelve officers had decided that they must tell the rest of the ship's crew about the disaster, for no purpose would be served by hiding the truth. Though the news agonized all, the Gehad reacted calmly and with dignity, in respect for their lost kin.

Although they could certainly never forget the horror of the destruction of their planet, the Gehad dulled their pain through preparations for the leap. This was just what Sesom had hoped would happen when he had suggested making the jump despite the tragedy, and doing so a week earlier. That moved the date to within forty-eight hours.

This course of action could also, Sesom knew, represent the last hope for their own survival. No inhabitable planet in their dimension was close enough to reach without hibernation chambers, which their ship did not contain. The dimension to which they had originally hoped to move their people presented the only chance.

Preparations continued at a swift pace as the Gehad worked with mechanical efficiency. Sesom spent his time in his quarters. He no longer watched the stars but instead peered over his leap calculations, time and time again, until his eyes blurred so much that they could no longer see clearly. He slapped his face hard, clearing his vision with the pain. Then he checked the computations one last time, finally admitting that no flaws remained in his figuring.

Theoretically, the jump should work. Theoretically is the key word, thought Sesom grimly, for we are the first to ever attempt such a thing. Desperately, he hoped that his numbers and reality would jibe. His heart stopped for a moment at the thought that they might not.

The captain's voice suddenly cut crisply through Sesom's thoughts, releasing the hand that had for a moment seemed to clutch his insides. "Thirty-minute countdown to leap. All workers to their cabins; strap yourselves securely to your seats. Repeat, half an hour to leap."

At this, many feet began to pound loudly outside of Sesom's cabin as the crew scrambled to comply with the order. Then on Sesom's private wall screen the captain appeared, looking much more tired than he had sounded a moment before. "Any final changes to the calculations, Sesom?"

Sesom sighed, praying that he was not dooming the entire ship with his answer. "No, the calculations work out perfectly," he replied.

The captain nodded, then tried to smile reassuringly at Sesom. When he found that he could not, he quickly cut the connection. Sesom understood the captain's inability to smile, for he too felt the icy darkness in his brain, rendering him incapable of optimism.

He slowly settled into his chair and belted himself so tightly that he could feel the metal frame of the back through its heavy cushioning. But the straps did not cause him any more trouble breathing than his thoughts.

The thirty minutes seemed like so many seconds, and the captain's voice returned. The numbers he spoke would perhaps be the last words he would ever hear. "Twenty-nine seconds, twenty-eight seconds . . . sixteen seconds, fifteen seconds . . . "

Sesom's body had gone numb. He could not taste the blood seeping from the lip which he was biting.

"Twelve seconds."

He could not feel the great pressure of the restraints across his body.

"Seven seconds."

His mind would not function.

"Four seconds."

Only one phrase seeped through his damned thoughts.

"Two seconds."

Let me live! Oh please, oh please let me live!

"One . . ." And the rest was lost in a crack that sounded like a thunderbolt multiplied a thousandfold.

Sesom smelled the electric stench of ozone and felt his eyes burn with the flash of blaring white light before a cloak of darkness and silence mercifully engulfed him.

Sesom struggled to move but found that he could not. His whole body seemed incapable of movement.

Opening his eyes, however, he thankfully discovered that what he had first thought to be paralysis was only the straps holding him in the chair. With a voice command, he released them, sliding to the floor from the sudden lack of support.

The result of the leap into another dimension is effectively described.

His body felt as if it had been pummeled by hundreds of hammers over every inch of his skin, and his nostrils caught the vaguely acrid smell of singed hair. Reaching to his head, he discovered that it was his own.

Then suddenly he remembered the jump. He had lived, but had the jump succeeded? Gingerly, he pulled himself upright, stumbled to his window, and looked outside.

Nothing.

Sesom shook his head sharply to clear his obviously still half-conscious mind. But when he peered outside again, he saw the same thing: nothingness.

"Migroth," he whispered to himself in disgust and despair. "We have succeeded and yet we have failed." Then he rushed from the room as fast as his weak legs could move.

At the control room, his fears were confirmed by the captain. "I am afraid it is so," he said dully. "As soon as the theoretical scientists awoke I had them look. They told me just what you have surmised. We have leaped into a blank dimension: no planets, no stars, no asteroids, no mass at all. The only thing in this place is pure energy, and we cannot build homes from that."

The midday meal was a dreary affair that day. The food that Sesom had ordered from the energy-mass converter was bland and tasteless in his mouth.

A machine that can produce anything from energy, thought Sesom, and the spiciest it can make does not overcome the numbness of my mind.

Something about the last thought bothered Sesom. A machine that can produce anything from energy . . . A dimension that is made solely of energy . . .

Of course! he thought. *What could make more sense!* Not even noticing that he had overturned his chair in his haste, he swiftly left for his cabin as numbers and figures fluttered like butterflies in his head.

It had taken two days to work out the basic steps behind an energy-to-mass chain reaction. He spent another week on the details.

As he labored in his cabin with only a few hours of sleep, the thoughts of the crew revolved around his silent figure. Every minute of the day they feared that they would receive word that Sesom had been wrong and that the figures showed the conversion could not take place.

When Sesom finally emerged from his cabin, the crew quickly gathered in the corridor to hear his verdict. Sesom's chin hung near his chest, as if exhaustion was a slowly growing weight upon his head. His arms hung limply at his sides, and new lines cut through his face.

His eyes, however, shone brightly with a light that had been absent for many weeks.

As he drew breath into his lungs to speak, every crew member did the same in anticipation.

He said simply, "It can and shall be done." Then, as the Gehad celebrated throughout the ship, Sesom stumbled back into his room and collapsed in sleep upon his bed.

The writer again delves into the realm of scientific possibilities with Sesom's conversion theory.

As the entire race of the Gehad watched from their windows, millions of tons of mass exploded like a legendary phoenix from the ship. In colors through the spectrum, they reminded Sesom of the stars which he had studied with such wonder at the beginning of their mission. Then, Sesom had stood in awe of a universe; now, he was creating one.

Crackling sounds permeated the ship's walls from the converter attached to the side of her hull. But as the mass catapulted outward, the noise was lost in the vacuum of space.

In a few hours the faint smell of burning receded as the computers shut off the supply of energy on which the converter had ravenously fed. Enough matter had been produced.

After weeks of studying the results of the new experiment, the scientists pronounced many livable planets in the new universe, but an unusual side effect as well.

"It seems," one explained excitedly to Sesom, "that the matter migrated to two separate planes, with one slightly higher and less dense than the other. It forms something like a stair-step effect."

The higher plane was dubbed the E'veins after the captain, and the lower was named the Areth in honor of their doomed planet. It was unanimously decided that they would settle in the E'veins in order to symbolically say good-bye to their home forever.

As the ship began to accelerate to the first possible planet, Sesom turned and walked away from his window. He lowered himself in front of the desk at which he had labored for this new life. As reconstruction would soon begin, he was now taking upon himself an important job: that of historian.

Sesom decided that this was the appropriate time to begin. At his word, a thin piece of hard, black plastic slid vertically from the desk to stare blankly at him.

The story ends in a surprising but familiar fashion.

As Sesom spoke softly to the screen, words began to appear:

In the beginning, the Gehad created the E'veins and the Areth . . .

Professional Model

Writer Bill Pronzini uses one of the best-known conventions of mystery writing in the following short story: the "locked room" puzzle. In this type of story, the writer focuses on the *how* of a crime, rather than the *who* or *why*. As you read this story, see if you can solve the crime along with the main characters. (Copyright © 1981 by Bill Pronzini. First published in *Ellery Queen's Mystery Magazine*. It is reprinted with permission.)

The Terrarium Principle

The setting for the characters' in-depth conversation is established.

Andrea Parker was on the back porch, working on her latest project—the planting of seeds in a bottle terrarium—when she heard Jerry's car in the driveway. She took off her gloves, brushed flecks of potting soil off her gardening shirt, and went into the kitchen to meet him as he opened the garage door.

There was a preoccupied scowl on Jerry's face. He looked rumpled, the way Columbo used to look on television. Which was unusual; her husband may have been a police lieutenant attached to the Homicide Division, but he definitely was not the Peter Falk type.

He brushed his lips over hers—not much of a kiss, Andrea thought—and said, "I could use a drink." He went straight to the refrigerator and began tugging out one of the ice trays.

"Rough day?" she asked him.

"You can say that again. Except that the operative word is frustrating. One of the most frustrating days I've ever spent."

"Why?"

"Because a man named Harding committed murder in a locked room this morning and I can't prove it. *That's* why."

"Want to talk about it?"

He made a face. But he said, "I might as well. It's going to be on my mind all evening anyway. You can help me brood."

Andrea took the ice tray away from him, shooed him into the living room, and made drinks for both of them. When she brought them in, Jerry was sitting on the couch with his legs crossed, elbow resting on one knee and chin cupped in his palm. He really did look like Columbo tonight. All he needed, she thought, was a trench coat and a cigar.

The mystery unfolds during the give-and-take of ideas.

She handed him his drink and sat down beside him. "So why can't you prove this man Harding committed murder? You did say it happened in a locked room, didn't you?"

"Well, more or less locked. And I can't prove it because we can't find the gun. Without it we just don't have a case."

"What exactly happened?"

"It's a pretty simple story, except for the missing gun. The classic kind of simple, I mean. Harding's uncle, Philip Granger, has—or had—a house out in Roehampton Estates; wealthy guy, made a lot of money in oil stocks over the years. Harding, on the other hand, is your typical black-sheep nephew—drinks too much, can't hold down a job, has a penchant for fast women and slow horses.

"This morning Harding went out to his uncle's house to see him. The housekeeper let him in. According to her, Harding seemed upset about something, angry. Granger's lawyer, Martin Sampson, happened to be there at the time, preparing some papers for Granger to sign, and he confirms the housekeeper's impression that Harding was upset.

"So Harding went into his uncle's study and either he or Granger locked the door. Fifteen minutes later both Sampson and the housekeeper heard a gunshot. They were sure it came from the study; they both ran straight for that door. But the door was locked, as I said. They pounded and shouted, and inside Harding yelled back that somebody had shot his uncle. Only he didn't open the door right away. It took him eight and one-half minutes by Sampson's watch to get around to it."

"Eight and a half minutes?" Andrea said. "What did he say he was doing all that time?"

"Looking out the window, first of all, for some sign of a phantom killer. Harding's claim is that window was open and Granger was shot through the window from outside; he says Sampson and the housekeeper must have been mistaken about where the shot came from. The rest of the time he was supposedly ministering to his uncle and didn't stop to open the door until the old man had died."

"But you think he spent that time hiding the gun somewhere in the room?"

Possible solutions to the crime are presented and rejected as the lieutenant and his wife discuss the evidence.

"I *know* that's what he was doing," Jerry said. "His story is implausible and he'd had arguments with his uncle before, always over money and sometimes to the point of violence. He's guilty as sin—I'm sure of it!"

"Couldn't he have just thrown the gun out the window?"

"No. We searched the grounds; we'd have found the gun if it had been out there."

"Well, maybe he climbed out the window, took it away somewhere, and hid it."

"No chance," Jerry said. "Remember the rain we had last night? There's a flower bed outside the study window and the ground there was muddy from the rain; nobody could have walked through it without leaving footprints. And it's too wide to jump over from the windowsill. No, the gun is in that room. He managed to hide it somewhere during those eight and one-half minutes. His uncle's stereo unit was playing, fairly loud, and if he made any noise the music covered it—Sampson and the housekeeper didn't hear anything unusual."

"Didn't one of them go outdoors to look in through the study window?"

"Sampson did, yes. But Harding had drawn the drapes. In case the phantom killer came back, he said."

"What's the study like?" Andrea asked.

"Big room with masculine decor: hunting prints, a stag's head, a wall full of books, overstuffed leather furniture, a large fireplace—"

"I guess you looked up the fireplace chimney," Andrea said.

He gave her a wry smile. "First thing. Nothing but soot."

"What else was in the room?"

"A desk that we went over from top to bottom. And model airplanes, a clipper ship in a bottle, a miniature train layout—all kinds of model stuff."

"Oh?"

"Evidently Granger built models in his spare time, as a hobby. There was also a small workbench along one wall."

The mystery is solved by the wife—deduced from the information she receives by questioning her detective husband.

Notice how the writer ties the solution to the opening lines of the story.

"I see."

"The only other thing in there was the stereo unit—radio, record player, tape deck. I thought Harding might have hidden the gun inside one of the speakers, but no soap."

Andrea was sitting very still, pondering. So still that Jerry frowned at her and then said, "What's the matter?"

"I just had an idea. Tell me, was there any strong glue on the workbench?"

"Glue?"

"Yes. The kind where you only need a few drops to make a bond and it dries instantly."

"I guess there was, sure. Why?"

"How about a glass cutter?"

"I suppose so. Andrea, what are you getting at?"

"I think I know what Harding was doing for those eight and a half minutes," she said. "And I think I know just where he hid the gun."

Jerry sat up straight. "Are you serious?"

"Of course I'm serious. Come on, I want to show you something." She led him out through the kitchen, onto the rear porch. "See that terrarium?"

"What about it?"

"Well, it's a big glass jar with a small opening at one end, right? Like a bottle. There's nothing in it now except soil and seeds, but pretty soon there'll be flowers and plants growing inside and people who don't know anything about terrariums will look at it and say, 'Now how in the world did you get those plants through that little opening?' It doesn't occur to them that you *didn't* put plants in there; you put seeds and they grew into plants."

"I don't see what that has to do with Harding—"

"But there's also a way to build a bottle terrarium using full-grown plants," she went on, "that almost never occurs to anybody. All you have to do is slice off the bottom of the container with a glass cutter . . ."

A light was beginning to dawn in Jerry's eyes. "Like we didn't look close enough at a certain item in Granger's study."

"The ship in the bottle," Andrea said, nodding. "I'll bet you that's where Harding put the gun—inside the ship that's inside the bottle."

"No bet," Jerry said. "If you're right, I'll buy you the fanciest steak dinner in town."

He hurried inside, no longer looking like Columbo, and telephoned police headquarters. When he was through talking he told Andrea that they would have word within an hour. And they did—exactly fifty-six minutes had passed when the telephone rang. Jerry took it, listened, then grinned.

"You were right," he said when he'd hung up. "The bottom of the bottle had been cut and glued back, the ship inside had been hollowed out, and the missing gun was inside the ship. We overlooked it because we automatically assumed nobody could put a gun through a bottle neck that small. It never occurred to us that Harding didn't *have* to put it through the neck to get it inside."

Andrea smiled. "The terrarium principle," she said.

"I guess that's a pretty good name for it. Come on, get your coat; we'll go have that steak dinner right now."

"With champagne, maybe?"

"Sweetheart," he said, "with a whole magnum." ▣

Professional Model

"Norma," by writer Sonia Sanchez, illustrates many of the elements that have come to be associated with urban fiction. As you read this model, ask yourself, what are the specific urban characteristics defining this story? For example, what role, if any, does the setting or environment play in this story? (This story is from *Homegirls & Handgrenades* by Sonia Sanchez. Copyright © 1984 by Sonia Sanchez. Used by permission of the publisher, Thunder's Mouth Press.)

Norma

The narrator's shyness and an ineffective teacher contrast with Norma's brilliance and compassion.

As a teenager I was very shy. I always felt so conspicuous that I talked with my head down, walked with my head down, and would have slept with my head down if sleeping had demanded a standing position. It was with difficulty that I mustered up courage to ask Mr. Castor again and again, "But how do you factor that equation? I don't understand how it's done."

And he kept pointing to the book and looking upward, as if the combination of those actions would give me the immediate joy of an answer.

A sound from the back of the class made me turn around. It was the "people"—the "people" who sat in the back and talked when they wanted to, ate their lunches when they wanted to, and paid attention when they wanted to. They were paying attention to Mr. Castor and me. And I shook. I always wanted to be inconspicuous around the "people."

The language used by certain classmates adds stark realism to the story.

Odessa screamed, "Sit down Mr. Castor. You don't know crap. Norma, go up front and teach that little 'pip-squeak' how to do this Algebra."

As Mr. Castor moved to the sidelines, like some dejected player, Norma got up and began her slow walk up to the blackboard.

Have you ever seen a river curve back on itself? That was Norma as she walked on the edge of the classroom. She was heavy with white petticoats as she questioned, "Whatcha wanna know Sonia?"

Indeed. What did I want to know? It was all so very simple. I just wanted to know how to factor the problems so I could do my homework. Nothing else. I had a father waiting for me at home who would take no excuses concerning homework. He said, "The teachers are there. If you don't know, ask them. They know the answers." He didn't know Mr. Castor though.

As I asked the question, she sighed, and explained the factoring process in such an easy manner. I wrote it all down and closed my math notebook. I could do my homework now. There would be no problem with the family.

Norma was still at the blackboard. She hadn't moved and I knew that she was waiting for Lewis to say something. Lewis was the other brain in the class. They were always discussing some complex math

Norma's and Lewis's intelligence provides a strong contrast to the hopelessness of their environment.

An anecdote illustrates Norma's brilliance, and her inability to conform.

problem. As if on cue, Lewis called out a more difficult question. She smiled. The smile ripened on her mouth like pomegranates.

Her fingers danced across the board. I watched her face. I was transfixed by her face that torpedoed the room with brilliance. She pirouetted problem after problem on the blackboard. We all thought genius. Norma is a mathematical genius.

I used to smile at Norma and sometimes she smiled back. She was the only one in the group who spoke to the "pip-squeaks" sitting up front. The others spoke, but it was usually a command of sorts. Norma would sometimes shake off her friends and sit down with the "pip-squeaks" and talk about the South. She was from Mississippi. She ordained us all with her red clay Mississippi talk. Her voice thawed us out from the merciless cold studding the hallways. Most of the time though, she laughed only with her teeth.

One day Norma called out a question in our French class. I understood part of the question. French was my favorite class. Mrs. LeFevebre was startled. She was a hunchback who swallowed her words so it was always difficult to understand her. But Norma's words were clear.

Mrs. LeFevebre spoke her well-digested English, "No rudeness, please Norma. You are being disrespectful. I shall not tolerate this."

Norma continued the conversation in French. Her accent was beautiful. I listened while her words fell like mangoes from her lips. The "people" laughed, "Talk that talk Norma. Go on girl. Keep on doin' it; whatever you're saying."

Mayhem. The smell of mayhem stalked the room. I wondered if the "people" would lock us all in the closet again.

Mrs. LeFevebre screamed, "Silence. Silence. Savages. How dare you ask me about my affliction. It is none of your business." As she talked, her huge owl-head bobbed up and down on her waist. I wondered if she had trouble each night taking off her black dress. Her head was so large.

Norma stood up and started to pack her books. The noise subsided. She walked to the door, turned and said, "I just wanted to talk to you in your own language so you wouldn't be so lonely. You always look so lonely up there behind your desk. But screw you, you old b _ _ _ _. You can go straight to hell for all I care. Hunchback and all."

She exited; the others followed, dragging their feet and mumbling black mourning words.

Mrs. LeFevebre stood still like a lizard gathering the sun.

I never liked that class after that. I still got good grades, but Norma, when she came to the French class, just sat and watched us struggle with our accents in amusement. I wondered what she did after school. I wondered if she ever studied.

George Washington High School was difficult. Our teachers had not prepared us for high school. The first year was catch-up time. My sister and I spent long nights in our small room, reading and studying our material.

I don't remember who it was. It was announced one day at lunchtime that Norma was pregnant. She had been dismissed from school. I had almost forgotten Norma. The mathematical genius. Norma. The linguist. The year had demanded so much work and old memories and faces had faded into the background.

Urban fiction, as evidenced in this story, is well grounded in the real world of contemporary city life.

I was rushing to the library. The library had become my refuge during the Summer of '55. As I turned the corner of 145th Street, I heard her hello. Her voice was like stale music in barrooms. There she stood. Norma. Eyelids heavy. Woman of four children, with tracks running on her legs and arms.

"How you be doing Norma? You're looking good, girl."

"I'm making it Sonia. You really do look good, girl. Heard you went to Hunter College. Glad you made it."

"You should have gone too, Norma. You were the genius. The linguist. You were the brain. We just studied and got good grades. You were the one who understood it all."

And I started to cry. On that summer afternoon, I heard a voice from very far away paddling me home to a country of incense. To a country of red clay. I heard her laughter dancing with fireflies.

Tongue-tied by time and drugs, she smiled a funny smile and introduced me to her girls. Four beautiful girls. Norma predicted that they would make it. They wouldn't be like their mother. They would begin with a single step, then they would jump mountains.

"Excuse me, do I know you? Do you know me? Yes, I do know you. You're the brother hanging on the corner with nothing to do." —Lisa Frederick

Statement Through Poetry

Writers may express their strongly felt beliefs in a number of different ways—in essays, stories, plays, poems, and so on. If they choose a poetic expression, the challenge is to create an effective balance between the statement of belief and the poetry itself.

More Than Pretty Words

Discussion: Write a poem expressing a strongly felt statement or belief. Focus on words and images that vividly convey the importance of your statement rather than on carefully developed points and arguments as you would do in an essay. Provide your reader with an opportunity to "feel" what you believe in your poem. Refer to the guidelines below and the models that follow to help you develop your work.

Searching and Selecting

1. **Selecting** • Think of things about which you have strong feelings or convictions. Remember that it will be the intensity and strength of your feelings that will be the driving force for your poem, so choose a meaningful topic.
2. **Reviewing** • If you have trouble coming up with a subject, refer to your journal entries for ideas. You could also complete a number of "I believe" statements, talk to your classmates, or refer to the models for ideas.

Generating the Text

3. **Noting** • Once you have a subject in mind, think of possible ways to develop it poetically. Again refer to the models for ideas. Also refer to poems you have studied in class or poems in other books, or simply rely on your creative instincts.
4. **Generating** • Get a feel for your subject by freely listing words and phrases related to it. Push yourself to form an extensive list. Afterward, as you review your list, underline vivid words and images that you might want to use in your poem, and look for a possible focus or emerging shape for your work. Continue collecting and experimenting as necessary. (See "Help File.")

Writing and Revising

5. **Writing** • As you develop your poem, try to keep your language and images sharp and precise. Each word and phrase is important; each one must add to the whole. (That "whole" may develop into a list poem, a prose poem, a sonnet, rap lyrics . . .)
6. **Revising** • Review the draft of your poem, reading it aloud several times. Have others read and react to it as well. Make changes accordingly. (When your poem seems to have a seamless, smooth quality to it, it's ready to share.)

Evaluating

Is there a statement of belief suggested in the poem?

Do all the pieces in the poem work together to form a unified whole?

Will readers appreciate the treatment of the subject in this poem?

Help File: You might find it helpful to develop your subject into a brief essay first, and then translate that writing into a poem.

Student Model

Poetry has acquired a bad reputation with many students. Poetry sometimes deals with this very opinion, as in the model below. This poem written by Travis Taylor raises some very interesting questions about poetry and poets, and their roles in our lives. (Note the rap beat established throughout the poem.)

The opening lines of the poem present some typical complaints about poetry.

The second half of the poem presents some advice to poets—in a rhythmic list of ideas.

Out on the Streets

I always thought poets were pretty weird.
Like a little old guy with a long white beard
hanging around his house all day
digging in the dictionary for a harder way to say
something everyone already knew anyway.
Writing stuff that no one read
until fifty years after he was dead.
Why didn't the dude get out on the streets,
Rap with his buddies, or go for some eats,
Hang on the corner, watch what went down,
Hop in the car, take a ride around town,
Look at some ladies, have a fine time?
Stick with the rhythm, forget about rhyme.
Cause it seems pretty plain to me,
you live your life, you make poetry.

Student Model

In this poem, Taylor Adams expresses a concern for those who have yet "To elicit from life / The elation of raindrops and sunshine." Pay careful attention to the specific words the poet uses as well as to the overall structure of the poem. (The epigram [in italics] is from Charles Bukowski, a contemporary poet.)

The poem poses a comparison between the freedom of nature and a confining civilized world.

An extended description of nature's wonders is presented.

The poet leaves readers with his own "awakening" experience.

IS DUSK, IS DAWN, IS DAY

"The sun was tired. And some of the cars went east
and some of the cars went west, and it dawned on me
that if everybody would only drive in the same direction
everything would be solved."
—Charles Bukowski

I realize that when a barefoot barbarian
Such as I
Stumbles in your world of shackles and shoes
He opens himself to the laughter and cries
That arise from misunderstanding.
Still, for those who have yet
To elicit from life
The elation of raindrops and sunshine,
For those who have yet to recognize
The magnificence of flowing trees and swaying rivers and bursting
clouds,
For those who have yet to experience
The simple joy of letting your feet breathe free,
For all of those
There will come a day when they shall feel the grass
Wet between their toes
And their souls shall be together
In meadows of barefooted bliss.
As for me, my days slip by too swiftly
To explain. For it only just occurred to me;
And this morning, as the sun rose calmly through the night,
The earth dawned on me.

Student Model

In "Tell Him Why" Lisa Frederick presents a forceful message that builds rhythmically in rap-lyric style. (The poem originally appeared in *New Youth Connections: The Magazine Written By and For New York Youth*, May 1992. It is reprinted with permission.)

Tell Him Why

Excuse me, do I know you? Do you know me?
Yes, I do know you. You're the brother hanging
on the corner with nothing to do.

Now you have nerve telling me about myself
When you have empty pockets on the right and emptier
pockets on the left

Just because I ignore your hisses, ain't no need for disses
I'll treat you like a mister if you treat me like a missus

I'm telling you this 'cause I'm sick and tired
There's a difference between being heckled
and being admired

You know what I'm talking about, you do it every day
You want the attention so be attentive to what you say

It's lewd, it's crude, it's downright rude

But in your head you're thinking, "What the heck"
And when a sista walks by you give her no respect

I'm a young female and I'm Black too
And in this day and age, that's two strikes against you.

So don't give me no stress because you fail to impress
If my own people give me nothing, others will give
me still less

Give us what we deserve: a lot of respect, a lot of love
'Cause you know I'm right when I say you need us
When you entered this world, it was a woman you saw first
Behind every good man stands a better woman
So give us what we ask, ain't no big task

And if you fall off the track we'll be there to pick up
the slack
With us you won't lack, 'cause sista's got your back

But I can't help you if you won't help yourself, so get those
want ads off the shelf

The opening lines of this poem immediately establish the female speaker's demand for respect—for herself and for her gender.

The use of internal and end rhyme helps create the poem's rhythm, or beat.

Don't get me wrong, honey, it's not all about the money
Whoever said life was a joke won't find this funny:

Think you look cute with a beeper and a Malcolm X hat
But I don't think Malcolm would speak to a sista like that

He would know that we're dignified, full of pride,
classified, bona fide and refined

He would've also stated that we're educated, complicated,
understated, underrated, and underestimated

The use of repetition ("understated, underrated . . .") and the poet's direct manner of addressing her male counterparts create a forceful expression.

Unashamed, unclaimed, untamed, unchanged,
understanding, undemanding . . . but still disrespected

We're used, bruised and left confused

So . . . my brown bag drinking, big mouth braggin, 1,000
gold chain wearing, imaginary B.M.W. driving, Jafarian
belt hoopin, bead wearing, Rastafarian talking, wannabe
down with culture brother
(you know it's true, at least one applies to you)

When you see us walking by and you say "hi"
Don't get mad 'cause we don't reply

It's just something in our culture that we miss
I know Isis and Nefertiti weren't spoken to like this

Oh, you don't see our crowns but we did come down from a
nation of queens and kings
Just think of us as royalty in jeans

A lot of love you can expect
If you just give your sista her respect

Professional Model

As you read William Stafford's poem, don't expect to find a clearly stated message. Instead, be prepared to read between the lines, to feel the message or "the one clear lesson." ("Learning to Like the New School" from *A Glass Face in the Rain* by William Stafford. Copyright © 1982 by William Stafford. Reprinted by permission of HarperCollins Publishers, Inc.)

Learning to Like the New School

They brought me where it was bright and said,
"Be bright." I couldn't even see. They tried
again: "Look up." I tried but it
was all sad to me. They turned and went
away. And then it all came on
to be a world like this—you learn only
the one clear lesson, "How It Is":
the rain falls, the wind blows,
and you are just there, alone, as yourself.
The world is no test—"So you got here, fine,"
any new place says. And you say, "Yes, I'm here."

Simple ideas and little bits of dialogue are presented in fast-paced fashion, so there is little time to reflect on any deep meaning.

"TONY: So you're good at runnin' numbers are ya?
BOB: Yes, I work very well with data processing systems. That's where I was before I began looking for a new job and saw your ad in the paper. I'm now ready to move on with my life. I'm looking to move up in the world.
TONY: Well, ya come ta da right place for dat. (He leans over, writing; Bob tugs on his collar.)"
—Nathan E. Slaughter and Jim Schweitzer

Playwriting

More than any other form of creative writing, a play can bring real or imaginary experiences to life. A play's effectiveness rests solely on the words and actions of the characters. So as a script develops, it is essential for the playwright to *get inside* and *know* the characters.

Act and Interact

Discussion: Write a one-act play exploring a specific conflict in the life of one or two main characters. Start with a few characters (in a particular setting, dealing with one problem) and see what develops as they interact. The personalities and/or temperaments of your characters should be revealed through their words and actions.

Searching and Selecting

1. **Searching** • A good one-act play is, first and foremost, a good story—a story involving two or more individuals dealing with a situation or problem in view of an audience (or reader). To write a good play, you must find a situation that is interesting and important enough to appeal to your audience; you must then create characters who are connected in some way to this situation. (Often these characters will have to help create tension or humor.)
2. **Selecting** • For starters, look at the situations around you (at home, in school, at work, in the news) for possible ideas. Maybe a local girl is trying to join the football team, or a classmate is trying to solve a community problem, or someone you know is facing a personal problem. Any situation or problem that is interesting and could be resolved on stage is a possible subject.

Generating the Text

3. **Exploring** • Once you have a suitable situation—one with dramatic possibilities—you must work out a basic scenario of what will happen as the play unfolds. You should also work on defining your characters (personalities, mannerisms, vocal patterns), perhaps by preparing a list or cluster for each character. These can be added to as you go along.
4. **Organizing** • Keeping the opening scenario in mind, allow your writing to take on a life of its own. Be flexible and creative, but try to remain clearly focused on the overall point or goal of your play—to entertain, to satirize, to solve a problem, etc.

Writing and Revising

5. **Writing** • Begin your play by revealing as much about the situation and characters as possible in the first few lines. Let your drama build naturally by both visualizing and listening to your characters as you write. Remember, too, that a play must have a middle, a point where the situation becomes complicated and appears to be headed toward a different outcome than the one you have planned. This will help create the suspense, tension, or humor needed for a strong climax.
6. **Refining** • As several classmates read your play, listen for gaps or choppiness in the dialogue and fine-tune accordingly. (Add stage directions as needed.)

Evaluating

?...?

Does the play focus on a single important conflict?

Is the dialogue realistic—does it sound like real people talking?

Is all of what the characters could/would/should do or say considered?

Does the play come to a strong, satisfying conclusion?

Student Model

This humorous one-act play represents the teamwork of student playwrights Nathan E. Slaughter and Jim Schweitzer. The playwrights rely on a common comic device—the simple misunderstanding—to create the humor in "The Mob Job."

The setting describes the stage and the opening scene.

The first speech reveals Tony as a husband and a busy businessman.

Bob's naive sincerity contrasts with Tony's "mob" mentality.

The Mob Job

Characters:
TONY "The Tiger" Vespucci, a gangster
BOB Ferris, an innocent job hunter

Setting: Scene opens in a plain room which has white walls with no decorations. Stage left a large black and white picture of Marlon Brando hangs above the door. A large, polished oak desk with a green carnival glass lamp stands right-center stage, facing the audience. A single chair is in front of the desk. In a second chair behind the desk is Tony Vespucci in a pin-striped suit, a black shirt, white tie, and expensive Italian loafers. Smoking a large cigar, he leans forward and pushes a button on his desk.

TONY: *(in a thick Italian accent)* Andrea, calla my wife and tell her ta hold da marinara sauce, I'm gonna be late tonight! An' den send in da next prospect. *(He puts his feet up on the desk, and there is a pause, broken when Bob timidly enters.)*

BOB: *(He stops and looks around a bit.)* I hope I'm in the right place. I'm here about a job posting in the paper.

TONY: *(taking feet from desktop and talking around cigar)* Yeah, yeah, yeah. Dis is da place all right. C'mon in an' have a seat.

BOB: *(adjusting his tie nervously)* Well, all right. *(He crosses to chair and sits. Pause.)*

TONY: So, what'sa ya name, kid?

BOB: *(smacking his head for forgetting)* Oh, I forgot . . . I'm Bob— *(reaches across table, takes Tony's hand, and shakes vigorously)* Bob Ferris.

TONY: Bob? Bob Ferris. Ferris . . . Bob . . . We can work wit dat I suppose.

BOB: Excuse me, sir?

TONY: Never mind. Hey, hey! Don't calla me sir, all right? It's Tony.

BOB: All right . . . Tony. Well, uh, your ad said you were looking for a goal-oriented young man with sharp sights and a lot of ambition. Well, I thought, Hey, that's me! Though I don't really know what this job is exactly.

TONY: How's about we's get ta dat later, hmm? Do ya have any, ya know, experience?

BOB: *(handing Tony a paper)* Uh, here's my résumé.

TONY: *(quickly looking it over)* Uh-hmmm . . . uh-hmmm . . . *(yelling loudly)* A-HA! *(Bob starts, almost falling out of chair.)* I see you're an accountin' major. Does dat meana you're good wit numbers?

BOB: Yes, I used to run number-crunching programs for the college I attended.

TONY: So you're good at runnin' numbers are ya?

BOB: Yes, I work very well with data processing systems. That's where I was before I began looking for a new job and saw your ad in the paper. I'm now ready to move on with my life. I'm looking to move up in the world.

TONY: Well, ya come ta da right place for dat. *(He leans over, writing; Bob tugs on his collar.)*

BOB: I feel kind of funny asking this question, but, let's say I get this job. What are some of the benefits? *(Tony pays no attention.)* You know, insurance plans, retirement funds?

TONY: *(stops writing, looks up)* Whaddya talkin' about?

BOB: Well, let's take insurance, for example. Say I was to fall or have an accident.

TONY: Oh, "accident," I got ya. Well, not only would we pay for ya hospital bills, but we'd senda some heavy muscle afta whoever's responsible.

BOB: You have good lawyers then.

TONY: *(turning quickly in fear)* Lawyers? Where, where? . . . *(He realizes what Bob meant.)* Oh, oh, lawyers. Well, I wasn't tinkin' about dem, but we got some. Somma da best lawyers . . . and judges money can buy!

BOB: Oh.

TONY: An' what was da other ting you mentioned?

Throughout the script, the writers use the question/answer interview format to set up the amusing dialogue.

BOB: Retirement funds?

TONY: Retirement? Well, ya can take da way of da weasel. Dat's da way many go. Ya see, ya go and talk ta da government, dey relocate ya, give ya a new name, an' a fresh start. Dey even pay ya! Oh, it's not as much as you'll be used ta, but no pension plan is perfect. Its official name is da W.P.P., but we call it our own "Social Security."

BOB: That's good. I am glad that you brought up the wages. What exactly would my pay be?

TONY: Well, ya don't have a specified wage per se, but you're well taken care of an' ya always have cash on hand.

BOB: Do you take out the taxes, or should I put it aside myself?

TONY: Taxes! We don't worry about taxes. Our organization is sorta "tax exempt" if ya know what I mean.

BOB: Oh, sure. Of course . . . You know, this job seems almost too good to be true! I suppose I even get my own company car! *(He looks across the table at Tony, half hopefully and half jokingly.)*

TONY: Well, I don't know about "company" car, but ya do get ya choice of Cadillacs.

BOB: *(ecstatic)* Are you serious?

TONY: Perfectly serious.

BOB: *(elated)* Where have you guys been?

TONY: Oh, around. We been around a long time.

BOB: Do I get the car for personal use?

TONY: Sure . . . but we do aska one ting, though.

BOB: I knew there had to be a catch.

TONY: Ya know, dere's a lotta room in dose cars. We only ask dat when ya take it out into da public sector dat dere are no stiffs in da back, if ya know what I mean.

BOB: *(very seriously)* Stiffs?

TONY: *(chuckling)* Hey, we'll get off dis dead subject. *(Tony laughs at his own joke, and Bob is confused.)*

BOB: Please do.

TONY: Is dere anyting else on ya mind?

BOB: Actually, there is. Don't I ever work days?

TONY: Whaddya mean? Whaddya talkin' about?

BOB: The newspaper ad says "must work nights."

TONY: It does? Where does it say dat?

Note that the help-wanted ad is filled with double meanings.

BOB: Right here. *(He pulls the article from his shirt pocket.)* It says, "Wanted. Goal-oriented young man for position with large organization. Must have sharp sights, good judgment, and blind ambition. Must work nights. Many advancement opportunities. Apply in person."

TONY: So it does . . . okay, what was ya question again?

BOB: I was wondering if there were any day hours available.

TONY: Whaddya mean?

BOB: I'm available nights, but I'd like to work some days.

TONY: It depends. Some jobs have ta be done at night. Da ones dat can't be done in da daylight.

BOB: This is all on the level, right? Nothing illegal.

TONY: Don't worry about it; da cops even help us. It's expensive, but dey do it. Let me ask ya one last question.

BOB: All right.

TONY: Have ya ever **removed** someone, ya know, gotten **rid** of anyone?

BOB: Yes, unfortunately.

TONY: *(happily)* Ah, ya have!

BOB: *(confused)* Yes . . . He had a wife and six kids, too. I felt just horrible about it.

TONY: *(smiling)* A wife an' six kids? You're ruthless!

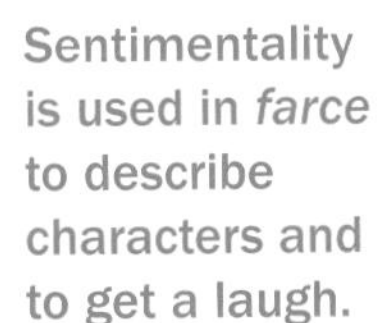

Sentimentality is used in *farce* to describe characters and to get a laugh.

BOB: *(weeping softly)* My last boss passed the buck on to me and made me hand him the pink slip.

TONY: *(thoughtfully)* Pink slip, eh? *(Bob is now blowing his nose.)* We usually use dead birds or horse heads.

BOB: Excuse me, did you say something about dead . . .

TONY: It's nothin', nothin' important.

BOB: I felt bad about doing it, but I couldn't allow it to get to me. Couldn't let it get personal. That's big business for you.

The stage direction indicating a pause often works as a transition for changing the subject.

Overreaction is common in melodrama and farce.

The climax occurs when Tony decides to hire Bob.

TONY: *(reaching across desk, patting Bob's hand)* Ya got it right dere, kid. Business is business.

BOB: I even liked the guy! But you have to do what you have to do. It's up to the boss.

TONY: Amen ta dat. Amen ta dat.

BOB: Well, I'm here now. *(He pauses to compose himself. Tony does this also.)* I would like to know more about the advancement opportunities the ad mentions.

TONY: *(very seriously)* Dat is a very touchy subject 'round here.

BOB: I'd like to advance rather quickly.

TONY: Well, ya have ta impress da boss. An' dose removals! You'd better get used ta dem if ya wanna advance.

BOB: Now, not that I'm trying to rush things, but what is the next position up from the one I'll be taking?

TONY: Well, let's see— *(calmly thinking, then suddenly standing up furiously)* Hey, hey, hey! It's mine! You'd better wait 'til I move up! Whaddya tryin' ta do? What'sa matter wit ya?

BOB: Huh?

TONY: Are ya bustin' me?

BOB: No, I wouldn't . . .

TONY: *(straightening tie)* Good, good. I didn't tink ya were dat kinda guy at all. I like ya! I like ya, Bobby! Ya don't mind if I call ya Bobby, do ya, Bobby?

BOB: Well, I . . .

TONY: Good. Bobby it is. Bobby Ferris. Ferris . . . Ferris . . . Ferrey . . . Ferret—AHA! *(Bob almost falls out of his chair.)* Bobby da Ferret! Dat's ya new name!

BOB: It is?

TONY: Of course it is! What'd ya tink? We was all born wit names like Johnny Roast Beef, Vito "The Vego-Matic," and Joe Bagman?

BOB: Well, what's yours?

TONY: Tony "The Tiger" Vespucci.

BOB: *(with a smile on his face)* Well, that's g-rr-eat!

TONY: *(upset)* Hey, hey, hey! *(He points angrily at Bob, then suddenly smiles.)* Hey, all right, now you're gettin' into it! They'll like ya!

BOB: Who's "they"?

TONY: *(going around the table to him)* Everybody! *(He puts his arm around him.)* C'mon, I'll introduce ya ta da boys. *(He leaves, Bob follows.)* One ting though: Don't tell Moe his nose is big, or he'll cut yours off. *(Tony slams the door behind them and the picture of Marlon Brando falls to the floor, spraying shattered glass everywhere.)*

FADE OUT

Student Model

Student playwrights Nathan E. Slaughter and Jim Schweitzer collaborate again, this time on a serious one-act play. Details of setting are minimal, so the focus remains on the characters. In a short time, the audience must learn enough about Mike, through his dialogue and actions, to make the play's dramatic developments believable.

When Time Dies

Characters:
DOCTOR, a psychologist
SUSAN GRUNWALD, a college student
MICHAEL P. LIEGL, a college student

Setting: Scene opens in a small room with one door that is stage right. The room is rather bleak looking and has two chairs in the middle. One is cushioned, the other is not. There is a large observation mirror stage left. The door opens and three characters enter together, the doctor behind the other two. He is dressed in a white coat and wears small, round glasses. The other two are dressed plainly and in the same colors. The doctor leads them to the chairs.

DOCTOR: Well, now. If you would have a seat in one of the chairs, we will begin the experiment.

The audience learns about the experiment along with the actors.

MIKE: Could you please explain one more time what will take place? There's no chance of physical trauma, is there?

DOCTOR: *(chuckles)* No, it is not set up to affect you physically. This is strictly a psychological experiment. We are interested in the human responses to external stimuli. We are here to study your minds. Body study takes place in anatomy labs . . . and on the beach. I assure you that you are safe.

MIKE: Good. Good. I'm glad.

DOCTOR: I'm sure you are. Now, please, sit down. *(Mike offers Susan the cushioned chair and she accepts. They sit down.)* We will be right on the other side of the mirror here *(motioning to the audience)*. Now, you, Susan, will be in here for five minutes. Every minute there will be a light letting you know that another minute has elapsed. At the end of the time period, I or one of my colleagues will reenter the room to let you know that your portion of the experiment has ended. Then, Michael, you will be left in here for another five minutes following Susan's exit. When your time has ended, I or a colleague will enter to notify you.

MIKE: All right.

SUSAN: Is there anything else we need to know?

DOCTOR: As a matter of fact, there is something I need. *(He points at their wrists.)* I need to take your watches to ensure the success of the experiment. *(They take off the watches and hand them to the doctor.)* Thank you. *(The doctor leaves. There is an ominous, echoing click as the door locks. Both people turn to look at it, then return to their original positions, nervously.)*

SUSAN: Well . . . this should be . . . uh . . . fun!

MIKE: Yeah, a real riot in L.A. A veritable scream.

SUSAN: *(uneasy)* Well, introductions are in order, I suppose.

MIKE: Yeah, sure. We're going to know each other for five minutes. Please, tell me your name!

SUSAN: *(sweetly ignoring his cynicism)* My name is Susan Grunwald.

MIKE: I'm Mike. Michael P. Liegl, to be exact.

SUSAN: What does the "P" stand for?

MIKE: I didn't ask your middle name.

SUSAN: It's Anne. Now, what does the "P" stand for?

MIKE: Protection. Privacy. Pretentious. Pick your poison.

In simple but consistent ways, Mike reveals some paranoid tendencies.

SUSAN: Look, you could be just a little nicer.

MIKE: I'm nervous enough as it is. I'm here to complete a bet, all right? This is not my idea of fun . . . , Sue.

SUSAN: Fine. *(A few seconds pass.)* So, I understand that you are a college student also.

MIKE: How did you know that?

SUSAN: The experiment is on college-age test subjects.

MIKE: Oh, yeah.

SUSAN: So where do you go?

MIKE: I go to—*(A red light flashes.)* What was that? Did you see that?

SUSAN: I think it was the light telling us that one minute has passed. Wow, that was rather quick. *(sarcastically)* I suppose time flies when you're having fun.

MIKE: I guess so. *(sarcastically)* Well, then, I suppose we'd better have more fun, so the time will pass even faster. So, what do you want to do when you get out of college?

SUSAN: To tell you the truth, I'm studying to teach German. The language is my favorite although I annoy my boyfriend by speaking it around him.

MIKE: Doesn't know it, huh? The language, I mean.

SUSAN: Not the slightest bit. I tried to teach him some, but he has a rather bad memory.

MIKE: Sounds kind of cruel if you ask me. I'll tell you, it would bother me if my girlfriend spoke a different language. Who knows what she would be saying behind my back.

SUSAN: Well, I don't talk about him behind his back, at least I don't say anything bad.

MIKE: Yeah, well, *(Red light flashes again.)* Wow. Another one. This is going rather quick. You'll be out of here before you know it. Then I'm still stuck in here, though. Time will probably slow down for me.

SUSAN: It won't if you don't worry about it.

MIKE: Right. You don't know my luck. My initials are M.L., and they might as well stand for Murphy's Law. If something bad could happen to me, it will. There's no getting around it. It's been that way all my life. Do you realize that I probably have not had one thing good happen to me? Bad luck and I have a very strong relationship: It attacks me and I fall.

SUSAN: Like how?

The dialogue establishes tension, building to the climax.

MIKE: What do you care? Why would I tell you? *(Red light flashes.)* Wait a minute! Already? It's been a minute?

SUSAN: Well, I suppose so; the light came on.

MIKE: You know what? I really want to know exactly what these external stimuli are that the good doctor was telling us about.

SUSAN: I don't know. Just relax and let things happen. Take a few deep breaths and calm down.

MIKE: Yeah, you're right. It's just that weird things always happen to me. Nothing ever goes the way I want it to.

SUSAN: Couldn't you be overreacting just a little bit? Just what in your life is so bad?

MIKE: I'm not opening myself to you! I don't even know you. Why don't you just keep your nose out of my business?

SUSAN: All right, I'm sorry. *(There is a long pause. Mike begins to calm down, and Susan just sits quietly.)*

MIKE: Look, I'm sorry. *(Red light flashes again.)* It has not been another minute! *(becoming nervous)* What is going on here? Why is that thing blinking so often?

SUSAN: What is wrong? What are you so insecure about?

MIKE: I am not insecure! Why does everyone think I'm insecure?

SUSAN: Because you obviously are!

MIKE: *(looking at Susan strangely)* You're part of the experiment aren't you? Aren't you? You are in on all this! That is why you keep asking me questions, isn't it? And that's why . . . you took the cushioned seat! Isn't it?

SUSAN: What! You—you offered me this seat. *(Mike freezes.)*

MIKE: *(calming down)* Oh, yeah. I'm very sorry. *(Red light flashes again.)* No. It has not been a minute. *(The doctor enters and walks to Susan.)*

DOCTOR: All right, your time is up. *(She stands up and begins to exit, then turns around.)*

SUSAN: It was nice meeting you, Mike.

MIKE: Yeah, likewise, Sue.

DOCTOR: You have five more minutes, Mike. I will return. *(Doctor and Susan exit through the door. Mike is left alone.)*

MIKE: Five more minutes. Good, I can't wait until this is over. *(He sits with his head resting on his hand. A few seconds pass, and it is obvious that he is already bored.)* Oh, boy. Okay, what to do for five minutes. *(He pauses and then sings.)* She'll be comin' 'round the mountain when she comes, she'll be comin' 'round the mountain when she comes, she'll be comin' 'round the mountain, she'll be comin' 'round the mountain, she'll be comin' 'round the mountain when she comes. *(He stops and looks at his wrist.)* Oh, I forgot he took my watch. I wonder how long it's been. I know it hasn't been a minute yet, but I wonder how long it's been. *(He looks up.)* C'mon. C'mon. Flash that red light.

As the play shifts to a series of monologues, the tension and action increase.

(All lights on stage go out.)

MIKE: Hey! What happened? Where are the lights? Hey, how am I to know that a minute's passed? I know you guys can hear me! Did the power go out? If it did, I would like to end the experiment now. Hurry and get the lights back on! How am I supposed to know if a minute has passed? Let's end the experiment, okay? This is supposed to be a controlled environment, so your experiment is no longer good, right? C'mon, Doc, you can answer me!

(Lights come back up.)

MIKE: Good, I hate the dark. *(looking at the mirror)* Am I done now? *(a pause)* I guess not. Did the light flash, I mean, was the light supposed to flash, because if it was I missed it and I would like to know if it did! Look, I know at least one minute has passed! Now where's that light? If I missed it, I want to see it. *(He pauses, looking up.)* Is this part of the experiment? I would like to know! . . . Where is that light? *(begins to become hysterical)* I know that light should have come on! It came on fast for Sue: Bam. Bam. Bam. Bam. Bam. Just like that and then she was out! Why isn't there a light for me yet? *(He begins advancing to the mirror.)* I know you are behind there, you pencil-necked—

Where's that light! If you guys are trying to pull some sort of prank here, I don't find this amusing! I want out of here and I want out now! NOW! *(He turns around, seemingly going crazy.)* Boy, Mike, they really knew how to get you mad. Put you in a room by yourself, lying, telling you they'll flash a light every minute, and then not doing it. *(He begins to get very angry again.)* They just make you upset. *(He pauses, getting an idea, then moving to his chair.)* Watch this! You'd better come in to try and stop me, or you better flash that light! *(He lifts up the chair and moves to the wall.)* I'll do it . . . I swear I'll do it! *(He pauses, then begins busting his chair against the wall.)* You'd better stop me! *(He beats it apart, then stops, breathing very hard.)*

(A blue light flashes. Mike looks up and tightens.)

MIKE: What is that? A BLUE light? What is a blue light for? *(He is now clearly irrational. He looks to the mirror.)* A blue light! That was a blue light! *(screaming at the top of his lungs now, after having gradually amplified his voice the entire time)* I want you to get me out of here! Do you hear me? Get me out of here! I'm sick of this! You're messin' with my mind, you psychotic—You people need help if this is what you do for pleasure! *(Still screaming, he moves back to the other chair.)* I'll bust this one, too! I swear I will! Watch me! *(He begins to lift it, but passes out before he even gets it off the ground. He collapses in extreme exhaustion beside the chair.)*

(The doctor reenters with a pen and paper. He examines the room.)

The doctor's final clinical comments provide an open-ended conclusion.

DOCTOR: *(ignoring Mike and reading from notes)* Male subject . . . age 20. Above average intelligence. Response to shifting patterns in external stimuli: irrational. Conclusion: none . . . Next subject please.

Professional Model

"A Woman Called Truth" is based loosely upon the life of Sojourner Truth, who was born into slavery in Ulster County, New York—one of the few pockets of slavery in the North. Playwright Sandy Asher chose to highlight several significant events in Sojourner's life, events that display the courage, wit, and determination for which this early abolition and women's rights advocate became known. In the following excerpt, Sojourner relates the story of her early years as a slave. (Excerpted from, *A Woman Called Truth: A Play in One Act Celebrating the Life of Sojourner Truth* by Sandra Fenichel Asher. Copyrighted 1989 by Sandra Fenichel Asher. Reprinted by permission of the Dramatic Publishing Company, Woodstock, Illinois.)

A Woman Called Truth

CHARACTERS

SOJOURNER TRUTH . . . also referred to as BELLE, a tall, muscular, handsome black woman with a forceful speaking and singing voice

OTHERS

Two women and three men play a variety of roles as follows:

FIRST WOMAN . . . black, also plays MAMA, SISSY, and OLD WOMAN

SECOND WOMAN . . . white, also plays MRS. NEELY, MARIA, MRS. GEDNEY, and MRS. WHITING

FIRST MAN . . . white, also plays BAUMFREY, NEELY, CATLIN, ISAAC, CHIP, OLD MAN, and FIRST REVEREND

SECOND MAN . . . white, also plays AUCTIONEER, DUMONT, GEDNEY, OFFICER, and SECOND REVEREND

THIRD MAN . . . black, also plays brother PETER, BOB, son PETE, and SLAVE BOY

TIME: Approximately 1810-1855

PLACE: In and around Ulster County, New York,
New York City, and Akron, Ohio.

The stage directions give actors and directors important clues for presenting the play. (Note that Asher uses a bare stage.)

AT RISE: *The stage is bare except for six cubes or stools, a lectern, a prop table, and hat racks. Five cubes are arranged U [upstage]. The lectern is DR [downstage right]; the sixth cube, DR of it. The table and racks are at the sides of stage and hold props and costume changes. OTHERS are seated on U cubes in shadow. FIRST WOMAN and THIRD MAN wear slave cloth; the rest, street dress suggesting the 1800's. SOJOURNER, also in slave cloth, a rough strip of undyed material with a neck hole, sits on DR cube in a pool of light. OTHERS' voices are heard out of darkness.*

FIRST WOMAN. Tell your story. It must be told.

SECOND WOMAN *(disdainfully)*. Well, wouldn't you just know it?

FIRST MAN. Is something wrong?

THIRD MAN. Tell your story.

SECOND WOMAN. Don't you see her? Sitting on the steps of the podium as if she owned the place? This is no woman's rights

The simple staging allows the play to go back and forth between the past and the present, weaving together the various strands of Sojourner's life.

convention. This is an abolitionist affair. Get her down from there.

FIRST WOMAN. Tell your story.

SOJOURNER. But who will listen? Who will hear?

FIRST WOMAN. They'll listen. They'll hear.

(SOJOURNER rises as OTHERS sing first verse of "Somebody Callin' my Name.")

OTHERS. **HUSH, HUSH, SOMEBODY CALLIN' MY NAME,**
HUSH, HUSH, SOMEBODY CALLIN' MY NAME,
HUSH, HUSH, SOMEBODY CALLIN' MY NAME,
OH, MY LORD, OH, MY LORD, WHAT SHALL I DO?

SOJOURNER *(moves behind lectern and begins her narrative in a mature but not overly aged voice)*. My name? *(Laughs, shakes her head.)* Which one is that, I wonder? Oh, I've had a bunch of them in my day. And a bunch of days for each of them. Yes, indeed, I've lived a life, I have. "What if there is no heaven?" a fellow once asked me. "What if you never get there? What'll you say then?" "I'll say, 'Bless the Lord,' " I told him, I had a good time thinking I would! *(OTHERS ad lib responses of "Amen," etc., as if at a lecture or tent meeting.)* I was born a slave in Ulster County, New York. Oh, yes, there were slaves up there, too. Not so many as in the south, and not so profitable, so there was talk going on about changing the laws. Took its time doing me any good. Must have been seventeen ninety-something I came into this world. On a bed of straw in the slave cellar. We were part of the livestock, Mama, Papa, my brother Peter, and me. There were other children, too, but I never knew them. All sold away. Mama called me Isabelle, but that got shortened to Belle. My last name belonged to my master, just like me. Belle Hardenburgh. Master Hardenburgh's Belle. Papa's name was Baumfrey, a Dutch word. Ulster County was Dutch country, you see. Everybody spoke Dutch up there, master and slave alike. Baumfrey means tall, strong tree.

MAMA *(in darkness)*. Where are you going, Baumfrey?

SOJOURNER *(continuing narrative)*. Master Hardenburgh was a kindly man, but he was getting old.

BAUMFREY *(in darkness)*. Up to the sickroom, Mama Betts. I've been called.

MAMA. Is Master that bad?

BAUMFREY. Bad, Mama Betts. Bad sick. I've got to go.

SOJOURNER. There was awful quiet in the slave cellar that night. Families huddled together, waiting. Peter and I fell asleep, but Mama kept watch.

Authentic slave songs, spirituals, and folk songs offer a sense of history and cultural roots.

The short lines in this section suggest a quick give-and-take of ideas.

(PETER comes forward into light as SOJOURNER moves in front of lectern. They huddle on floor, asleep. OTHERS sing following verse of "Somebody Callin' My Name.")

OTHERS. **EARLY ONE MORNIN', DEATH CAME KNOCKIN' AT MY DOOR,**
EARLY ONE MORNIN', DEATH CAME KNOCKIN' AT MY DOOR,
EARLY ONE MORNIN', DEATH CAME KNOCKIN' AT MY DOOR,
OH, MY LORD, OH, MY LORD, WHAT SHALL I DO?

(MAMA hurries forward into light, whispering.)

MAMA. Isabelle! Peter! Wake up.

SOJOURNER *(in a child's voice)*. Mama? What is it?

MAMA. Just listen to me, child. Pay attention now. I want you to show me you remember everything I've been teaching you.

PETER. I'm tired, Mama. I want to sleep.

MAMA. No time for that now. You must swear to me that you will never lie.

SOJOURNER. Mama, why are you—

MAMA. Isabelle, do as I say!

SOJOURNER. Yes, Mama.

MAMA. Will you ever lie?

SOJOURNER and PETER. No, Mama.

MAMA. And you will never steal?

SOJOURNER and PETER. No, Mama.

MAMA. And you will always obey your master?

SOJOURNER and PETER. Yes, Mama.

MAMA. Good. Now, children, listen hard to what I tell you tonight, even if I have told it all before. I want you to remember it always, because you will be told many things after I am gone.

SOJOURNER. Where are you going, Mama?

MAMA. Just listen. There is a God, and he sees everything and he knows everything. You must never forget him, you hear? He lives in the sky, high, high up in the sky. And if ever you are beaten or cruelly treated—

SOJOURNER. Master doesn't beat us, Mama.

MAMA. Isabelle, will you hush? *Listen to me.*

SOJOURNER. Yes, Mama.

The mother prepares Sojourner and Peter for their fate by giving them the only gift she can offer—her faith.

MAMA.	Whenever you fall into any kind of trouble, you must ask God for help. Talk to him. Listen to him. He will always hear you and help you, if you remember to ask. Will you?
PETER.	Yes, Mama.
SOJOURNER.	I'll remember.
MAMA.	Good. Now, look. Look up at the stars. Do you see them?
SOJOURNER.	I see them.
MAMA.	Those are the same stars that shine down on your brothers and sisters, the very stars they see as they look up, though they are far away from us and from each other. Remember them. Remember us here, right now, warm and close. No matter where we go, when we look up at those stars, we will be together.

[The rest of Asher's play describes Sojourner's life following the death of Master Hardenburgh and how it was that Isabelle Hardenburgh became known as Sojourner Truth.]

Reflective Writing

"On our way to bed one night we stopped to pose for this next picture. One of our favorite games growing up was to pretend we were old. Dressed in robes, tottering around calling each other Esther and Albert, we listened to our wind-up radios." —Amy Serang

Essay of Reflection

In an essay of reflection, a writer focuses on an important aspect of his or her past experience. Instead of simply trying to re-create this experience, the writer works more closely with the subject, carefully examining it in order to form new understandings about its significance.

"It seems to me . . ."

Discussion: In a reflective essay, explore your thoughts and feelings about an important time or personal relationship in your life. Think of this activity as an opportunity to put a specific aspect of your experience into better perspective. Carefully reflecting upon a subject naturally leads to new understandings about it. Refer to the model essays that follow and the writing guidelines below to help you develop your work.

Searching and Selecting

1. **Searching** • Choosing a subject for your work should not be difficult. Start with an inventory of all the people who, for better or worse, have made a difference in your life. Also think of the many important times *(starting high school)*, events *(family get-togethers)*, and activities *(neighborhood games)* in your past experience.
2. **Reviewing** • Continue your subject search, if necessary, by reviewing your special skills or interests. Are you an accomplished artist or basketball player? Do you enjoy playing a musical instrument or working on cars? (There is always a story to be told about a special talent.) Also review your journal entries for ideas, and talk about possible subjects with your classmates.

Generating the Text

3. **Collecting** • With a worthy subject in mind, collect your initial thoughts and feelings about it through free writing, clustering, cubing, or dialogue writing.
4. **Assessing** • Assess your initial thinking and writing. Have you identified the important details related to your subject and formed any new thoughts about it? (Remember that reflecting involves exploring and examining ideas and experiences.) Continue collecting as necessary.
5. **Shaping** • The most common way to shape a reflective essay is to tell a story or re-create a time or experience, and along the way, reflect upon different parts of it. If this story structure doesn't work for you, shape your essay along more traditional lines.

Writing and Revising

6. **Writing** • Develop your first draft freely as an important story that needs to be told—or according to other planning and organizing you may have done.
7. **Revising** • As you review your work, look for important details that might be missing or any gaps in thought. Also make sure any new understandings you have formed are clearly expressed. Revise and refine accordingly.

Evaluating

Does the writing form a meaningful whole, moving smoothly and clearly from start to finish?

Does the writing display qualities associated with reflective writing (examining, exploring, reconsidering, etc.)?

Will readers appreciate the treatment of this subject?

Student Model

In this essay, Will Tillman reflects upon the death of a special friend. This model is a good example of an important story that needed to be told. (This essay first appeared in the June 1992 commemorative issue of the *High School Writer*. It is reprinted with permission.)

A Short Story of an Unknown Man

The purpose (or need) for the essay is clearly established in the opening paragraph.

Mr. Montgomery was 56 when he died. It felt strange to see his picture there on the obituary page. What was more bizarre than that was seeing his last name. Montgomery. All I had ever known him as was Thomas. He was a gentle man, one of the best people I have ever known. His hair and beard were long, down to his chest, and flecked with white, which gave him the appearance of an Indian guru. His whole life was a page right out of the hippie era. The hair, the incense, everything he did typified hippiedom. But now he was gone. His passing left a terrible void in my life that has yet to be filled.

The writer highlights important aspects of his subject's lifestyle.

Thomas was much more than a neighbor. He was a friend to the point of almost being a relative. He had lived in the house across the street from us long before we had moved into our house on Marks Place. Since he had lived there, he had turned his house into his own personal sanctuary. It was dark, but not gloomy. The animals he kept gave the house a pleasantly uncaged feel. Only his guinea pigs and birds were confined, but even they had a whole room. But, that was how Thomas lived. Free and easy. I guess that is why I loved him so much. He was the grandfather I never had, and that is why his death hurt me so badly. Only now do I recognize what a dear and trusted friend he was.

Thomas knew he was dying. The doctors did not have to tell him he had cancer spreading through his body like wildfire. He knew. But this knowledge did not stop his life. He worked until he was too weak to perform his job. He was never bedridden.

The last time I saw Thomas he was cleaning house, just like nothing was wrong. I remember our last conversation. It was about school, my parents, just the things we had always talked about. The only thing different was the sense of urgency when he asked me to come back and see him. I almost cried that day. He and I both knew the end was near. It was just a question of time. I swore I would come and see him again. I swore it.

As I walked across his yard and into the street, I somehow knew that this was the last time I would see Thomas. I knew it in my mind, but I just could not accept it in my heart.

In the end, the writer attempts to come to terms with the passing of his friend.

I lost more than a friend that day in November of 1986. I lost a man I dearly loved. I did not see Thomas after I left that day. He died in his sleep the next night. I have had to live with that unkept promise for the past five years. I feel like somehow I let him down. When I think about it, I cry. I hope I will be able to face death with as much bravery as he did. I miss him very much. Thomas, I love you.

Student Model

In this essay, Amy Serang reflects upon her close relationship with her younger brother Andrew. Note that a series of old photographs prompts the writer's initial reflections. (This essay first appeared in the June 1992 commemorative issue of the *High School Writer*. It is reprinted with permission.)

My Brother, My Best Friend

The "gray, icy rain" puts the writer in a reflective mood.

It is raining. A heavy, gray, icy rain. The kind of rain that brings tears to my eyes and sends worry pulsing through my veins. The kind of rain that makes me long to be five years old again.

When I got home from school, I got out my old photo album. Feeling the soft cover in my fingers, I slumped onto my bed and began glancing over the familiar shots of my brother and myself. His name is Andrew, but I've called him "Boo" ever since he was born, right before my second birthday. I couldn't pronounce "brother" properly, so I referred to him as my "little booner." Eventually abbreviated to "Boo," the name stuck. By the time he was three he responded to nothing else.

Imagining his tanned face today, I am amazed by how miniature and helpless the picture makes him look, lying in his tiny wooden cradle. I smile to think that someone six-foot-three ever slept in a cradle two feet long. To see him sleeping so peacefully makes me realize how vulnerable he was, and to an extent, still is.

The descriptions of the photographs focus on the special relationship between Serang and her brother.

Snapshots of my fifth birthday party are on the next page. All of my best kindergarten friends were there, but it was Boo beside me. He always got the first invitation. Most years he was even allowed to open one of my gifts.

On our way to bed one night we stopped to pose for this next picture. One of our favorite games growing up was to pretend we were old. Dressed in robes, tottering around calling each other Esther and Albert, we listened to our wind-up radios. We always wished that we were already old. Looking back now, though, I want nothing more than to be young again.

One of our greatest weaknesses has always been keeping secrets from each other. This picture was taken three days before Christmas —when we exchanged gifts. We were never able to stand the suspense. Last year I had to go out Christmas Eve to buy him a gift, so I would have something to give him the next morning.

Swimming is something we have always been able to share but at the same time couldn't. It all started in our inflatable pool in the backyard. The picture of us perched on the red, yellow, and blue plastic sliding board brings back a flood of warm summer memories. Sitting there grinning in our saggy racing suits, we felt ready to conquer the world. The expression on his face in the picture is the same one I'll see this summer as I look across the pool from my lifeguard stand to his.

The writer provides an effective mixture of specific details and personal reflection throughout the essay.

When swimming lessons rolled around, though, he was a lot more hesitant than I was. But as soon as the four women pried his fingers from the chain-link fence, he was ripping up the water. I remember a similar situation arising when registration for swim team was held a few years later. Every morning my mom and I had to bribe him to go to practice. That was until his first ribbon. Today, as a record-holding All-American who practices 30 hours a week, he still cringes to hear how he got his start from a desire for a McDonald's baseball cap. It seems ironic that a one-dollar-and-fifty-cent bribe made ten years ago could soon be worth a couple-thousand-dollar scholarship.

Most people assume that we are twins. We look similar, finish each other's sentences, and carry on conversations without words. When he sleepwalks and hides things, our parents come to me to find out where he put them. When he is tired and mumbles, they ask me what he is saying. When he is depressed, they ask me to talk to him.

The last time I was depressed I bought a pound of M&Ms and two liters of Pepsi. I sat on my bed feasting away (in hopes of extricating myself from my rut) until there was a knock on my door. In he came to tell me how much he hates Latin and how terrible geometry is. I poured half of the bag onto the bed in front of him and handed him the bottle.

The significance of leaving home for college and being "really alone" is the focus of the writer's closing reflections.

On the way in tonight I collected the college brochures from the mailbox and carried them to my room with me. I usually enjoy poring over every detail about every college, but today I can't even open the envelopes. The closer I get to leaving for college the more anxious I become. However, on days like today, I can't face the realization that I will be alone. Really alone. I can't face the fact that when I leave home next year, I will be leaving a part of myself behind. For the first time he won't be there for me. Through four moves, seven schools, and eight "best friends," he was there for me. My only best friend. Who will I drive to the bus stop or rent movies with? Who will share my midnight snacks? Who will pack my lunch and call me Esther and beat me at Ping-Pong? Who could take his place? ▣

Student Model

In this essay, Ferentz Lafargue reflects upon his boyhood friends—first as close childhood playmates and now as struggling young adults. (This essay first appeared in the November 1992 issue of *New Youth Connections: The Magazine Written By and For New York Youth*. It is reprinted with permission.)

The Crew from the Parking Lot

Highlights of the crew's boyhood activities are provided in the first section of the essay.

The parking lot behind Wertheimer's department store on Jamaica Avenue was once a place where a lot of boyhood dreams were born. Dreams of growing up and playing for the Yankees or Giants someday, dreams of meeting that girl, the one you knew was out there, the one that was made for you. My friends and I used to spend the whole afternoon there playing baseball, football, man hunt, and practically anything else you could think of.

One day we noticed a piece of wood in the corner of the lot. We found a rock to prop it up and made ourselves a bicycle ramp. We practiced jumping for a week or two until the wood broke and it was back to playing bike tag and waiting for the next thing to come along.

Every winter when it snowed, there would be huge piles of snow in the corners of the lot. We would start out by doing some light skiing to get warmed up and soften up the snow. (The skis were made of the finest cardboard we could find.) But we all know what happens when you put a bunch of guys somewhere with snow . . . SNOWFIGHT!!

The rules were simple: whichever mountain you were on was your territory and whoever was with you was your team. We would fight until one team captured the other team's mountain or the teams split up and everyone started fighting amongst themselves. When that happened, it was every man for himself. We would go home looking like we had just climbed Mt. Everest, and sometimes I think that would have been easier.

WE WERE A TEAM

We also shared a lot of disappointments in the parking lot. We felt bad for Ed when he didn't make the varsity basketball team. We felt sorry when Devon's girl Wendy moved away. (They were the royal couple of the parking lot.) When Abner and Carlos were sent to fight in the Persian Gulf War, we all kept an eye on the news. There weren't any me's or I's in the parking lot—we were a team.

The essay is organized around a special order of time: how the crew operated before and how they operate now.

But these days the parking lot is just used for parking cars. We don't even keep in touch like we used to. Rarely will you see two of us together. Some have moved away; the rest just feel like they're miles away. At least to me they do. The only thing we all have in common is that we grew up.

When I look around now and see people that I used to be down with back in those days, I feel really sorry for some of these guys.

Devon was the superstar of the parking lot. He could throw, run, catch—the whole nine. We used to think he was the total package. We thought he would play high-school baseball or football, then get drafted or get a scholarship, and go on to become a major leaguer. But instead of going out for one of the teams, he opted to be down with the fellas, hanging out and doing things like robbing people, stealing chains, or getting caught up in stupid gang battles.

RIKER'S, HERE I COME

Now he's one of the people who comes up to me and talks about how he messed up, how he should have stayed in school. Now the only things he strives for are his own apartment, a G.E.D., a job, and a car. Devon's only 18 and has been sent to Riker's two times already. The sad thing is he has no fear of going back.

The writer reflects upon the lives of a few individual crew members.

Devon's younger brother John was a pretty good ball player too, but more importantly, he was a B+ student and a born leader. He was never afraid of being team captain. In fact, he thrived on it. He used to talk about joining the Marines and getting his M-14. Now John is 17 and has a kid, and he's not even close to a high-school diploma. He was hardly ever in school last year. The word is that John is dealing guns. An M-14 is probably child's play compared to some of the guns he's come in contact with.

Then there's Angel. Angel used to be my best friend, and in a way he always will be. Angel had drive and determination. One summer he lost his glove and, being that he was the only lefty in the parking lot, he had no one to lend him one. But Angel decided not to let that keep him on the sidelines. He found a right-handed glove and for about a year and a half he tried to be right-handed. He started doing almost everything right-handed.

Eventually he got another left-handed glove. But even after that you could occasionally see him tricking an opposing batter with a wicked right-handed curve ball. Angel hasn't dropped out yet, not officially, but I doubt he goes to school more than five full days a year. When he does go, he usually cuts out early in the day. Now Angel's dealing drugs. He used to have determination, but these days the only thing he seems determined to do is mess up his life.

ROLE MODEL?

The tragic significance of one fallen friend is examined.

The sad thing is that these are the guys that little kids look up to. The other day one of my friends and I were walking down 89th Avenue and one of my little brother's friends came up to us with a fake blunt that he had rolled up, and was telling us how good it was. This kid is 10 years old at most. But you really can't blame him. That's what's considered cool.

The ones that plan to go on to college go so that as soon as they're finished and have some money in the bank, they can move as far away from the neighborhood as fast as they can. My homeboy Abner, for example, hasn't even graduated from college yet, and he's already beginning the process. He recently moved to Forest Hills, and if it weren't for his parents, you'd never see his face around the block at all.

He even started to forget people's names. There's one girl he's known for about 10 or 15 years now, and the other day he couldn't come up with her name. It made me wonder if he remembers mine.

I'M THEIR LAST, BEST HOPE

Then there's me. I was the youngest kid in the parking lot, which meant I was last to get picked for the teams and the first to get picked on. I was like everyone's little brother. I never made it to the forefront; I just stood back and watched everyone else. I looked up to these guys. But I knew the real them. I was smart enough to learn from their mistakes.

They still keep an eye out for me. Every time one of them sees one of my articles or hears about me doing anything else good, he's always ready to congratulate me and tell me to keep it up. It's almost like I'm their last hope of success: if I come out okay, then they'll honestly be able to say they had a hand in raising me.

I intend to go to college and study communications and advertising. Hopefully one day I'll be writing for a big-time newspaper (no offense NYC) or working for an advertising company. Then I'd like to make sure my little brother gets his act together, help fix up my neighborhood, and do whatever I can to help out some of my old friends. But whatever I end up doing, one thing I won't do is let those guys down and mess up my life.

The writer's closing comments suggest that through this writing, he was able to form new understandings about his relationship with the parking lot crew.

Writing this article, I discovered I'm a pretty lucky guy after all. Remembering all those good times we had in the parking lot was enough to make me cry. I hope everyone has a parking lot in his or her life. What good is a tree without roots?

Student Model

In this model, Joe Fletcher reflects upon a special teacher he had when he was in middle school. Note that the writer directs his comments specifically to this teacher in a thoughtful and personal letter.

The writer recalls in detail, and with great respect, Mr. Schyvinck's special style of teaching.

Dear Mr. Schyvinck,

Throughout life, people are always influenced in some way by others. This influence is what causes individuals to grow mentally. It has been no different for me. I have met a wide variety of people in my life and have learned from each of them. The one person that sticks out in my mind as having had the most influence on me, however, is you.

I liked you from the first day I had you for seventh-grade English class, and it is easy to see why. You were a teacher with a great sense of humor—not what I was accustomed to. That first day, all you did was sit there and talk with us, sharing your feelings. You even joked with us about how one day, someone in another class had had really bad body odor. Our class could sense we had someone special for a teacher.

One reason why I took such a strong liking to you is that my parents had recently gotten a divorce, and I was coming out of a turbulent sixth-grade year. I needed something to fill the emptiness I was feeling. You were there for me. You had a way of making me feel good about myself, who I was and what I did. The little talks that you had with us really touched on some things that I needed to hear. I remember one day you told us that we should not be overly concerned when people ridicule us. You said that the important thing is that we like who we are. You restored some confidence in me that I had thought I had lost for good.

One of your better qualities was your ability to connect a story with a meaningful lesson in life. You told us about your son who was trying out for some major league baseball team. During the tryouts, he went out of his way for a fly ball and ended up crashing into the fence. I think he hurt himself, but because of the extra effort he put forth, he made the team. You had many stories like this that inspired us to do our best.

You worked with all of us to make us better students, never leaving anyone out. You would make sure that everyone answered a question or added something to class each day. You would go around the room and ask each student a question or how he or she felt about something. You showed that you really did care if we learned. You would always stress doing more than just an average job, that we would not get very far if we were not willing to put forth that extra effort.

You told us to realize that when we did well, we could take things even further and turn our effort into an even better job. You constantly reminded us, "Don't Just Get By." I remember in October when we had to take preposition tests. You had us list as many prepositions as we could. We took about three of these tests. On the first two I listed about 70 prepositions; they were easily "A" tests. You encouraged us to learn even more, so on the third test I listed nearly 100 prepositions: around, besides, through, into, beneath . . . . This totally broke your curve and you said it was a new record. The surprising thing was I still felt that I could have done better.

Throughout the year you remained a great teacher, always fair. You

There is a directness and clarity of expression in this letter that can only come from careful writing and rewriting.

A natural method of development—before, during, and after having Mr. Schyvinck as a teacher—provides the necessary structure for the writing.

pushed us to do our homework and do it better. You could not stand students being lazy (which I was before I had you). If kids in the class would not do anything, you would make them work (unlike most teachers today who don't care and will just let them sit there not learning anything). You would ask the students questions and have them diagram sentences as a class until you were sure they knew what they were doing. Remember Paul? He was not necessarily stupid, but he just did not want to work. One day while we were diagraming sentences, you noticed him staring out the window. You made Paul diagram the next sentence on the chalkboard, incorporating him into the class. You worked with him and in a way made it fun so that he would want to work. This impressed me.

At the end of the year, we were all anxious to see what our grades were. You gave us these index cards that had our grades on them. I looked at mine, and then I turned the card over and read the words, "Don't Just Get By!" You told us to bring the cards back senior year when we graduate and you would give us a dollar.

Before I had you as a teacher, I was just an average student. Then I started applying what you were teaching us to all of my classes. I started trying harder to do the best that I could, and my grades improved significantly. Ever since our year together, I have been a 4.0 student or close to it.

Your approach affected not only my grades, but my whole outlook on life. You told us that we live life only once so we should try to live it to the fullest. Before I had you, I was a lazy, chubby kid, content to spend my free time, even in the summer, just staying inside and watching TV. You told us that if we did not like the way our lives were going that we should change them. I did not like the way mine was going so I changed it. The summer after I had you I became more active. I stayed outside a lot more and went to my friends' houses more often. I began riding my bike often, and I slimmed down and gained muscle (you probably would have made a great exercise instructor).

Ever since our seventh-grade year, I have looked at that time as a turning point in my life. I credit most of those changes to you and your indispensable advice. Without your constant encouragement, I am sure that I would still be just getting by. Many years from now, I will still look back on my childhood and reflect on the timeless lessons that you were generous enough to share with me.

I'm looking forward to graduating next year and moving on to college, but I am especially anxious to meet with you and cash in on that card that I have been hanging on to for the last four years. Along with this letter, I will finally get the chance to thank you in person for giving me the desire to do the best I can.

Best wishes,
Joe Fletcher

Professional Model

In the following excerpt from *Move On*, writer and television news personality Linda Ellerbee reflects upon her life as a contemporary American adult. Note that this model covers a great deal of time in a very short space. (This excerpt first appeared in *Move On: Adventures in the Real World* by Linda Ellerbee. Reprinted by permission of the Putnam Publishing Group for *Move On* by Linda Ellerbee. Copyright © 1991 by Linda Ellerbee.)

Adventures in the Real World

In the opening paragraph (one long sentence), the writer lists the different things she has lived through.

. . . I've lived and bled my way through *The Power of Positive Thinking*, the poodle skirt, *The Catcher in the Rye*, the first date, the way of Zen, the New Frontier, the Great Society, one giant step for mankind, the light at the end of the tunnel, our long national nightmare, the energy crisis, the "me" generation, the Cinderella Syndrome, the farmer in the White House, the actor in the White House, the Rainbow Coalition, the decade of greed, dead dreams, live television, and, yes, five networks, four marriages and two children.

Ellerbee develops another list in the second paragraph, this one counting the many blessings in her life.

And I'm still counting. What's more, as crusty but lovable Benjamin Disraeli once said, I feel a very unusual sensation—if it's not indigestion, I think it must be gratitude. I count my blessings. I'm grateful George Bush continues to breathe uninterrupted and that nobody ever died from a fractured syntax, and that on the worst day of his life Robert Redford never looked like Dan Quayle. I'm grateful Jessica loved Roger Rabbit for his soul and Ed Meese found another line of work. I'm grateful Mickey Mouse can still boogie at sixty. If Mickey can, I will. I'm grateful ET is alive and able to phone home from inside my VCR. I'm grateful for Steven Spielberg. Also Garry Trudeau, Ella Fitzgerald and NPR. I'm grateful I live in America, where a kid can grow up dreaming that one day Imelda Marcos and Leona Helmsley will share a cell somewhere. I'm grateful Jim Henson lived at all and that Kermit will live always. I'm grateful that (so far) I still have enough canned goods in the pantry to afford to say no to producers who tell me what I ought to do is host A Talk Show With Substance. Finally, I'm grateful steroids don't make you write faster. One can just say no to just so much in this life.

In closing, the writer reflects upon what she has learned in her full life.

I'm grateful for so much, but what do I know now that I didn't know then? What have I learned through all these changes in and around me? I've learned to do things my own way, even if I'm wrong, which often I am, but only dead fish swim with the stream. I've learned that if you don't want to get old, don't mellow. I've learned always to set a place in life for the unexpected guest. And to be content with questions. I was right all along; questions are better.

Most of all, I've learned that a good time to laugh is any time you can. ▣

"Mike discovered he had the disease last June. After breaking out in as rash, he underwent a series of tests, including one for HIV. The HIV test came back positive, and his near-perfect life was changed forever. 'It has affected every area of my life,' Mike says about the virus which inhabits his body." —*Amy Taylor*

Essay of Speculation

When someone writes informatively about the future, he or she is writing an essay of speculation. A writer's speculations must take into account as many variables as possible—including past patterns and experiences, current research and trends, and logical assumptions and outcomes.

What if . . .

Discussion: Write about the "future," something that hasn't happened. See what intriguing thoughts come to mind with the question, "What if . . . ?" In writing an essay of speculation you must think carefully about something in the present and make an educated guess about its future. You could address global issues, or make projections (of science fiction proportion) about a specific arena of life. Examine a current trend, cultural attitude, or present-day technology and consider what effect it might have in the future. Read the models to see how other writers handled essays of speculation. Then consult the guidelines below to help you develop your essay.

Searching and Selecting

1. **Searching** • What if we suddenly ran out of . . . ? What if cars . . . ? What if . . . ? Consider all the possibilities; then select a topic you really do have an interest in. Speculation requires a personal investment of energy in thoughtful reflection. Notice that the model essay writers all speak with personal conviction.
2. **Selecting** • If no subjects come readily to mind, try reading publications such as *Prevention Magazine*, *Men's Health*, *National Geographic*, *Discovery*, and *Omni* for possible ideas.

Generating the Text

3. **Collecting** • Have you got all the facts you need? (In the models notice the environmental facts, AIDS statistics, and the Huck quotations and dates, all supporting the authors' points.)
4. **Focusing** • Have you narrowed your topic? If you have a large issue, do you have a plan to tie everything together? Have you thought about the possible domino effect of your "what if . . ."? One change often causes another change. Will you make your point through an illustrating story or an interview (AIDS), by building a case almost like an attorney (Huck), or by using a voice of humor or satire (environment)?

Writing and Revising

5. **Writing** • After finding a topic you know and care about, begin writing. You can expect new ideas to evolve as you write. Address any roadblock (such as faulty logic) that will trouble your readers if you don't catch it.
6. **Refining** • Hold mock trials to test your speculation's logic. In a small group, you (the defense attorney) read your essay to your peers (the prosecuting attorneys). They will question *only* your logic, using statements like, "If you say that, how can this be . . . ?"

Evaluating

?...?

Have sufficient background and factual information been established?

Does the speculation (the projected effect) follow logically from its cause?

Is the "what if . . ." stated clearly?

Is "so what" adequately addressed?

Will readers sense a personal investment in this essay?

Student Model

In this essay, student writer Amy Taylor speculates on the devastating consequences of the question, What if young people do not receive, or choose to ignore, information about AIDS? (This essay first appeared in the March 20, 1992, issue of *MHS Today*, the Milton [WI] High School student newspaper.)

The essay focuses on the story of an AIDS victim and his wife; the writer provides background information and explanations as needed.

AIDS Can Happen Here!

"The difference between good people and bad people is good people learn from their mistakes. You shouldn't have to pay for your mistakes with your life."

Unfortunately, Mike Johnson of Milton, Wisconsin, will pay for his mistake with his life.

At first glance, Mike, 29, appears to be a typical up-and-coming businessman. He is well dressed, highly intelligent, articulate, and healthy in appearance. However, he is not your typical businessman. Mike Johnson has AIDS.

He was infected at least six years ago by a former girlfriend. Unaware that he had been exposed to the HIV virus, Mike married. His wife, Sherie, has also tested positive for HIV.

Mike discovered he had the disease last June. After breaking out in a rash, he underwent a series of tests, including one for HIV. The HIV test came back positive, and his near-perfect life was changed forever.

"It has affected every area of my life," Mike says about the virus which inhabits his body.

But Mike is a positive person.

"There's always a reason to be depressed," Mike says. "I choose not to be. I am faced with my imminent demise; therefore, life becomes a very precious thing. Self-pity is not a very productive state of emotion, so why do it?"

Mike and Sherie were living in Dallas, Texas, when they tested positive for HIV. They moved back to Milton to be near their families and friends.

Since moving back to Milton, Mike and Sherie have been speaking at schools throughout the state, believing the only way to overcome the epidemic is for people to fight against AIDS.

Since teenagers are currently the highest risk group, the Johnsons are especially concerned with educating teens.

"We have been trying to let people know that HIV is a behavior-oriented disease, and you can absolutely eliminate the risk of HIV by modifying the way you behave," Mike says.

They also encourage members of the communities they visit to give teens all the facts.

"People who are afraid to be pro-active in the fight against HIV are going to have to answer to the parents two years from now who

One-third of the world's population destroyed? That statistic is speculation, based on current projections of the spread of AIDS.

say, 'Why didn't you do something when you had the chance? Now my child is dying!' " Mike added.

Mike and Sherie are doing their best to give teens all the facts and encourage them to practice abstinence.

"We have 5,000 kids sitting there, and you can hear a pin drop. We make them laugh, we make them cry, and we tell them the truth," Mike says.

The truths that they share are scary. If a cure is not found for AIDS, overpopulation will not be a problem in the future because more than one-third of the population will die of it.

"AIDS is everybody's problem," Mike explains. "Even if you're not sexually active, someone you know or care about is."

Except for taking AZT, a drug which slows the HIV virus, and Bactrim, an anti-pneumonia drug, Mike does not take many precautions to protect his health. He's too busy trying to reach as many people as possible while there is still time.

"This disease will probably kill me," Mike says. "Ironically, I have the potential to do more good than I ever would have had before."

Student Model

In this model, writer Andrew Chrisomalis questions everyone's concern about the environment. "Why the big fuss?" he says. However, once you read this essay, it's easy to see that Mr. Chrisomalis is playing with mirrors. The environment is a big deal to him; he's simply making his point through indirection (and sarcasm)—stating the opposite of what he really believes. (This model first appeared in the December/January 1991 issue of *Merlyn's Pen: The National Magazine of Student Writing*. It is reprinted with permission.)

The Environment Can Take Care of Itself

The maintenance and the survival of our environment have become sensitive and disputable issues. Various groups make different claims, from the possible near end of life as we know it, to assertions that the environment is still safe and stable. Well, I know that the environment is safe and stable.

The writer's use of indirection and understatement creates awareness of perhaps the biggest environmental problem—the attitude that there is no problem.

Why the big fuss about oil in our water? It mixes in eventually; anyone with common sense knows that. And there is plenty of water on this earth, so why get into such a stew about it? Someone is bound to invent something to solve the problem . . . it always works out in the end.

And all that ocean pollution everybody is getting so uptight about, especially in the summer: I'm more worried about the sand! Messy stuff, it just gets stuck in my hair spray and caught in my bologna sandwich when I'm trying to enjoy a relaxing beach picnic. My solution? Build more swimming pools. Such a big hullabaloo about 11 million gallons of oil that blanketed Prince William Sound. Personally, I don't relate to all those fish and ocean creatures: what did they ever do for me? Should I care that it took 22 minutes for the crew to report that they had run aground? Who's counting? They eventually did call in. People keep criticizing Exxon for having inadequate cleanup gear, just enough for a 1,000-2,000-barrel spill. Hey, at least they had something! Exxon actually did a very good job of cleaning up. I wouldn't have wasted my time recovering 2.5 million gallons of oil from the water, much less 11 million. The Exxon crews recovered almost 23 percent before they decided to call it quits. To tell you the truth, I feel sorry for Exxon. They're the poor fish that lost 200,000 barrels of oil.

The writer jumps from issue to issue, quickly dispatching each one regardless of its magnitude.

And speaking of problem solving in the good old H_2O, what about those whales? Everybody loved the book *Moby Dick*, and awesome old Ahab hunted a whale for heaven's sake! A big white one, grandfather of them all! Nowadays, these "Greenpeace" characters get all bent out of shape when people hunt those clumsy sea monsters. They call them an "endangered species" and breathe heavily at the thought of losing them. But what about us? Human beings will be an endangered species, too, if we can't eat or do anything else natural to us . . . like killing animals. Nobody criticized Daniel Boone or Davy Crockett when they hunted animals for their fur—they were our frontier heroes! Nowadays we treat furriers like Chapter 11 people. Mustn't "mistreat animals" or cause them any itsy-bitsy pain! Isn't it just as cruel for my aunt to be left shivering on a cold day?

Another one of my gripes is this recycling. Who has time to separate the green glass from the clear glass from the newspapers from the aluminum cans? My grandfather's generation didn't have to take all that trouble, so why should I? Realists like me can leave that to the "environmentalists." Or let the next generation worry about it.

And one other thing: this ozone layer business. I mean, what's it to me, as long as my Big Mac is hot? I'd breathe a lot easier if all those environmental hotheads just cooled off.

The devil-may-care final remark brings this essay to an effective conclusion.

Well, it's time for my daily run. After all, I have to maintain my body so I can enjoy life on this planet in all its beauty and diversity!

Professional Model

The writer reveals the groundbreaking research that led Twain scholar Shelley Fisher Fishkin to suggest that the source of Huckleberry Finn's voice was a young black servant named Jimmy. Because this suggestion cannot be proven, it remains scholarly speculation. This essay appeared in the *Milwaukee Journal* (July 7, 1992) as a news service release. (Copyright © 1992 by the New York Times Company. Reprinted by permission.)

Opening lines imitating Huckleberry Finn's voice attract the reader's curiosity and interest.

Twain's 'Huck' May Have Been Based on Black Youth's Voice

You don't know about this without you have read a book by the name of *The Adventures of Huckleberry Finn*; but that ain't no matter. Mr. Mark Twain wrote it and he got considerable praise for using a boy's voice to tell a tangled story about race and about America, and nobody kin say for sure where that voice come from.

Now a Twain scholar has linked Huck's voice to a 10-year-old black servant Twain met just before starting work on the book. Twain described the boy in an almost-forgotten article in the *New York Times* in 1874 as "the most artless, sociable and exhaustless talker I ever came across."

Shelley Fisher Fishkin, an associate professor of American studies at the University of Texas, shows that the speech patterns of the black boy, whom Twain calls Jimmy, and of Huck Finn are similar and in some ways identical.

But more important, given that the entire book is told by Huck, she shows how both voices mixed sassiness with satire, a point of view that helped make Twain's book one of the most important American novels. Fishkin lays out the theory in a book to be published in 1993 by Oxford University Press called *Was Huck Black? Mark Twain and African-American Voices*.

"For Professor Fishkin to come up with this," said T. Walter Herbert, a professor of English at Southwestern University in Georgetown, Texas, and an expert on 19th-century authors, "does not refute Hemingway's line that 'All modern American literature comes from one book by Mark Twain called *Huckleberry Finn*.' It simply complicates and enriches that claim."

The main part of the essay provides valuable background information and expert analysis.

A New Perspective

Uncovering the roots of Twain's art could lead to a reconsideration of the author and his most important work, which has been banned in some places because of its attitudes and language.

Twain's defenders always have argued that Huck's language was satiric and meant to expose his late 19th-century audience to its own hypocrisy and intolerance.

Tracing Huck's voice to a black source also could change the way the book is taught.

"This shows a real black root in a white consciousness," said David Sloane, a professor of English at the University of New Haven and president of the Mark Twain Circle of America.

Fishkin said she was not arguing that Twain envisioned Huck as a black child, but that "his voice in key ways was modeled on black speakers."

The heart of Fiskin's argument rests with "Sociable Jimmy," which appeared on page 7 of a 12-page issue of the *New York Times* on Sunday, Nov. 29, 1874. The page on which it ran also included obituaries, advertisements and brief news items.

In his introduction to the article, which was Twain's first published work dominated by the voice of a child, he said he had been enthralled by Jimmy's unpretentious performance.

"He did not tell me a single remarkable thing, or one that was worth remembering," Twain wrote, "and yet he was himself so interested in his small marvels, and they flowed so naturally and comfortably from his lips that his talk got the upper hand of my interest, too, and I listened as one who receives a revelation."

The writer summarizes Fishkin's argument and offers a Twain quotation to support the speculation.

After coming across it in her research for another book on Twain, Fishkin was struck by Jimmy's voice. She reread *Huckleberry Finn* 20 times and reread "Sociable Jimmy" more often, as well as examining much of Twain's writing for similar clues. She found passages in both the article and *Huckleberry Finn* that shared the same linguistic roots.

Fishkin found that Huck and Jimmy constantly repeat the same words, make frequent use of present participles, and often make the same mistakes. The two boys often use the same adjectives in place of adverbs. Jimmy says "He's powerful sick." Huck says "I was most most powerful thirsty."

The boys are alike in other ways, too, she says.

The only real family each has is "Pa," and both fathers drink too much. The boys are entranced by a particular clock, both consider themselves judges of good taste, and they are comfortable around dead animals, especially dead cats.

While they disagree about how much of Huck derives from Jimmy, all the scholars who have read the manuscript said it demonstrates—for the first time—strong black roots in Huck's speech.

"If Robert Johnson's career lends credence to the legend that the blues belong to the devil, Blind Willie Johnson stands as proof to the contrary. One of the greatest of the guitar evangelists, Blind Willie wrote songs that spoke of divine deeds, scriptures and salvation . . ."

—J. D. Considine

Extended Literary Analysis

In this form of analysis, a writer displays a critical understanding of a literary work. An effective literary analysis is based first and foremost on the writer's interpretation of a text. References to secondary sources are made to support a writer's main points, or to offer alternative points of view.

After Careful Reflection

Discussion: Share the results of your extended analysis of a literary subject in a carefully developed essay. You might, for example, match your reading or interpretation of a specific text with the viewpoints of an important critic or two. Or, you might provide a careful analysis of two or more works by the same author, or compare the work of two different authors. Then again, you might want to examine a film adaptation of a novel, and so on. The focus of your analysis must be on your own understanding of your subject. Secondary sources should be used to support the points you've already made or to provide alternative interpretations. Refer to the models that follow and the guidelines below to help you develop your essay.

Special Note: While these guidelines specifically discuss the analysis of a *literary* subject, feel free to explore an artistic or a musical subject if that makes more sense to you.

Searching and Selecting

1. **Searching** • Think of authors or texts that appeal to you, that anger you, or even confuse you. (Why a particular text confuses you can be an excellent starting point for analysis.) Focus on writers and texts you already know something about. If one form of analysis appeals to you (say, for example, a film adaptation of a novel), search for possible subjects related to that form.

Generating the Text

2. **Collecting** • Once you decide upon your subject, establish a thorough understanding of it by carefully reexamining the appropriate works, by clarifying your own thoughts about your subject, by reviewing class notes, by referring to secondary sources, and so on.
3. **Focusing** • Decide upon a suitable focus for your essay once you have established a good critical understanding of your subject. (You might have discovered an interesting point of comparison between two writers or simply have developed a new understanding about a particular work or writer.) Plan and organize your writing accordingly.

Writing and Revising

4. **Writing** • Shape your first draft according to your planning and organizing. Develop and clarify each main point in as much detail as possible, making sure to work in direct references to the text(s) and to secondary sources (if they are used) when appropriate.
5. **Revising** • Review your work carefully for clarity, coherence, depth, and style. Also make sure that all direct references to the text and direct quotes from secondary sources are properly cited. Revise and refine accordingly.

Evaluating

Does the writing demonstrate an extended understanding of a subject?

Is the writing focused, clear, and organized?

Are direct references/quotations properly cited?

Will readers appreciate the treatment of this subject?

Student Model

In this analysis, student writer Melissa Meuzelaar demonstrates an extended understanding of the film *Fantasia*. As you will soon see, Ms. Meuzelaar speaks with authority; her thoughts and feelings about the film are clearly expressed and thoroughly researched.

The essay's focus is clearly presented: *Fantasia* is a "work of art" that redefines animation.

The writer draws parallels between the music and the animation, supporting the theory that in *Fantasia* the two are intertwined.

Flight of Fancy

Don't buy *Fantasia* because it is an animated movie. Buy it because it is a masterpiece. *Fantasia* is more than just a Saturday morning cartoon or a feature-length fairy tale for small children. It is a work of art that will delight anyone who has an active imagination and loves classical music. However, it is not a movie for people who don't enjoy classical music or for people who want a well-defined plot and dialogue. *Fantasia* is a classic piece of cinematography that redefines the role of animation and reinterprets classical music in a way that delights the viewer.

James Taylor, the host of the movie, introduces *Fantasia* as a new form of entertainment. It is, he says, the "design, picture, and stories that music inspired in a group of artists." The music that inspired the artists is two hours of classical music written by some of the world's greatest composers. However, the animators did not discuss what the music meant with a music theoretician or with the composers themselves. They simply listened to the music and drew the images that it brought to their minds. Consequently, the animators' inspired interpretation appeals to the average person.

When they drew pictures for Bach's "Toccata and Fugue in D Minor," the animators created abstract images and shapes because this piece is pure music with no meaning. It is music for the sake of music. The composer probably had no theme in mind when he wrote the music. The title of the piece has no meaning other than describing the type of music. However, when the animators drew pictures for Paul Dukas' "The Sorcerer's Apprentice," they illustrated a story based on what the title suggests. Other times, they simply took an idea from a composer's statement and developed it. For example, Igor Stravinsky said that his ballet *Rite of Spring* represents primitive urges and dances, so the animators drew the birth of the world according to Darwin's theory of evolution.

The artwork in *Fantasia* has made a lasting impact on all the animation that has followed. Many animated characters created in *Fantasia* have been used by Disney Studios, other movie studios, and toy companies. In his movie *Land Before Time*, Stephen Spielberg created a menagerie of dinosaurs that look as if they migrated directly from the *Rite of Spring* sequence with only a few evolutionary changes. Mattel imitated the little pastel horses from "The Pastorale Symphony" for their toy "My Little Pony." Disney Studios has used animated characters from *Fantasia* more than any other studio. Almost every Disney movie created after *Fantasia* uses at least one character type from *Fantasia*. The elephants in the sequence "Pink Elephants on Parade" from the movie *Dumbo* are blushing imitations of the ballerinas in "Dance of the Hours."

Fantasia is the best animation ever done by Disney Studios, or any other studio, except for the newly developed computer animation. In computer

Meuzelaar assesses the animation in the film and compares it with other Disney projects.

animation, a picture is drawn on the computer and then manipulated screen by screen to create a more accurate picture than can be done with hand animation. Disney's *The Little Mermaid* and *Beauty and the Beast* outclass *Fantasia* only because they use computer animation.

The soundtrack of *Fantasia* is extremely important since the movie has no dialogue and little plot. The animators recognized this importance in a tribute called "The Soundtrack." Animators drew visual representations of the sounds produced by each section of the orchestra. For example, they made rounded images for deep, mellow instruments like the bassoon. For percussion instruments, the animators created jagged, sharp shapes. The tribute to the soundtrack is a clever way of recognizing an essential part of this type of movie.

Both the positive and negative aspects of the film are presented, resulting in a balanced and thorough analysis.

Fantasia is a piece of imaginative animation and a delightful visual representation of classical music. However, it is inconsistent in one way. The movie presents at least four separate world views. In *Rite of Spring*, Taylor describes our "lonely, tormented, little planet spinning through a sea of nothingness" before it begins the evolutionary process; whereas, in "The Pastorale Symphony," the Greek gods and legends come to life. In "Night on Bald Mountain," demons are hopelessly dancing before their master on All Hallows' Eve. The last piece, "Ave Maria," is Disney's attempt at making multiple world views sacred. It is as if Walt Disney attempts to justify a mixed world view with a sacred piece. The movie needs more consistency in this area; the variety of world views only confuses the audience.

The inconsistency in *Fantasia* might concern parents who buy it for their children. They should watch this movie as a family in order to explain to children that the world didn't evolve from funny little shapes and that God doesn't throw lightning bolts at people who have parties.

Fantasia belongs in every private movie collection because it is a landmark in animation that entertains adults and children. The inconsistencies should not hinder enjoyment of a wonderful piece of cinematography. *Fantasia* allows the imagination room to explore; it's nothing like most television programming which numbs people with saucy dialogue and shallow plots. *Fantasia* opens the door to the mind—with a flourish—and sets the imagination free. ▣

Student Model

Student writer Jamison Smith explores three major works of Henrik Ibsen. According to his thesis, the playwright often plays the anarchist that "chips away at the established order."

In the first paragraph, the writer provides convincing background information as he introduces his thesis.

This analysis effectively combines plot summaries and direct quotations from the play with primary and secondary interpretations.

Permission to Fire

"With pleasure I will torpedo [*sic*] the Ark!" Such unprovoked violence is the anarchist's tool. With it, he chips away at the established order. Such a man will compromise for nothing—not even the propagation of his own ideals. His stance is a stance against the group. Henrik Ibsen is such an individual. His desire to decimate the Ark has evoked this analysis: "Intoxicated by an uncompromising vision of absolute freedom and purity through a total purge of existing life, [Ibsen] announces what he sees as his own part of the revolution" (Brustein 37). Ibsen sets himself apart from most anarchists in that he doesn't set bombs in government buildings. Ibsen lays his incendiaries in the pages of his literature. Ibsen's words are dynamite incarnate. Ibsen's instrument is the rebel. It is through this rebel that Ibsen launches his attack.

"*The Wild Duck* . . . contains the harshest criticism Ibsen ever directed against himself" (Brustein 73). The main character is Gregers Werle, an idealist—Ibsen's self-portrait. He values truth above all else; thus, he forces his hosts, the Ekdals, to uncover the hidden secret involving them and Gregers' wealthy father. Opening the doors of everyone's past, Gregers expects the Ekdals to achieve a "great rapport . . . a life, a companionship in truth with no more deception" (Ibsen 185). Instead, Gregers' idealism "succeeds only in mutilating" (Brustein 73) what he has tried to purify. Hjalmar Ekdal despises the falseness upon which his family is based. Hjalmar withdraws his love for his daughter which drives her to suicide. Such is the "baleful effect on the lives of others when . . . certain truths . . . are put into practice." *The Wild Duck* is Ibsen's tragic commentary about "the ideologist in himself—that indignant moralist who would smash human happiness for the sake of ennobling mankind" (Brustein 74).

Similar to *The Wild Duck*, Ibsen's play *A Doll's House* involves idealism and rebellion. This time, however, Ibsen's criticism isn't directed at the rebel. In *A Doll's House*, Ibsen's protagonist is a typical eighteenth-century woman. She is her husband's little lark who dutifully does his bidding. As in *The Wild Duck*, tension arises when a dark secret of Nora's surfaces. Years prior, Nora saved her husband's life; but in doing so, she forged her father's signature on a loan document. Upon discovering Nora's transgression, Torvald verbally attacks her. Prefaced by years of subjugation, Torvald's tirade incites Nora to lash back. As George Bernard Shaw writes, "the woman's eyes are opened . . . her husband [is] left staring at her, helpless, bound thenceforth either to do without her . . . or else treat her as a human being . . . " (539). Torvald tries to assuage Nora, but he can not undo the damage. Nora has stopped loving Torvald, and she leaves him with a "slam of the door . . . more momentous than the cannon of Waterloo" (Shaw 540). In *A Doll's House*, Ibsen uses the rebel, Nora, to show the injustice of the male ego.

With the third play, the writer follows a familiar pattern, offering a brief summary followed by a discussion of the rebel theme.

More fiery than Nora or Gregers, Halvard Solness rebels against God in *The Master Builder*. Appropriately, Solness's rebellion begins with a fire. In a blaze, he loses his home and his two sons. His wife sickens with grief, and Halvard, too, feels robbed of his happiness. Solness blames his loss on God's intention to intensify his church-building efforts. Instead of immersing himself in his work, Solness revolts. At the top of a scaffolding for the first time, Solness puts a wreathe on his last church at Lysanger. He is sick with vertigo, yet high above the earth, Solness renounces God by refusing to build more churches and dedicating himself to constructing homes for human beings. From down below, a young girl watches and admires the master builder. This girl Hilda grows up to be a beautiful young woman and later calls on Solness to prove his "will, virility, and potency" (Brustein 75). To gain Hilda's fancy, he once again rises on a scaffolding despite his vertigo, this time to hang a wreathe upon the weather vane. Solness, even with his ego-filled "balloon," can not supersede God, and he falls onto the rocks below. However, in hanging the wreathe upon the vane, Solness succeeds in defying God in his own way.

The conclusion injects new information about Ibsen's private life and the transcendent nature of his work.

Ibsen uses the rebel to illustrate how ideals, inequality, and individuality can destroy happiness. Ibsen is a radical, an anarchist. He rejects comfort for higher ideals. Ironically, Ibsen is an author, not a militant subversive; his family never experienced the trauma that he vividly describes in his works; and he never torpedoed the Ark. Ibsen is able to transcend this missing experience to communicate his ideas to an audience—a feat worth applauding.

Smith

Works Cited

Brustein, Robert. The Theatre of Revolt. Boston: Little, Brown and Company, 1964.

Ibsen, Henrik. The Wild Duck. Ibsen: Four Major Plays. Trans. Rolf Fjelde. New York: Penguin Books, 1965. 119-216.

Shaw, Bernard. "A Doll's House Again." The Saturday Review 83 (1897): 539-541. Rpt. in Twentieth-Century Literary Criticism. Vol. 8. Detroit: Gale Research Company, 1982. 143.

Professional Model

Professional writer J. D. Considine wears the hat of music critic in this essay about 1920's guitarist Blind Willie Johnson, an unorthodox but successful blues and spiritual guitarist. The writer's familiarity with past and current musicians enables him to speak with authority about his subject. (By J. D. Considine, from *Rolling Stone*, April 18, 1991. By Straight Arrow Publishers, Inc., 1992. All rights reserved. Reprinted with permission.)

The Vision of Blind Willie Johnson

The writer immediately sets Blind Willie apart from other blues artists.

If Robert Johnson's career lends credence to the legend that the blues belong to the devil, Blind Willie Johnson stands as proof to the contrary. One of the greatest of the guitar evangelists, Blind Willie wrote songs that spoke of divine deeds, scriptures and salvation, not drunken debauchery, sex and sin. You'd never hear him utter a line like "Hello, Satan, I believe it's time to go." Yet the heavenly focus of Blind Willie's lyrics never took away from the earthiness of his music; if anything, it lent a certain respectability to the rhythmic insistence of his slide guitar.

All of which made Blind Willie a sensation in the late Twenties and early Thirties. Although he was hardly a prolific record maker—his output consists of a mere thirty songs, cut between 1927 and 1930—he was phenomenally successful, for a time outselling even such secular stars as Barbecue Bob and Bessie Smith. Moreover, his music endured. Not only were his biggest hits regularly reissued on the gospel market, but his influence could be heard in a diverse range of performers, from Fred McDowell and Muddy Waters to Bob Dylan and Alex Chilton.

Throughout the essay, Considine shares specific details and facts about Blind Willie and other musicians.

Nor is it hard to hear why. Johnson may have been extremely idiosyncratic, but there's no denying the power of his performances. His growling "false bass" voice takes some getting used to—said to derive from the preaching of sanctified ministers, it recalls to modern ears the "groaning" basso style of *mbaqanga* star Mahlathini—but his bullfrog delivery fairly bristles with power and authority. And though he was never a particularly accomplished guitarist, his playing was full of drama and energy. He knew how to write a riff (just ask Led Zeppelin, whose version of "Nobody's Fault but Mine" adds little to Johnson's original) and put as much grit into gospel standards like "Let Your Light Shine on Me" as he did into bluesy originals like "You're Gonna Need Somebody on Your Bond."

Listen to *The Slide Guitar: Bottles, Knives & Steel* and it's obvious Blind Willie Johnson was an original: Not only is his ghostly, quivering vibrato nothing like the more liquid tone preferred by Robert Johnson or Tampa Red, but he also seemed to be after an entirely different effect. Rather than use the slide to energize the beat, Blind Willie employed it as a counterpoint, so that on "God Don't Never Change"

The writer also provides critical comments on various songs by Johnson, revealing a close and careful understanding of this musician and his work.

it moves across the basic rhythm like the Holy Spirit over the world. That's one reason why his slide work, the focus of Yazoo's *Praise God I'm Satisfied*, continues to fascinate, from the driving "Jesus Make Up My Dying Bed" to the otherworldy "Dark Was the Night—Cold Was the Ground."

Despite the eloquence of the instrumental bits, the focus of Johnson's recordings was preaching, not playing. That hardly made them less bluesy, of course. In the context of *News & the Blues: Telling It Like It Is*, a collection of blues songs on public issues and events, Johnson's "If I Had My Way I'd Tear the Building Down" makes the struggle of Samson seem every bit as contemporary as the fight in Jack Kelly's "Joe Louis Special," which is also included on the volume. But Johnson's real genius was in applying the physicality of the blues to his spirituals. That's what gives *Sweeter As the Years Go By*, a second compilation of Johnson's songs, its kick, from the call and response of "John the Revelator" to the thumping pulse that ignites "Let Your Light Shine on Me," and that is why Johnson's music seems vigorous, vital and moving even now. ▣

Professional Model

An extended literary analysis may assess and critique works by two different writers. In the following analysis, Anne-Marie Oomen examines books of poetry written by two award-winning African-American poets who share a common culture and theme. The writer uses her own poetry-writing experience, as well as her own deep appreciation for both volumes of poetry, as the basis for her ideas. As you will see, no secondary sources of information are cited.

For Better or Worse

The opening lines introduce the subjects of the analysis and establish their basic similarities.

Poets Rita Dove and Naomi Long Madgett have written books of poetry using family and marital narratives written in the tradition of "voices." When I chose these collections for analysis, I knew Rita Dove had won a Pulitzer for her work, and Naomi Long Madgett had won a Hopwood Award. The collections are highly regarded and worthy of analysis. Both women were writing important narrative stories inspired by parallel African-American cultural experiences. One writer, however, offers the reader greater brilliance.

Naomi Madgett's early "Octavia" poems are impressive. Her identity with the long-lost aunt, Octavia, is haunting, especially in the prologue poems where she establishes her own personality as a heritage from this ancestor. Her father speaks the telling lines. " 'You outgrew the likeness,' he told me, / 'but by then, it was too late. / Reincarnated in my blood/ you were determined not to die.' " These poems emphasize the author's need to understand what happened to Octavia, and also establish her own identity, thus putting Octavia to rest at last.

Throughout the essay, Oomen makes direct references to each poet's work to illustrate her points.

Madgett tells her story in an interesting way. At times, she incorporates letters from her family's correspondence into the poetry as dialogue or simply uses the letter as a whole, establishing line breaks to make a rhythm that works in loose free verse. The poems in which she uses the letters have the strongest voice, carrying that kind of stilted tone "older" letter writers often assumed in their language. For example: "Dear son, / I am up now but not able to work. / I gave up my school two weeks ago. / Most of my salary last month / went to pay someone for teaching in my place, / doctors' bills and medicine." The effect is cumulative and endearing. The historical link adds credibility to the characters in the poems and captivates the reader's empathy.

As good as the material is, however, and as intrigued as I am with the unfolding story of the family and Octavia, the author often gets in her own way by telling us too much about what her characters feel. "The basic preparation that normal school would give / was not enough. You yearned for deeper learning, more for yourself than for the children / you would teach." These lines inform too much by telling the reader how to feel.

A more serious weakness seems to be the occasional mawkish tone in these poems. About Octavia's father, Madgett writes: "How your rebellious words / flung from my mouth / must have grieved my father! / Yet his transcendent love / for both of us / always forgave." The approach here is too direct, too preachy, and Madgett gives no startling or revealing picture to go with the sentiment.

Weaknesses in Madgett's collection could have been avoided by more careful editing and revising. However, the author's ideas work well

Both the strengths and weaknesses of Madgett's poetry are identified and then compared with the work of Dove.

thematically, and the poems are important for their historical and personal testimony about an era and a family; consequently, the collection as a whole has merit.

In contrast to Madgett's overwriting, Rita Dove's poems seem spare to the point of starvation. So much has been left out that one experiences an enjoyable "hunger." There is always something underfoot, some powerful undercurrent that leaves the reader asking for more.

In her narrative poems, Dove selects a few formative events as the underlying structure. She reviews the marriage from Thomas' point of view, then Beulah's, capturing the essence of their lives in brief moments of testing and trial. Poems like "Aircraft" reverberate through the years, though Dove speaks of only one day—one moment. She uses abstraction more skillfully than does Madgett, perhaps because she uses it less and with greater impact. After building Thomas' experience as a riveter, she tosses out one line, "Reflection is such / a bloodless light." Because of the sensory experience detailed in the previous lines, this abstraction reveals and highlights what has happened—his life is bloodless even in the moment he reflects on it.

Dove's narrative is tightened in one poem by allusions to events that happen in another poem. Her powerful opening poem, "The Event," describes the death by drowning of Thomas' friend Lem, and explains how Thomas claims the mandolin, the instrument that will lead him to all the other "events." In one of the last "Thomas" poems, "The Stroke," she writes, "He knows it was Lem all along: / Lem's knuckles tapping on his chest in passing, / Lem's heart for safekeeping, / he shores up in his arms." Returning to Lem at the point where Thomas has his first serious encounter with his own mortality unites the early and the later poems, fills out the biography, and answers the unanswered question in that first poem—so what about Lem?

As well as this graceful sense of unity, Dove's imagery is startling and beautiful. In "Straw Hat," the lines "He used to sleep like a glass of water; / held up in the hand of a very young girl" are impressive. This kind of writing does not merely absorb the reader; it inspires with its fresh metaphors.

The brilliance of the "Thomas" poems contrasts with the quiet voice in the second part of this book. The "Beulah" poems build and emphasize the story of despair, of lives being lived out. Her poems are less linked to specific events and more to the ordinary day, her mothering and pregnancies. However, Dove unites both sets of poems by sharing the imagery in both. For example, after cataloging his work in the aircraft factory, the next lines for Beulah read: "Last week they had taken a bus at dawn / to the new airdock. The hanger slid open in segments / and the zeppelin nosed forward . . . Beulah felt just that large and placid, a lake . . ."

In conclusion, the writer expresses what she has learned about her subjects and herself from this analysis.

While Rita Dove's work is superior to Madgett's, both help the careful reader to become a better judge of poetry. Rita Dove's work is exceptional. Reading two texts deriving from the same cultural tradition enabled me to more clearly see Dove's poetic brilliance and to realize how my judgment has evolved and grown. ▣

SOURCE TEXTS

Dove, Rita. Thomas and Beulah. Pittsburgh: Carnegie-Melon University Press, 1986.

Madgett, Naomi Long. Octavia and Other Poems. Chicago: Third World Press, 1988.

"When Congress passed the Gun Control Act, it didn't anticipate that Americans would desire to own civilian semiautomatic versions of military automatic weapons. Thus, the law allows the Russian-designed AK-47 to be categorized as a 'rifle' even though the weapon can easily be altered for automatic firing." —Michael Pollock

Position Paper

In a position paper, a writer takes an assertive and authoritative stand on a significant issue. A position paper is a form of argumentative writing, offering reasons for the writer's position, entertaining alternative points of view, and, in closing, reaffirming the initial position.

Heavy on My Mind

Discussion: Present your position on a significant issue of local, national, or global importance. Develop your paper so readers can clearly follow your train of thought—from your opening claim(s) to any background information you offer, from your analysis of the issue to the facts and details supporting your position. Provided below are basic guidelines to help you develop your paper. Also note the model papers following these guidelines.

Searching and Selecting

1. **Selecting** • Think of current developments in the news (decisions, trends, laws, advancements, or controversial issues) that will be of interest to you and your readers. Also study newspapers, magazines, journal entries, class notes, etc., for ideas.
2. **Reviewing** • If need be, review a current issue of the *Readers' Guide to Periodical Literature* for subjects as well as other guides or indexes in the library. Think about possible ideas as you read for pleasure or for a particular class, as you observe the normal course of events in your community, or as you overhear conversations in the cafeteria line.

Generating the Text

3. **Noting** • Determine what you already know about your subject and your initial position on it—perhaps through a freely written exploratory draft. Also state what you hope to find out during your investigation of the issue.
4. **Investigating** • Collect as many facts and details as you can to help you develop your work. While reading may be your most important source of information, also consider conducting interviews, writing letters, gaining firsthand experiences, and so on.
5. **Assessing** • Reassess (or state) your position on your subject now that you have thoroughly researched it, and then determine how you can most effectively present and support it. Plan accordingly. (Think of a position paper as a form of argumentation offering the reasons for your initial claim, entertaining one or two alternative points of view, reaffirming your position, and so on.)

Writing and Revising

6. **Writing** • Write your first draft freely, working in facts and details as they come naturally to you—or according to your planning and organizing.
7. **Revising** • Carefully review your writing; have at least two of your classmates read and react to your work as well. Revise and refine your writing accordingly. (Refer to the Proofreader's Guide when you are ready to proofread your work.)

Evaluating

Does the paper present an in-depth discussion of a timely issue?

Has a position been effectively presented and supported?

Will readers appreciate the treatment of the subject?

Student Model

The following essay presents student writer Cristina Lehman's position on the issue of religion in public schools. The essay unfolds clearly and logically, and avoids the common mistake of basing one's position on emotion rather than on fact.

The opening scenario presents the writer's position and introduces the basis of her argument.

The writer concedes a point to the opposition and then explains why this concession does not alter her position.

Examples establish the writer's "authority" and further clarify her argument.

Continued Debate on Religion in Public Schools

Picture this—after a long day in public school, the students learn that a guest speaker is coming tomorrow. Excited, they find out it is not the local weatherman, but a priest from the nearby Catholic church. Then, in the few remaining minutes of class, the students pick up their Bibles and read a few passages. As one might have already guessed, all of this would be strange indeed. Thankfully, this kind of education is not allowed in public school systems. One of the reasons can be inferred from Eunice Edgar's statement: "A religious program will make people in minority religions or without affiliation feel uncomfortable" (Dodge 2). This brings one to think that if one religion were allowed in public schools, the result would be resentment of other religions, or conformity under pressure. Therefore, religion should be kept out of public schools.

It is true that Americans have the right to practice whatever religion they want. But the issue of whether it should be permissible in public schools touches sensitive ground. To begin with, religion in public schools goes against the Constitution of the United States. Debate on this issue is based on the Constitution's amendments. The First Amendment clearly states its desire to leave religion out of public schooling. The establishment clause says there can be no official religion (Arbetman, ART. 95). The free-exercise clause relates how one can practice whatever religion one chooses (95). If religious education were to be mandated in public schools, both of these rights would be violated. In addition, the First Amendment is interpreted to prevent government agencies from giving support to religion in public schools (Peach, ART. 81). The First Amendment, however, is not the only one which deals with this issue. The Fourteenth Amendment contains an equal protection clause which states the separation of church and state (Arbetman, ART. 95). The Supreme Court has also voiced its opinion that having religion affiliated with public schooling is unconstitutional (95). Also, the American Civil Liberties Union feels that the wishes of the majority are not as important as constitutional law (Dodge 2). All in all, one can see how religion in public schools directly goes against the Constitution of the United States.

Granted, having religion in public schools might lead students down a more religious path of life. But it might also lead to chaos, disbelief, and confusion. The United States courts already feel this chaos. Many have used the courts to fight for their rights concerning this issue, but have failed. The public support to have religion in public schools has been as high as 81 percent, consisting primarily of Catholics (Thompson 1-2).

The "Students for Voluntary Prayer" is a specific example of failure. This group tried to have prayer meetings in public classrooms on the school campus. Yet, after much time and effort in dealing with the courts, the case was dismissed (Arbetman, ART. 95). In another example, President Reagan went as far as to propose a constitutional amendment that would permit

The final section offers compromises and alternatives to practicing religion in the public schools.

voluntary group prayer in schools (Thompson 1). His proposal would allow the government to dictate certain religious exercises and let the students participate voluntarily (2). Fortunately, Reagan's plan was rejected. People ranging from young students to the president have persistently fought to affiliate religion with the public schools, but to no avail.

Instead of continuing the fight against the courts and the Constitution, protestors should start to accept the compromises and alternatives that governments and schools have made. First of all, an "equal access" policy allows the state to create an open forum on campus (Arbetman, ART. 95). In addition, some schools permit prayers, invocations, or benedictions during graduation ceremonies. Many schools, such as Pulaski High School in Wisconsin, allow prayers which do not promote a particular religion. Also, some schools permit a moment of silence to respect all religious views. This also avoids legal fights (Dodge 2). Another compromise is allowing education "about" religion. This includes classes such as Biblical Literature, in which the teacher teaches in an objective, historical, and non-devotional manner. The courts also allow "release time" for students to attend classes of religious instruction (Peach, ART. 81). These alternatives allow some leeway, yet also avoid confusion.

Religion should be kept out of public schools. It is such a personal issue that people should not have to feel pressured to practice their faith the way others wish them to. Since people feel so strongly about religion, there will always be tension concerning this issue. Thus, no matter how our government treats this issue, some people will always be disappointed. So, to allow children their freedom of religion and to obey the law, the guest speaker from the nearby Catholic church will not be coming in tomorrow or anytime in the near future. ▣

Works Cited

Arbetman, Lee. "Religion in the Public Schools: The Debate Goes On." Street Law News Fall 1983: 4-7. Rpt. in School, Vol. 2. Ed. Eleanor C. Goldstein. Boca Raton, FL: Social Issues Resources Series, 1984. ART. 95.

Dodge, Gary. "Many Area Graduations Still Will Open With Prayer." Green Bay Press-Gazette 1 June 1990: 1-2.

Peach, Lucinda J. "Why Do I Have to Go to School?" Update on Law-Related Education Winter 1988: 23+. Rpt. in School, Vol. 3. Ed. Eleanor C. Goldstein. Boca Raton, FL: Social Issues Resources Series, Inc., 1989. ART. 81.

Thompson, Roger. "School Prayer." News Brief. Editorial Research Reports 16 Sept. 1983: 1-2.

Student Model

Student writer Michael Pollock presents his position on gun control in this forceful paper. Throughout the writing, Mr. Pollock employs anecdotes, facts, specific details, and analysis to state his position. (This essay originally appeared in the October/November 1990 issue of *Merlyn's Pen: The National Magazine of Student Writing*. All of the quotations appeared first in "The Right to Bear and Die by Arms," a story by Fred Bruning in the June 19, 1989, issue of *Maclean's* magazine. It is reprinted by permission of *Merlyn's Pen*.)

Peace on Earth

The opening scenario immediately catches the reader's attention and serves as a lead-in to the writer's position on gun control.

The door to the bank shatters as a Volkswagen van sails through and comes to a halt inside the lobby. The man dressed in black and wearing a pig mask jumps out of the van holding anAK-47 semiautomatic rifle. He immediately opens fire, spraying bullets all over the room. Customers are being shot and falling to the floor as what feel like magicians' swords tear at their organs. With screams and cries, they crumple to the floor like jelly, holding their chests.

This is one event that can happen to anyone if action is not taken to decrease the number of semiautomatic weapons being bought and used in America today.

We started our history with an armed revolt, and the West, North, South, and even East were won by black powder and well-placed slugs. Our Constitution speaks to the bearing of arms, although it is quite certain that the leaders of yesteryear did not anticipate that centuries later their descendants would exhibit a zeal for guns that verges on the psychopathic. How could Jefferson and Franklin have known that, in 1990, schools would install metal detectors to ferret out students carrying pistols, or that ordinary citizens could drop by their local gun shop and walk away with enough firepower to restage the Revolution? Little did the politicians of old know that in 1990 something called the National Rifle Association would function almost as a fourth branch of government. In the past, the NRA has been able to outshoot gun control advocates and coerce members of Congress, but lately the organization looks as if it is losing ground and becoming less formidable.

Details recalling a specific experience support the writer's position.

Trouble began early in 1989 when a gunman killed five children and wounded twenty-nine others and one adult in Stockton, California. The weapon of choice was a Chinese-made AK-47 assault rifle, which is able to fire nearly 100 shots without reloading. Almost immediately, it occurred to citizens of California and elsewhere that the AK-47 should not be as easy to buy as a loaf of bread. Predictably, the NRA disagreed. "Outlaw the assault rifle," said the organization, "and you tamper with America's soul."

George Bush, an NRA member himself, hesitated at first, but when fury over the Stockton incident grew like a raging inferno, the president banned imported assault rifles and called for prohibitions on high-capacity ammunition magazines manufactured in the U.S. and overseas. The NRA was livid. The NRA got more bad news when Colt Industries suspended commercial sales of the AR-15 semiautomatic rifle. Another setback came to

The writer concedes that assault weaponry has a specific purpose and use.

The writer's analysis of the Gun Control Act adds further support to his argument.

In closing, the writer's position is clearly reaffirmed—and a call to action is made.

the NRA when the California legislature voted to ban manufacture and marketing of all semiautomatic assault weapons. Setbacks like these are unusual for the NRA and may signal that gun control activists are making progress.

There are certain situations in which extreme forms of weaponry, such as submachine guns, are useful. But these situations rarely involve ordinary citizens. Sawed-off shotguns were purchased by the U.S. government and used in World War I as "trench guns" and later in World War II and the Vietnam War. In 1939 the Supreme Court, in *U.S. vs Miller*, sustained the National Firearms Act of 1934, which required their registration.

When Congress passed the Gun Control Act, it didn't anticipate that Americans would desire to own civilian semiautomatic versions of military automatic weapons. Thus, the law allows the Russian-designed AK-47 to be categorized as a "rifle" even though the weapon can easily be altered for automatic firing. Typically, such weapons, which are often used by gangs and drug dealers, can fire 300 to 1,200 rounds a minute. Their bullets penetrate cars, walls, police officers' vests, and maybe even your body. Law enforcement officials have sought for a long time to outlaw assault rifles. The NRA insists tenaciously that the AK-47 and other assault rifles are used for "hunting" by thousands of "sportsmen." I've yet to meet a hunter who would rather have a shredded elk rack from an assault rifle than a whole rack from an elk shot with a single-shot rifle. The "sportsmen" the NRA is talking about are gang members and drug dealers who are "hunting" police officers and other people.

It's time America made a choice. Either we follow the letter of the Constitution and let anyone have possession of a mass murdering tool, or we pass laws to regulate and decrease the sale of semiautomatic "hunting rifles." If enough young people learn of this life or death dispute, they can put pressure on the politicians, and action will be taken. I hope my descendants will hunt only wild animals—with a rifle that shoots only one deadly piece of lead at a time. ▣

Professional Model

In the following "memo," writer Stephen Budiansky offers his views on recent attempts to limit immigration to the United States. He urges readers to consider the following scenario: What if the first Americans had behaved like our government has and told the new arrivals to go home? (Reprinted from the June 7, 1992, issue of *U.S. News & World Report* with permission. Copyright 1992, *U.S. News & World Report*.)

1620 to 1992: Long Ago but Not So Far Away

TO: Massasoit, Chief, Wampanoag tribe

FROM: Squanto

RE: Immigration interview report, 26 DEC 1620

The writer puts himself in the shoes of a Native American reporting on the recent influx of Europeans.

One hundred so-called boat people filing claims for political asylum were interviewed. The vast majority of these claims are nonsensical. None could show a justifiable, immediate fear for their lives if they returned to Holland and/or that they had held a sensitive position in a persecuted political or religious organization. In fact, several admitted that they had only several years earlier voluntarily relocated to Holland specifically because it was an open society that would tolerate their sect ("the Separatists"). The obvious contradictions in their stories suggest that these are not bona fide political refugees but rather economic refugees, merely out to better their lives.

By referring to the arrivals as "boat people," he establishes a link between early European immigrants and contemporary refugees.

Their claim to permanent residency status based on special skills or professional training is likewise unsubstantiated. Most lack even the most basic job skills, as the earlier wave of boat people who were admitted to Jamestown has unfortunately demonstrated. Most of those immigrants were listed on the ship's manifest as "Gentleman," which they themselves define as "whosoever can live without manual labor." They are lazy, prone to acts of violence and unable or unwilling to become productive members of society. Established residents of the area complain of a rash of petty thefts and of being accosted by immigrants begging for food. Even when faced with outright starvation—and more than two thirds already have starved to death—they are unwilling to find gainful employment. In one well-documented incident, the immigrants chopped down their own houses for firewood. It is perhaps relevant that several prominent authorities in England have explicitly encouraged emigration to America as a way to rid their country of "idle and worthless" persons.

Reasons for denying the Europeans access to America are presented in the final portion of the memo.

The conditions aboard these boats are horrendous. Interviewees report that five persons in fact died in transit. Smallpox, scurvy and typhus are rampant aboard these crowded ships, which allot a space of only 7 feet by 2-1/2 feet, below decks, for each passenger. More than 150 boat people died of disease on one ship that arrived in Virginia two years ago. The ships are also in poor physical condition. Interviewees reported that a second boat, the *Speedwell*, was forced to turn back twice because of leaks and eventually abandoned the voyage. Firm action now can effectively discourage other Englishmen from taking to unseaworthy vessels, which will only lead to a further unnecessary and tragic loss of life. . . .

Recommendation on applications for asylum: DENY.

Academic Writing

"Overcrowding can also contribute to the dropout rate. Students feel neglected and may want to leave school and not return. The EPP report found that schools with the greatest number of students at risk of dropping out are also the most overcrowded."

—Monica Bermudez

Problem/Solution Essay

A skillfully written problem/solution essay provides readers with a detailed analysis of the subject—from a clear statement of the problem to the discussion of possible solutions. It is essential that a writer carefully examines the subject from a number of different angles before proposing any solutions.

"A problem well stated is a problem half solved."

Discussion: Write an essay in which you analyze a problem and present one or more solutions. Choose a problem in your own life, and explore it thoroughly, proposing possible solutions (or reporting an actual solution). Or take a problem in the world around you, and analyze it completely before suggesting possible solutions or recording what is already being done.

Searching and Selecting

1. **Searching** • Think about the things students complain most about: crowded classrooms, peer pressure, school spirit, jobs, grades, discrimination, safety. Could you discover a solution for any of these problems? What about a problem that developed around your neighborhood, at your school, or in your personal life? What about environmental issues, politics, or other areas that affect your world? What is being done to address these problems? Do you have suggestions, solutions?
2. **Selecting** • As a class, list ten top problems or concerns for seniors. Could you analyze and propose a solution for one of these problems? Do you know someone who solved a difficult problem in a unique way? Have you resolved a problem in your own life or been part of the solution to a problem?

Generating the Text

3. **Forming** • After you've selected a problem, write it out in the form of a clear statement. Then analyze it thoroughly, exploring the problem's parts, history, and causes. Weigh possible solutions. Try listing reasons why solutions might work, or why they might not. (Use the "Mapping the Problem" graphic organizer to help you analyze your subject.)
4. **Assessing** • Are you dealing with a manageable problem for your essay? If not, could you address just one aspect of the larger problem? Have you got enough background material? Do you need facts and statistics to clearly establish the problem? Do you have illustrations of the problem? Anecdotes? Powerful and convincing examples and details?

Writing and Revising

5. **Writing** • Once you have analyzed and assessed the problem, write your first draft. Organize your information so it will be clear to any readers unfamiliar with the problem.
6. **Refining** • What anecdote, statistic, or detail could you develop into an exciting lead? Could you use dramatic dialogue or a powerful quotation? For readers to care about your solution, they must first care about the problem. What details could make your problem/solution engaging for readers?

Evaluating

Is a real solution offered for a real problem?

Is the writing interesting? The lead engaging? The conclusion logical?

Will readers understand and appreciate the essay?

Mapping the Problem

A. **The Problem:**
- Write the specific **Problem** in the center of the map.
- List as many **Causes of the Problem** as you can.
- List the **Parts of the Problem:** its history, different aspects of problem, etc.

B. **The Solution:**
- List as many **Possible Solutions** as you can.

C. **The Future:**
- Consider the **Future Implications** of each solution.

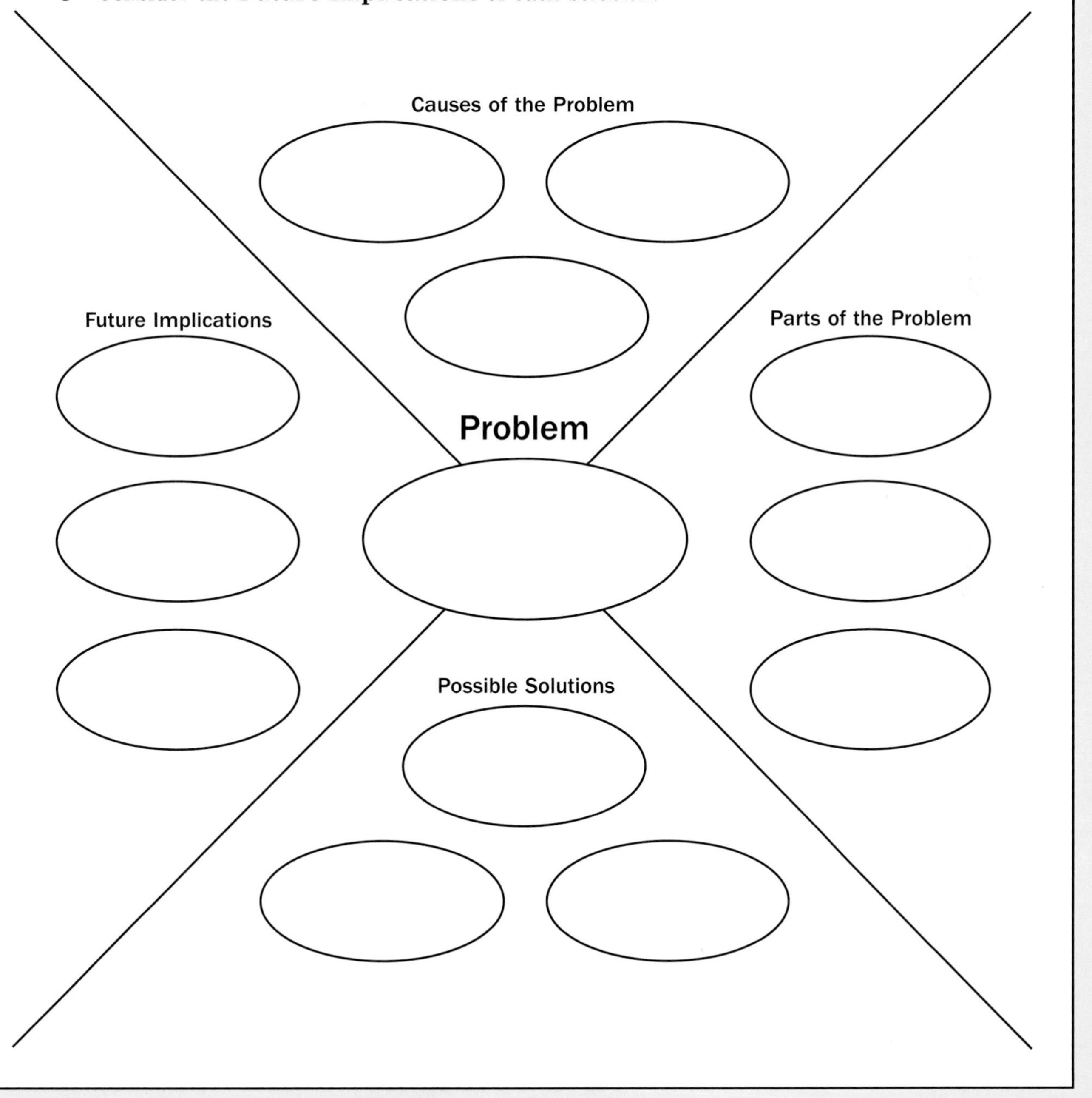

Student Model

In this essay Monica Bermudez discusses the problem of overcrowded classrooms. Some people believe that schools alone hold the key to solving this problem, but as this writer suggests, everyone needs to become involved. (This article is reprinted with permission from *New Youth Connections: The Magazine Written By and For New York Youth*, December 1991.)

Overcrowded Classrooms: Do You Ever Feel Like a Teen Sardine?

The writer describes the scene in overcrowded classrooms (the problem) and suggests two main causes.

You know the scene, the first week of school and your classes are packed. You walk in a little late only to find that all the seats have been taken, so you have to stand. Usually they manage to find a seat for you by the second week (even if they have to take it from another overcrowded class).

Sometimes it's because the program office has screwed up and [has] accidentally given you a class you took last term or a class you didn't ask for. But most of the time there are just too many students and not enough teachers or classrooms. Immigration is one big factor in why schools are so jammed. But the main reason is that there is no money.

At Humanities HS, for instance, Jan Zubiarr, 15, has 38 people in his math class, four over the limit set by the teachers' union contract.

"Lots of people don't have seats," he said. "It's not fair."

The school has room for 1702 students but last year 1860 registered. This means that the school was at what the board of education calls "109% utilization." (If 1702 had registered it would have been 100% utilized—full to capacity.)

No Place to Sit Down

Effects of overcrowding are discussed.

Students from several high schools all had the same complaint: with so many kids in one room, the time for learning is being taken up just getting the class together. "We deserve 41 minutes [of education]," said Nancy Alfaro, 16, of Grover Cleveland HS, "and not [to] spend half of it finding out where people sit."

Students also complained that there aren't enough supplies to go around. Amy Herget, 16, also from Cleveland, says in her classes not only are people always standing, there aren't enough books either. (Cleveland is 111% utilized.)

Another problem is that with so many people in one class, the teacher just doesn't have time for all of them.

Claudia Ramos, a senior at Richmond Hill HS (129% utilized), is planning to pursue a career in the fashion industry. With 40 people in her fashion design class, she says it's hard to get the teacher to look at her work. "It bothers me. I feel I'm getting less attention . . . a lot of kids are getting short-changed on their education."

Overcrowding Causes Tension and Violence

Noreen Connell, executive director of the Educational Priorities Panel (EPP), an organization working to improve public education in New York City, says, "Overcrowding also affects morale."

A 1989 EPP report on overcrowding said that "the school's atmosphere can become tense and, in some cases, violent."

Overcrowding can also contribute to the dropout rate. Students feel neglected and may want to leave school and not return. The EPP report found that schools with the greatest number of students at risk of dropping out are also the most overcrowded. And schools which are predominately Black and Latino are consistently more crowded than those with a large white population.

The writer shows that the impact of overcrowding affects everyone.

Many schools have tried to adapt by creating "double sessions." At Bushwick HS, which is 170% utilized—serving almost twice as many students as it should be—this means that the 11th and 12th grades start their day at 7:50 and end at 2:00. The 9th and 10th grades start at 9:15 and finish at 3:30. But this often prevents students from participating in after-school activities.

Temporary Solutions

Rose T. Diamond, director of strategic planning at the New York City Board of Education's division of School Facilities, said some schools are moving administrative offices out of their buildings to make more space for students. During our interview, Diamond got a phone call about two school districts fighting over classroom space. Her solution was to use another place such as the auditorium or gym. This has been the common remedy around the city, and not a great one, many teens say.

Present solutions offer little relief. Successful solutions will involve the students themselves.

The EPP report goes on to say that the schools that aren't overcrowded should try to create special programs to draw students away from those that are. It also suggested that schools that were closed be reopened and other alternative spaces be found in office buildings for example.

Meanwhile, the board of education has a five-year plan to build new schools and add and lease new space. By the year 1995, they say they will need to make room for almost 50,000 more students. In Queens they will be building West Queens HS which will accommodate 2500 students. Townsend Harris (also Queens) will house 1000 students. In Port Richmond HS, on Staten Island, there will be room for 800 more.

"Solving this problem," Ms. Diamond says, "is the chancellor's top priority." In the meantime, she says we should "try to be patient and understand."

But Connell doesn't think so. She says that teens are a great "political force" and they should write letters to their legislators and invite them to "observe overcrowding firsthand." She recommends that teens "tell as many people as possible how bad things really are." ▣

Student Model

Student writer Zeba A. Khann tackles a big problem—air pollution in New York—by focusing specifically on two organizations that promote solutions. (This essay is reprinted with permission from *New Youth Connections: The Magazine Written By and For New York Youth*, September/October 1991.)

Transportation Alternatives: Take a Hike, Ride a Bike . . . Clear the Air

Every time you decide to walk, ride a bike, or take public transportation instead of driving, you're doing something positive for the environment.

Currently, New York City has the second worst air pollution in the country, after Los Angeles. According to Joseph Rappaport, Coordinator of the Straphangers' Campaign of the New York Public Interest Research Group (NYPIRG), "People in L.A. live and die by the car . . . we don't, and it should stay that way."

A dramatic quotation highlights New York's pollution problem.

Automobile exhaust is one of the main causes of air pollution. Not only is air pollution a leading cause of asthma, it also reduces lung capacity, aggravates heart problems, and can even cause cancer.

The Straphangers' Campaign promotes mass transportation as an alternative to cars. They believe that mass transit means cleaner air. To help make public transportation more attractive to riders, the Straphangers' Campaign fights for better, more reliable subway and bus service. It tries to get the state to pay for new subway cars, track work, and programs to make the subway safer. After successfully fighting state budget cuts last spring, the campaign is now doing everything it can to stop the 35-cent fare hike the Transit Authority has proposed for next year.

Transportation Alternatives is another group working to decrease people's dependence on cars in order to reduce air pollution. But Transportation Alternatives puts a greater emphasis on bicycling and walking than on mass transit. It fought for better bike lanes on the Brooklyn and George Washington bridges as well as on many other roadways. With easier access, the group expects more people to bike instead of drive.

People who walk, bike, or take mass transit generally find commuting more enjoyable than people who drive, says John Orcutt, Executive Director of Transportation Alternatives. They don't spend long hours stuck in traffic. They get exercise, read, or talk to other people. The end result is also less air pollution.

The writer addresses this problem from a position of authority, citing names, providing direct quotations, and offering relevant statistics.

Even with new pollution-control devices being installed on cars, the level of air pollution continues to rise simply because there are more cars on the road. The number of drivers has doubled since the early 1970's. Meanwhile, the number of subway riders has been declining. In 1948, the subway system carried two billion people per year. Now, just a little over a billion people ride the subways each year.

NYPIRG has 17 chapters located at colleges and universities in New York, and a student board headed by a student chairperson. Transportation Alternatives' Auto-Free Committee has 1,500 members, many of the most active ones being teenagers. In fact, teens play an active role in both organization, as volunteers and as interns.

Student Model

In this essay, Tristan Ching addresses a rather universal problem: there just aren't enough hours in the day. This writer finds a unique solution to this problem without compromising her love of ballet or learning.

Backseat Driver

I've spent half my high school life buckled up in the backseat of a car. Nestled comfortably on those gray leather seats, I eat dinner, do my homework, and sleep. The car isn't just a means of transportation anymore; it has become a home away from home.

The primary methods of development in this writing are personal narrative and analysis.

I haven't always spent so much time in the car. I began the three-hour commute to Santa Monica for ballet classes four years ago. When I chugged along the Pacific Coast Highway that first time, I had no idea what I was getting myself into. The Westside Ballet School, with its world famous teachers and talented students, opened the door to technical skill and artistry. Ironically, it also opened the door to the unpleasant realities of ballet. Although I was expressive and musical, I didn't have the ideal body for ballet. While I accepted the fact that I was too short and too dark to blend in with a *corps de ballet*, I also reached another conclusion. If I couldn't blend in, then I would work until I was good enough to stand out as a soloist in a company.

While other people entertain friends in their living rooms, I have had some of my most memorable discussions in the car. I have carpooled with several dancers, but Kirsten has been the most influential of the group. She showed me the degree of sacrifice, determination, and devotion needed to succeed, not just in ballet, but in life. I began to study videotapes of ballets to see what made dancers like Gelsey Kirkland and Makarova truly outstanding. I read books, magazines, and anything remotely related to ballet. I was addicted.

Kirsten helped me develop a love for ballet. Unwittingly, she also helped me appreciate school. She had dropped out of high school and did independent study instead. She insisted that independent study was just as good as a traditional education, but I wasn't convinced. How could in-class discussions about *The Scarlet Letter* or *The Great Gatsby* be replaced with a textbook? By defending the importance of school, I discovered that I really did believe that education should be an essential part of everyone's life. When I refused to skip school to go to an extra rehearsal, Kirsten said, "Tristan, you have to make the choice between ballet and school." I didn't agree; I was going to do my best in both.

The writer points out that what works for one person does not necessarily work for another.

"Doing my best in both" was similar to juggling. At first, I dropped a lot of balls. Finally, I learned that if I ate dinner and did homework in the car, I could maintain a balance between school and ballet. Looking back, I understand Kirsten's point of view better. Devoting herself entirely to ballet was all right for her because all she ever wanted to do was dance. For me, just dancing isn't enough. I want more than performing someone else's work, I want to create something of my own.

The gray Mazda has taken me down the road of self-discovery. I used to think the three-hour commute was a waste of time. How wrong I was! Riding beside the ocean and the sunset, I settle back and envision the life ahead.

Professional Model

In this model, writer Beth Brophy describes an exciting program in Washington, D.C., designed "to do more than throw money at the homeless problem." (This article first appeared in *U.S. News & World Report*, April 19, 1993. It is reprinted by permission of *U.S. News & World Report*.)

Feeding Those Who Are Hungry

A description of one day in the D.C. Central Kitchen naturally draws readers into the essay.

WASHINGTON, D.C.—The D.C. Central Kitchen looks like any professional kitchen—clean, well-lighted, with plenty of pantry and counter space. One recent day, Mary Richter, the energetic, redheaded chef of the trendy local restaurant Cities, demonstrated cooking techniques to six aspiring chefs. Hands washed, in clean white aprons, they listened to Richter explain how to tell leafy from woody herbs as they made pesto.

But the students of D.C. Central Kitchen are unusual: They're homeless people who live in a shelter in the same building. Since 1990, 70 people have graduated from the 12-week job-training program, which is partially funded by the hunger-relief organization Share Our Strength. Six hours a day, five days a week, trainees learn the ins and outs of professional kitchens and, perhaps more important, tips for keeping a job, such as showing up on time.

The writer incorporates many important facts about Central Kitchen into her essay.

The program, which costs about $18,000 a year for 32 students, aims to do more than throw money at the homeless problem. According to the Bureau of Labor Statistics, the number of food-service jobs in the United States will jump 35 percent over the next 15 years. "Not jobs flipping hamburgers," notes Robert Egger, D.C. Central Kitchen's executive director, "but skilled work that pays $6.50 to $8.50 an hour at first and then gets more lucrative."

The second paycheck. Egger has a not-so-hidden agenda. His guest lecturers are local chefs who learn a lesson themselves: Homeless people are worth employing. Once the trainees graduate, Central Kitchen taps an extensive network of restaurant and food-service contacts for jobs. Of the program's 70 graduates, 40 remain employed, 16 of whom live and work on their own.

As noted here, solutions often create new problems.

But some have further problems. Richter, for example, has seen mixed results; the first graduate she hired disappeared after one paycheck, the second found the job too stressful and the third did well and then left for a bakery job. Recently, Richter hired another graduate, a 41-year-old widow, and devoted a month to teaching her how to prepare pizzas and other appetizers while helping her search for an apartment. But the woman, who had had a drinking problem, earned her first paycheck and then never returned. "Going through our program and getting a job is the easy part," explains Egger. "Maintaining the job, and making it past the second paycheck, is the hard part."

In the wake of the most recent defection, Egger plans to revamp the program by June to exclude those who haven't completed drug and alcohol rehabilitation programs and aren't living in halfway houses. Yet despite the frustrations, Egger hopes to replicate D.C. Central Kitchen's program in 15 other cities such as Minneapolis, Kansas City and San Francisco. The kitchen, says Richter, is where she can do her best work to improve the world: "Cooking is nurturing. Feeding people, whether they make $100,000 a year or $1,000, involves taking hungry people and making them not hungry." ▣

"For as long as I can remember, I have always wished I could become Laura Ingalls. I have longed to go running through golden wheat fields wearing a calico dress and sunbonnet." —*Lisa Cochrum*

Essay of Evaluation

In an essay of evaluation, a writer acts like a roving critic, exploring the value or significance of a personal experience, casual observation, current trend, new product, and so on. The tone of such an essay varies, depending upon the subject. The evaluation of a traumatic experience, for example, may be intense and emotional, while the evaluation of a new product may be objective and to the point.

"I'm almost glad it happened."

Discussion: Judge the worth of a particular event, incident, project, class, idea, person, or enterprise (business) in an essay of evaluation. The manner in which you develop your writing depends on your subject. An evaluation of a personal incident or performance will quite naturally be very personal in nature—a self-evaluation, if you will. An evaluation of a class, a group activity, or an enterprise will be more public in nature and speak to a wider audience. An evaluation of a product may result in a very objective report. Think in terms of your subject's value, impact, and significance; its strengths and weaknesses; its place in the scheme of things; and so on. Provided below are basic guidelines to help you develop your writing. Also note the sample essays following these guidelines.

Searching and Selecting

1. **Listing** • If you have trouble thinking of a subject to evaluate, write *people*, *places*, *events*, *objects*, and/or *ideas* on a piece of paper turned lengthwise. Then freely list ideas under each heading. Somewhere along the way, you should hit upon a subject or two.
2. **Selecting** • You may also try one or more of the selecting activities listed in the handbook to help you find a subject. (Refer to "Selecting a subject" in the index for this information.) If needed, enlist the help of friends and family members. (Point to consider: to evaluate a subject, you must know it well.)

Generating the Text

3. **Recording** • Once you have an idea in mind, write freely about your subject for at least 8 minutes, recording as many thoughts, feelings, and ideas as possible.
4. **Assessing** • Carefully review your exploratory writing—noting the important points you've made, deciding what more needs to be said, and so on. (Remember that you are trying to put your subject into perspective, to rate it, to measure it.)
5. **Focusing** • State a focus for your work—a sentence (or two) expressing a dominant impression or feeling you want to express in your writing. Then make some preliminary decisions about the arrangement of ideas in your writing.

Writing and Revising

6. **Writing** • Write your first draft freely, working in facts and details as they naturally come to mind or according to your planning and organizing.
7. **Revising** • Review, revise, and refine your writing until it says what you want it to say—and it's ready to share with your readers. (Refer to the Proofreader's Guide in the handbook when you are ready to proofread your work.)

Evaluating

Does the writing form a meaningful whole, moving forward with a clear sense of order and purpose?

Is some form of evaluation or assessment taking place in the essay?

Will readers appreciate the treatment of the subject?

Student Model

In this essay of evaluation by Gail Scott, we learn about the importance of a brief but unforgettable moment in her life. The writer re-creates her memory with clarity and intensity, making it seem very real. (Reprinted with permission from *New Youth Connections: The Magazine Written By and For New York Youth*, November 1991.)

I Thought I Was White

Readers are naturally drawn into the essay in the first paragraph.

When I was a little girl, I thought that all Blacks were dark-skinned and anyone lighter than that was White. It wasn't until I was about 5 or 6 years old that I learned otherwise. I didn't mean to start any trouble, but I said something that got the whole family ready to bite my head off.

We were all at my grandparents' house—my parents, my grandparents, my sister Lorene, Cousin Alice, Uncle David, and his girlfriend Billie. It must have been some sort of holiday since we were all together like that. The big dinner table was set up and everyone was milling around the living room, waiting for dinner to be served. For some reason Lorene and I began discussing our difference in skin color. Although we share similarities in our appearance, she is darker than me. I announced to her that we didn't really look alike at all because I was White and she was Black.

My Grandmother Yelled at Me

The intensity of the moment is effectively re-created through the grandmother's words and actions.

Before Lorene had a chance to agree or disagree with me, my grandmother, who had overheard, shouted, "Don't you ever say that!"

All action came to a halt. Everyone, including me, turned around to look at her. Her eyes, which were blazing with fury, stared into my big, brown, innocent eyes. "You are Black," she told me. "Maybe you're not that dark, but you're still Black. Your mother is light and she's Black, just like you."

Whispers of "What happened, what did she say?" filled the room. Grandma repeated my words and I received confused looks from the other adults. I remember someone telling my grandmother, "Calm down, she didn't mean any harm." I still had no idea why Grandma was so angry.

The description of the moment after the grandmother's outburst adds drama to the essay.

I looked to my mother and my sister for help, hoping they would save me from another humiliating lecture. Lorene glanced at me for a moment, then she focused her eyes on the floor. My mother just looked at me and then at my grandmother as though she didn't know what to say, and that's just what happened—my mother didn't say a word, either to scold me or defend me.

I Felt Terrible

I remember having this terrible feeling, like I had said a swear-word or knocked over and broken an expensive plate. I felt all alone and for a 5-year-old, that's an awful feeling. I didn't understand what was going on or why they were making me feel this way. All I knew was that I had made the mistake of opening my mouth in the first place.

My memory of that day ends with the entire room looking at me as though I had murdered someone. I never mentioned the incident after it happened for fear of the angry memories it would spark.

The writer's thoughtful evaluation of the experience helps her see her grandmother's actions as necessary and important.

Now that I am older, I can understand why my grandmother was so upset. She didn't want me growing up with a false image of myself. I feel that being Black means being proud of where you come from. My saying that I was White made it seem as though I was denying my heritage. Grandma was only pointing that out and setting me straight.

Of course, Grandma didn't have to yell at me, but I guess if she hadn't, then the moment would not have been as powerful. I might even have forgotten about it. Instead, I have always kept that day in the back of my mind to keep me from losing sight of who I am. I'm almost glad that it happened because that was my first step in learning about myself as a Black person.

Student Model

In this essay, Lisa Cochrum assesses her feelings about a favorite childhood TV character—Laura Ingalls Wilder—from an older and wiser perspective. Note how clearly the writer makes her assessment, moving smoothly from one main point to the next. Also note how effectively she supports her main thoughts with references from an Ingalls biography.

Oh to Have a Sunbonnet

Throughout my childhood, Monday nights were always an event in my household. All work and play stopped and we would plop ourselves in front of the TV, gluing ourselves to the screen for the next hour. The object of our most fixed attention was *Little House on the Prairie*. Centered around the small-town activities of Walnut Grove, Minnesota, it depicted the life of the prairie settlers in the 1800's. . . .

The focus, or thesis, stated at the end of the second paragraph sets the tone and direction for the essay.

For as long as I can remember, I have always wished I could become Laura Ingalls. I have longed to go running through golden wheat fields wearing a calico dress and sunbonnet. How rich her life seemed, filled with nature, a sense of community and the utmost respect for other people and her God. Yet, as I have gotten older and have read about the life of the real Laura Ingalls Wilder, many of my idealistic images have been altered.

The true Laura Ingalls Wilder was born Feb. 7, 1867, in Wisconsin. Her early childhood was spent in Pepin, Wisconsin, in a little house at the edge of a big woods. In the years that followed, her family made several moves by means of a covered wagon. First to Independence, Kansas; then Plum Creek, Minnesota; Burr Oak, Iowa; Walnut Grove, Minnesota; and finally DeSmet, South Dakota. Throughout these years, Laura kept a personal diary in yellow school notebooks. It is upon these accounts of her life [and how she wrote about them in her *Little House on the Prairie* books] that the television series was based. Most of the main characters and large events of her life were not altered in the depiction on TV, but the overall picture was. As I said earlier, most of the problems that came Laura's way could usually be solved in the hour show, yet in the diary of the real Laura Ingalls, she told of the many hardships that couldn't ever be solved. In her biography, the author, Donald Zochert, recounted the many blizzards, plagues, droughts, fires, and severe illnesses that threatened her family's financial and physical existence.

What follows is the writer's perceptive evaluation of the made-for-TV Laura Ingalls Wilder as compared to the real person.

While in Plum Creek, Minnesota, the Ingalls family faced one of their most tragic trials, a seasonal occurrence of grasshopper plagues. Laura later describes it in the following way:

> *With the coming of summer, Pa's little patch of wheat was washed with a faint green. The wheat sprouts were coming up. But at the same time, the grasshoppers hatched. The ground squirmed with grasshoppers, as they marched and ate and tried their wings. They ate everything. Pa watched them sadly, but he didn't fight them. He knew what was going to happen and he was helpless to stop it. The first hot winds off the prairies to the west brought more grasshoppers, drifted across Dakota and Minnesota. The air filled with the sound of angry buzzing and Pa knew that his days on Plum Creek were over. With the small wheat crop devoured even before it*

> *had grown, there would be nothing to live on. In the prairie evenings Pa sat with Ma on the doorstep of the little house. In silence they watched the sun move slowly toward the dark edge of the western prairie. That was where Pa's heart was—west with the setting sun and the wide spaces and the high silences. But now to the west were grasshoppers, devouring dreams and lives as well as crops.*

With their livelihood gone, the family was forced to move to Burr Oak, Iowa, and begin a new life managing a hotel there. Yet, they all longed to return to the country and eventually moved back to Minnesota, but this time to Walnut Grove. The television series used this town as the basis for their show. Upon reading Wilder's biography, I found many of the same people and places that had become so dear to me on *Little House on the Prairie*. But again, the biography revealed that there were many hardships associated with life in that time. The blinding blizzards that would overtake the area were a constant threat to the people that lived there. Donald Zochert described one account that Laura wrote about in her diary.

Excerpts from Wilder's biography effectively support and authenticate the writer's main points and make for very interesting reading.

> *Winter storms sometimes kept Laura and Mary and Carrie home from school. Blizzards struck quickly and without warning, and the girls knew that the safest thing to do was to stay in one place. Not everyone followed this sensible rule, however. One day after a blizzard had blown itself out, word spread around town that some children were missing from their house, three miles out in the country. . . . Pa was one of the men who helped search for them. The children were finally found buried in a snowdrift; they had left the safety of the house and wandered into the fury of the storm. Three of them, two boys and a girl, were frozen to death. The oldest child, a girl Laura's age, was badly frozen but still alive. She had kept the baby of the family inside her coat all the time they were out in the storm and the heat of her own body kept the baby alive. But one of the girl's own legs was frozen so badly the doctor had to cut it off. Pa told Laura about this, and no doubt used it as a lesson on what not to do in a blizzard.*

One of the things *Little House on the Prairie* depicted correctly was Laura's marriage to a local farm boy named Almanzo Wilder. What they didn't show was that their first year of marriage was very difficult. Laura would later refer to her married life as the years of "sunshine and shadow." Laura and Almanzo were living in DeSmet, South Dakota, trying to establish their first farm. They were desolate times and when Laura wrote about them, anguish echoed in her words:

> *They were dry years in the Dakotas when we were beginning our life together. How heart breaking it was to watch the grain we had sown with such high hopes wither and yellow in the hot winds! And it was back breaking as well as heart breaking to carry water from the well to my garden and see it dry up despite all my efforts.*

In closing, the writer reaffirms her position . . . but not without feeling a little bit of the magic of her childhood dream.

In the years that followed they lost several crops, their house and barn burned down, and their second child died only twelve days after she was born. In fact, Laura and Almanzo would only have one child in their sixty-four years of marriage, a daughter, Rose, born during their first year together. They were also struck by ill health. Two years into their marriage, Almanzo and Laura contracted diphtheria. They lay sick in bed for several weeks, fighting an illness that was near-fatal for both of them. Almanzo had always been a fighter, and unfortunately he fought too hard this time. He forced himself up from his bed and suffered a stroke that left him paralyzed. Though he was able to regain most of his lost movement, he never fully recovered. He was only thirty years old, and he couldn't do a whole day's work. For the rest of his long life he shuffled as he walked.

Although *Little House on the Prairie* depicted some of the sorrows that touched Laura's life, like her sister's blindness that resulted from a fever, and the death of the only son that her parents bore, it painted a very rosy picture of Laura's life on the prairie. Upon reading her biography, I began to see the true life of a woman on the plains. Laura was strong, persevering, and flexible; she had to be because her environment was physically draining and emotionally trying. The true story of her life made me realize what the human spirit can do when it is pushed to the limit, but it also made me see that my dream of becoming Laura Ingalls Wilder was one based on fantasy. But there is still a part of me that longs to go running through golden wheat fields wearing a calico dress and sunbonnet. ▣

Professional Model

Jill Robinson, the speaker in this excerpt from "Fantasia," evaluates the effects of growing up in Hollywood as a member of a family closely tied to the movie industry. (From *American Dreams* by Studs Terkel. Copyright © 1980 by Studs Terkel. Reprinted by permission of Pantheon Books, a division of Random House, Inc.)

"Fantasia"

Note that this model is part of a transcription (written version) of an interview.

. . . Out of the corner of my eye, I knew there were people watching who seemed smarter than we were. These would be the writers, who were cynical. They didn't believe it was all gonna work out all right. They didn't believe all movies were wonderful. I sensed this coming. I think the snake in the Garden of Eden was my growing awareness. The reality was always there. I chose not to see it. The thing that terrified me most was my own intelligence and power of observation. The more I saw, the more I tried not to see.

Couldn't bear it, the reality. Couldn't bear to feel my father was wrong. Couldn't bear the idea that it was not the best of all possible worlds. Couldn't bear the idea that there was a living to be made. That punishment does not always come to those that deserve it. That good people die in the end.

The triumph of the small man was another wonderful Hollywood myth, very popular in the mid forties. Once that dream went, once that illusion went, we all began to suspect what was really going on. Once we became conscious, that was the snake. It was the awareness of the power, awareness that war was not a parade, awareness of reality. This is what killed the old movies. It was the consciousness of the extras, and I became one of the extras.

The speaker talks pessimistically and forcefully about the American myth.

I think we're all skidding away, we're destroying. California is just a little bit of it. The more bleak I become, the more—I live in Connecticut, okay? I read somewhere Connecticut has the highest incidence of intestinal cancer in the world. I think that's because we eat ourselves alive there. We're filled with despair, and it just rots us away. Where I live looks exactly like the MGM back-lot idea of a small New England town. There's no pressure in Connecticut, it's all okay. Nobody is working much, there aren't many jobs, a lot of businesses are failing. But it looks so sweet. It looks endearing. During the blizzard, you would have thought that Currier and Ives came in there. That several people I know lost everything they own in that blizzard, nobody really thinks about that. It looks like the American Dream.

Okay, we found Connecticut, and it doesn't work either. They go out to retirement homes in California, and they still get sick. And they worry about earthquakes. We always knew there'd be an earthquake. I loved the people who were trying to make it happen in the sixties.

The speaker's evaluation extends from one coast to the other, from California to Connecticut.

They were down there, on the Andreas Fault, with chisels and hammers, a whole group of fanatics, trying to saw it off. They needed the ending to make the earthquake happen. They predicted it and, fearful that it would not come true, they actually went up there. They really believed that God needed help. I say He's never needed help with that. Even my God is a movie god. He really runs the studio. Into the ground, as my grandmother would have said.

The Hollywood dream has driven us crazy, but no more than any other mythology. Religious orders that govern whole states and decide what they should believe. Greek and Roman gods and goddesses. Catholicism. Hollywood is just another draft, a more polished version.

What else are we gonna live by if not dreams? We need to believe in something. What would really drive us crazy is to believe this reality we run into every day is all there is. If I don't believe there's that happy ending out there—that will-you-marry-me in the sky—I can't keep working today. That's true, I think, for all of us. ▣

Part II

Writing Workshops

Searching and Selecting

Gearing Up for Writing

This is a chance for you to take stock of your writing experiences and abilities at the beginning of the year. Consider each question carefully before answering it, and word your answers clearly and carefully. This information will make it easier for your teacher to advise you about your writing, and it will make it easier for you to evaluate your writing progress later in the year when you refer back to this survey.

1. What are the last pieces of writing you have completed? (Identify two or three.)

2. What forms of writing are you most familiar with? (*Reports*, *essays*, *paragraphs*, *reviews*, *stories*, *poems*, *essay-test answers*, and so on.)

3. What is the most successful or meaningful paper you've written in the past year or two? Briefly describe it.

4. Do you usually write on subjects of your own choosing or on assigned topics? Which do you like better and why?

5. What is your greatest strength as a writer? Explain.

6. What stage in the writing process gives you the most trouble? (*Getting started*, *focusing my efforts*, *organizing*, *drafting*, *revising*, *editing*, etc.) Explain.

7. Do you follow a set revising strategy? What sorts of changes do you normally make when you revise?

8. What type of writing gives you the most problems? What type of writing would you like to learn more about? What specific writing skills would you like to practice?

inside info

Review this survey each quarter to see how your writing attitudes, skills, and interests evolve throughout the school year.

Writers on the Block

READ: Read and enjoy the following quotations from a variety of famous writers about the process of writing.

"A really good writing class or workshop can give us some shadow of what musicians have all the time—the excitement of a group working together, so that each member outdoes himself."

—Ursula K. LeGuin

"Writing is the only thing that, when I do it, I don't feel I should be doing something else."

—Gloria Steinem

"To write about people you have to know people, to write about bloodhounds you have to know bloodhounds, to write about the Loch Ness monster you have to find out about it."

—James Thurber

". . . as soon as you connect with your true subject you will write."

—Joyce Carol Oates

"Easy writing makes hard reading."

—Ernest Hemingway

"The real writing takes place between the first miserable, crude draft and the finished thing."

—Gloria Naylor

"You always feel when you look it straight in the eye that you could have put more into it, could have let yourself go and dug harder."

—Emily Carr

REACT: Select one of the quotations that matches up well with your own writing experience. Explain the connection in a freely written exploratory draft. (Use your own paper.)

extend Write your own pithy statement about writing to be posted in the classroom. Review "Understanding the Process" in the handbook if you're having trouble coming up with ideas. (Refer to "Writing process, Understanding the process" in the index.)

Selecting Strategies in Review

"There are few experiences quite so satisfying as getting a good idea . . . You're pleased with it, and feel good. It may not be right, but at least you try it out."

How do you get good ideas for your writing? Are they just waiting to be picked like so many heavy, ripe peaches? Or are they the result of your conscious effort, the process of putting pen to paper (or fingers to the keyboard)? Unless you think, eat, and sleep writing, selecting a subject is undoubtedly more work for you than it is play, more searching and sorting than plucking.

REVIEW: Review the "Guidelines for Selecting a Subject" in your handbook. (Refer to "Guidelines, Selecting a topic" in the index for this information.) Identify two or three old reliables—activities listed in this section that you regularly employ when searching for a writing idea. Also identify any unreliables—activities that you have tried once or twice without much success. And lastly, note any additional selecting practices you use, perhaps creations of your own ingenuity and experience. (Share your results.)

(Answers will vary.)

- Old Reliables

- Unreliables

- Additional Selecting Practices

APPLY: Let's suppose you are assigned to write an essay of advice in which you offer advice (of course) on any subject you wish, to any audience you wish (classmate, pet, yourself, . . .). Select a subject for this essay using the "Essentials of Life Checklist," the last piece of information presented under the "Guidelines for Selecting a Subject." This checklist provides an incredible variety of writing possibilities. Unfortunately, too few writers use it. Now's your chance. (Do your sorting and thinking on another sheet of paper. List the subject you select on the line provided here.)

Subject: ....

extend Write nonstop for 8 to 10 minutes on this subject, recording whatever comes to mind as you go along. Afterward, take note of any ideas that surprise you, that seem perceptive and clear, that would be worthy of further development if you were to continue working with this subject.

Talking Heads

Creating **imaginary dialogues** can help you develop possible ideas for writing assignments. It's a way to get thoughts out of your head and onto paper where you can roll them around and build on them. Give this strategy a chance! You'll be surprised at the way your ideas (and possible subjects for writing) will begin to develop.

DIALOGUE: Complete the following comic strip by filling in the dialogue bubble in each frame. (Also consider drawing additional frames.)

(Sample dialogue starter)

extend Begin a short personal essay on a writing idea that has emerged from your dialogue. If, for example, your dialogue turned out to be about getting along or working together—like how it's necessary in families, or in small writing groups, or how you're terrible at it—that can be your starting point. (Share the results of your writing.)

Generating Texts

How Do You Shape Up?

You know by now that there are quite a few steps in the writing process. You can't go from picking a subject to writing a final draft with no work in between. Most successful writers spend time shaping their writing subjects, and they also have their own preferences about the activities they use along the way. In this workshop, you are going to take stock of your own writing preferences when it comes to searching and shaping a subject.

REFLECT: How do you narrow a subject down? How do you gather supporting details? How do you decide what to focus on and how to start the first draft? In short, how do you usually work a subject into proper shape? Explain your searching and shaping process on your own paper.

(Possible responses)
List key words
Free-write
Write journal reflections
Cluster
Find an angle
Start in the middle
Write an instant version

RETHINK: Your handbook offers many suggestions for shaping a subject. Review the handbook section "Guidelines for Searching and Shaping a Subject," and see what we mean. (Refer to "Writing process, Guidelines for shaping a subject" in the index.) Think about how you might incorporate some of the activities listed there into your own processes of working with a writing subject.

TRY OUT an activity from the handbook—either *Offbeat Questions* or *Audience Appeal*. These two activities are sometimes overlooked as ways of shaping a subject, but they're surprisingly effective and quite fun. Say you're writing an essay of reflection about an important time in your life. See what you can discover about your subject using one of the three activities mentioned above. *Note:* If you're having trouble identifying a subject, try completing the sentence starter that follows.

The most important period of my schooling occurred when I entered middle school
....

Essays of reflection require reflective details, but you should incorporate other types of details as well. (For more information about the different types of details, refer to "Details, Kinds of" in your handbook's index.)

Six Faces

READ: If you've already picked a topic, use the writing method called "cubing" to search your mind for more of what you already know. How many sides on a cube? That's easy: six. (Think of dice. The sides are numbered for you.) You can use the six sides of a cube to remind you of six major ways to explore your topic. Suppose you've decided to write about the TV coverage of a major sporting event. Here is how you might "cube" your topic.

Side 1: Describe It

For 5 minutes, write at top speed about the sights and sounds (and maybe the tastes, smells, and physical feelings) that you connect with the TV broadcast. Describe it so that a reader feels he or she has been there.

> They put a camera right on the woman's skis while she was doing the slalom. I could hear the ripping sound of the edges of her skis through the ice crystals. The snow was spraying onto the camera lens and making circle rainbows . . .

Side 2: Compare It

For 5 minutes, write a comparison between the telecast you watched and something comparable to it: for example, a related personal experience or another channel's coverage of the same event.

> Because of the way the camera got down to the snow level and made you feel and hear every cut and hump and whoosh and stuff, I got more excited watching this broadcast than I did the one time I went skiing in person. When I went skiing, I couldn't hear much because I had a rotten earache from the wind, and I couldn't feel much because the boots and stuff were killing my feet. I was totally numb . . .

Side 3: Associate It

For 5 more minutes, write about something that in some odd way you connect in your mind with the telecast. Maybe it reminds you of an afternoon nap, or a carnival sideshow, or a really bad play.

> The telecast was like, let's see, okay, like a half-dream, when your mind is swirling with wild images part of the time but somebody keeps breaking in talking the rest of the time and spoiling the mood. These jerky announcers thought their jokes were worth more airtime than the skiing, but I wanted to stay caught up in the dream . . .

Side 4: Analyze It

For 5 more minutes, write about the different identifiable parts of the telecast.

> I could count about four or five parts to the broadcast. Or maybe not parts but layers. There was the obvious commercial layer, which kept breaking in about every seven or eight minutes. Then there was the chitchat layer, where the announcers talked about themselves, mostly . . .

Side 5: Apply It

For 5 more minutes, write about what the telecast is good for, what its results are, how it could be used, etc.

> Parts of this broadcast would work well for a ski school, since they showed some of the fine points about how a skier balances and absorbs shocks with the knees. Or a tape of the broadcast could be used in journalism school, to analyze the structure (and the faults!) of a typical sports broadcast . . .

Side 6: Argue for or Against It

For 5 more minutes, make a case pro or con—to keep the telecast or to dump it, to change it or to leave it the same. Argue for its style of presentation, or against its length, or whatever.

> I want to argue that sports broadcasters should change the ratio between their talk and the amount of footage they show of the actual sport in action. The ideal, from my perspective, would be about five minutes of action footage for every one minute of talk. And the talk should concentrate on what the athlete is doing and why, not on who went to what college, who's from what Swiss village, who's got a collection of beer coasters, and that kind of junk.

There. That's a little over one half-hour's work. By the time you're through, you'll know a lot more about what you already knew. You're practically guaranteed to come up with some new ideas in the process of cubing. You'll be surprised! Then you can take that new material and channel it into an improved draft of your writing.

WRITE: Select an appealing topic from the "Writing Topics" section in your handbook. (Refer to "Topics, Sample" in the index for this information.) First, free-write about this topic for about 5-8 minutes. Then search your mind for more ideas about your topic by cubing it. Or, if you have already written a poem, a story, an editorial, or an essay, cube that for new ideas. (Refer to "Writing process, Guidelines for shaping a subject" in the handbook index to help you get started.) Underline any thoughts or phrases you especially like in your free writing and cubing.

Psst! If you can't make a cube, simply write about three or four of the instructions that interest you.

Note: Cubing is an extremely powerful technique for developing writing or discovering a focus. Urge your students to discipline themselves so they will get the full value from the exercise. Urge them to make cubing part of the very structure of their thinking.

Ready, Set, CHOOSE

Are you just about ready to write? Have you listed facts, details, examples, or key words? Have you tried clustering or free writing? Have you noted your best ideas?

At this point, some writers blast ahead. They write the first thing that comes to mind. Who knows? That might work for you. But if you want to get the feeling, the form, and the thrust of your writing more under your control, here is something that may help: a **Choice Chart**. Apply it to your next writing assignment.

(Sample responses follow. Student responses will vary.)

Choice Chart

My broad subject: Soccer

My specific topic: How to head the ball

Type of writing:	Comments:
...... Personal Narrative	I want to give instructions but make the reading enjoyable too.
✔ Subject (Expository)	
...... Creative	
...... Fiction	
...... Poetry	
...... Drama	
...... Reflective/Persuasive Essay	
...... Academic	

If new or experimental, then

New angle ✔ What?	From the coach's point of view
New form ...... What?	
New method ...... What?	
New style and language ...... What?	

I want to focus on	Comments:
✔ Emotion	I want to show a connection between safety factors and
...... Ideas	fear of getting hurt.
...... Convictions	

If focusing on emotion, then

✔ Fear .... Pride .... Joy .... Other (Specify)

.... Longing .... Jealousy .... Love

.... Compassion .... Anger .... Hate

Comments: ....

What to do with the emotion:

.... Relive it .... Relieve it .... Build it ✔ Transform it

Comments: I want to show how fear can be turned into boldness.

If focusing on ideas, then

.... Narrate .... Analyze .... Evaluate .... Explain

.... Describe .... Classify .... Argue .... Combine several approaches

.... Define .... Compare .... Illustrate

Comments: ....

Start from

.... Conventional ✔ Unconventional .... Truly offbeat ✔ Other (Specify)

Comments: I could describe the strange way a soccer ball looks when I fear it and how much more comfortable it feels when I'm confident.

If focusing on convictions, then

.... My usual ones (or) .... Some new ones

.... Consider .... Test .... Recommend .... Reject

Psst! Well, have you made as many choices for your writing as you can? If some of them don't come easily, save them for later. They'll come to you, along with plenty of other choices. But if you're ready, why waste time talking? Get writing!

Focus Pocus

The focus of a piece of writing may be plainly stated near the beginning, or it may be postponed until later—or it may not be stated at all. How can a person tell what the focus of a piece of writing is? And how can you create a clearer focus in your next piece of writing?

Start with this general formula. A focus is the specific combination of the following elements:

1. a central subject
2. a specific aspect of the subject
3. an idea and/or a feeling about that aspect

For the writing to be clearly focused, all of these elements should be present, although they may not need to be directly stated. (*Note:* Compare this formula with the formula for a topic sentence found in your handbook. See "Topic sentence" in the index.)

READ & REACT: Read over the beginnings of the essays below. All come from an issue of *Life Magazine* that focused on the American family. Each has the same general subject, but each has a different focus. Some state their focus more openly than others. Try to identify the different elements that make up the focus in each passage. (You won't necessarily be able to comment on each element; just do the best you can.) Afterward, share your results.

> Dozens of cereal boxes. Piles of unread mail. Stacks of magazines. Toilet paper tumbling from the linen closet. And a family room with no room for the family. Such was life at the Raffels' suburban New York home.
>
> —"Now You See It . . . Now You Don't" by Naomi Cutner

Central Subject: *Life at the Raffels' home*

Specific Aspect: *The home's appearance*

Idea: *Life at the Raffels' home was full of clutter.*

Feeling: *Good humor and affection*

Our child is due in six weeks. A host of our friends have told us that we should start now, singing lullabies. They mean it. Babies hear things in the womb, they say. My husband, who finds this silly, has nonetheless lit upon a ritual all his own. At night with a fairly straight face, he whispers the rules of baseball to my belly. "You'll be wanting to know about tagging up," he says.

—"Family Talk" by Lisa Grunwald

Central Subject: Building a family

Specific Aspect: Talking to a baby in the womb

Idea: Adults act silly around their unborn children.

Feeling: Fondness

In my family most of the people are storytellers. Combine that with growing up in Hampton, Virginia—small towns make you aware of your ties to a place—and my romantic quest to find out more about my family makes sense. William Roscoe Davis, my great-grandfather, was the first African-American on the Davis side. His father was an English sea captain and his mother, Liza, an African-born slave. My father's older brothers knew their great-grandmother; their memory was that she had a taste for French finery, especially things like perfume. In 1861 William's family became free when they escaped to the Union Army's Fort Monroe, near Hampton. William soon traveled to New York, under the auspices of the American Missionary Association, to lecture and raise money for the 1,500 blacks who were living around the fort. I found a January 14, 1862, story in The *New York Times* describing him as "a fine, intelligent-looking mulatto."

—"American Album" by Thulani Davis

Central Subject: Ms. Davis' "Roots"

Specific Aspect: The variety of her relatives

Idea: Much is known about her ancestors.

Feeling: Fascination

REFLECT: Which of these paragraphs do you enjoy the most? Which one seems most clearly focused? Which one states its focus most plainly? Which one has the most implicit (unstated) focus?

As you write about your own family life, or any other subject, keep the basic elements of a focus clearly in mind.

Write Angles

READ: Feature writers often talk about the importance of finding an angle for each of their stories. They know from experience that their readers are impatient and fickle. If a story doesn't immediately catch their attention with an interesting or engaging angle, they will quickly move on to another one.

The same holds true for the essays, reports, and articles you write. If you haven't found that special angle or focus for a particular writing project, your readers will have a hard time maintaining interest in your work (not to mention the fact that you will have a hard time developing it).

Psst! Review what your handbook has to say about developing a focus, or an angle, for writing. (Refer to "Focus" in the index.) Also study feature articles in magazines and newspapers to see how professionals focus their efforts into effective finished pieces.

REACT: Let's suppose you were assigned to write a profile of a specific enterprise or business. (A profile is the product of a writer's in-depth investigation.) This business happens to make and sell authentic East Indian gourmet meals to specialty stores. Review your notes on this business listed below. (These notes are based on a newspaper article about an actual business.)

- Indian Groceries & Spices, which started as a small shop selling spices, has started a line of frozen dishes.
- Thirteen dishes (all vegetarian) were quietly put on the market last month.
- One of the dishes is lentils and eggplant.
- A main feature of many of the dishes is curry, a popular Indian spice that at times can be very hot.
- The dishes are spicy and sometimes fiery.
- All of the dishes are microwavable.
- The meals retail for about $2.99 each.
- In New York the first shipment of 300 cases sold out in six weeks.
- The recipes for the dishes were developed by Shirish Sanghavi, who has been involved in the business since it was the small grocery store.
- In addition to frozen foods, the company sells 150 other products including mint chutney and mango pickles.
- Annual sales now top $10 million.
- One hundred employees work in the operation.
- The two brothers who run the business were originally chemical engineers.
- Many smaller competitors are starting in the field.
- The brothers are confident about their products because of the fine quality of ingredients the products contain.

WRITE: Now decide on a special angle, or focus, for your writing so you can begin developing your profile. (List two or three potential angles for your work.)

Psst! The leads (openings) in the drafting section of your handbook might trigger some ideas. (See "Openings" in the index.)

Angle 1 I could focus on how affordable the meals are.

Angle 2 how unusual the ingredients are.

Angle 3 the spicy hotness of the food.

EXTEND: Write the first part of your profile, focusing on one of the angles you've just written. Make sure that your opening grabs your reader's attention. (Write a number of versions of your opening until you hit upon one that you like.) Share your results. Then, if you're so inclined, write the complete profile, adding details of your own making if necessary.

(Sample opening)
At Indian Groceries & Spices, your mouth has a choice between a two-alarm fire or a three-alarm fire . . .

inside info

Always write with your readers in mind. Satisfy their need to learn something and to enjoy themselves by giving proper attention to your subject and the way you write about it (the angle).

Hooking Your Reader

Consider the fishhook. Why does it work? It's got a curve to make it catch, a point to make it sink in, and a barb to make it stick. Oh yes, and there's the bait.

What can fishhooks teach you about writing? Many writers speak of the need for a "hook" in their writing. The audience is the sea in which they fish. The reader is the fish they want to catch. The subject is the bait. The angle of approach is that curving hook. The surprise in the opening is the point that sinks in. And that little extra touch, that idea left open or that hint of things to come, is the barb that won't let the "hook" slip out.

READ: Here are the opening sentences or paragraphs from a number of published essays. As you read through these openings, see if you can catch on to the hook and barb in each one. (Share your thoughts.)

According to the projections, crime was supposed to be under control by now. The postwar baby-boom generation, which moved into its crime-prone years during the early 1960's, has grown up, yielding its place to the (proportionately) less numerous baby-bust generation. With relatively fewer 18-year-olds around, we should all be walking safer streets.

—James Q. Wilson and John J. DiIulio, Jr.,
"Crackdown: Treating the Symptoms of the Drug Problem"

(*Hint:* What is the effect of the word "should" in the last sentence?)
[Note: It implies that a "but . . . " is coming in a moment.]

My, my, girls, what's all the fuss over the new "mommy test"? Hundreds of eager young female job seekers have written to me in the last few weeks alone, confident of being able to pass the drug test, the polygraph test, Exxon's new breathalyzer test—but panicked over the mommy test. Well, the first thing you have to grasp if you hope to enter the ranks of management is that corporations have a perfect right to separate the thieves from the decent folk, the straights from the druggies, and, of course, the women from the mommies.

—Barbara Ehrenreich, "The Mommy Test"

(*Hint:* Can you tell that this opening is sticky with sarcasm?)
[Note: Sarcasm is most obvious.]

In government circles it's called the "NIMBY problem." Whether the proposal is for AIDS clinics, halfway houses for prison parolees or dumps for toxic and nuclear waste, it is usually met by the opposition of citizens' groups who shout NIMBY—"not in my backyard!"

—Ted Peters, "The Waste-Disposal Crisis"

(*Hint:* What is your emotional response immediately after you read the final phrase?)
[Note: Don't you want to say, "Well, it has to be in somebody's backyard"?]

The end of the world is coming—again: 989 years ago, as the odometer of Western history approached its first millennium, the whole of Europe was seized by a paroxysm of preapocalyptic shivers.

—Bill Lawren, "Apocalypse Now?"

(*Hint:* What is the tone of the word "again" in the first line?)
[Note: It suggests that most predictions of the end are premature.]

A very, very long time ago (about three or four years) I took a certain secure and righteous pleasure in saying the things that women are supposed to say.

—Gloria Steinem, "Sisterhood"

(*Hint:* Where do you suspect that the writer is leading? What makes you think so?)
[Note: Her stress on "very, very long time" and on "righteous" suggests things have changed.]

REFLECT: How do you think the writers go from these openings to the next paragraphs? In many cases, there is some kind of turn—a *but*, or *yet*, or *nevertheless*, or *still*. (The writer does that when she or he knows the "hook" is set, and it's time to start reeling in the fish.)

WRITE: Here is a chance to practice writing "hooks" for three different kinds of essays: personal, subject (expository), and reflective.

1. **Personal** Write an opening sentence or two with a "hook" about an aspect of your life that you think might be fascinating to a reader.

   Nothing was a better preparation for success in love than my failure at sports.

2. **Subject** Write a "hook" opening to an essay in which you communicate some specialized knowledge you already possess.

   Ragtime is so peppy, yet taking it slow is the key to this music.

3. **Reflective** Write a "hook" opening to an essay in which you propose how to correct the number one irritant in your life. (Be sure you have a proper audience in mind.)

   Cashiers of the world, look at me. No, not at the next cashier. At me. Over here. I'm your customer.

Hey, kiddo, let me tell you something . . .

When one of my many, many relatives wants to give me advice (something they all love to do), I'll get the infamous introductory remark: "Hey, kiddo, let me tell you something." Based on my experiences as a writer and as a member of a large family, I'd have to say that the essay of advice is the essential essay form.

REACT: Writing an essay of advice is almost always based on personal experience. It is, in a sense, one step up from an essay of experience. You not only speak *of* an experience, you also speak *from* experience and provide your readers with helpful advice and tips. Let me show you how it's done . . . kiddo.

Essay topic: Grandparents

Narrowed topic: Spending time with grandparents

Angle (Advice): If you have grandparents, spend time with them.

Three points of experience that support my angle:

1. I don't have any grandparents left (alive), and I envy people who do.
2. I never liked to visit my grandparents when I was in middle school.
3. I realize they were often right and always acted out of love for me.

APPLY: Now that you are nearing graduation, you should be qualified to give advice about getting through high school. Suppose you were asked to advise next year's incoming freshmen on that subject. Plan your writing in the space provided below. (Use the model above as your guide.)

Essay topic: High school

Narrowed topic: Teachers as real people

Angle (Advice): Talk to your teachers person to person.

Three points of experience that support my angle:

1. I discovered that my trigonometry teacher actually smiles outside of class.
2. I discovered that my art teacher collects baseball cards, just like I do.
3. My history teacher shared her love of history with me when I challenged her after class.

extend Write a first draft of your essay to see what develops.

Crunch Time

Some impromptu writing is free, fast, and wild. The only mistake you can make is to quit. But some impromptu writing has to be focused, organized, and clear. And you might be graded on it when you're through! GULP.

What should you do? You could go in there with fourteen #2 pencils, rub their erasers down, gnaw on your wrist bone, and blast out a half hour later, heavy with sweat. Or you could do this workshop to get a better idea of how to clear your head and make the best of your short writing time.

Suppose your teacher has given you an assignment to compose an essay in class for a grade. You may prepare for it outside of class, but you may not use notes while writing the essay. You will have 40 minutes to write and revise the essay. One way to prepare for those 40-minute crunch times would be to train a little voice in your head to kick in with the right suggestions at the right time.

REACT: With the help of a classmate (or writing group) plan an impromptu writing strategy, an essential checklist of helpful hints and reminders that you could refer to for this type of writing. Include some of the ideas listed on this page as well as additional ideas you find in the handbook or create on your own. (Make sure that the items in your list are arranged in a logical order. The length of the list is up to you.)

Impromptu Writing Strategy

(Answers will vary.)

give details
connect the parts
consult your memory
check your work
stick to your topic
start where you feel the most power
avoid wasting time
follow through with what you start
make each word count
have every sentence do something
build a structure
calm down
stop and plan
go back later and fix it
jot an outline on scratch paper
keep parts in proportion
get to the point
ask what your reader wants
give something extra
say it clearly
hang in there

Developing Texts

Hold Your Position

If everyone agreed on all important questions, we wouldn't have to explain or defend our positions. We could walk around uttering blanket statements. But since we don't all buy the same ideas, we have to develop our points using the best methods of development at our disposal. We can, among other things, describe, analyze, compare, or classify our ideas as we go along. (Refer to "Selecting a Method of Development" in the opening chapter of the handbook for more information.)

READ: The student who wrote the position paper below uses many different methods of development to explain her thoughts about the gradual destruction of the oceans. Read the paper carefully to appreciate the position she builds.

The Ocean Blue
by Kara Watkins

Take a swim in the ocean. Chances are you'll come across pop cans, bottles, assorted plastics, maybe even a syringe or two. We have made the sea our dumping ground, thinking its great expanse will absorb whatever we put in it. Unfortunately, most of what we put into the oceans stays there. We have not taken out the garbage, just rearranged it. The ocean is part of our world, just as the land is. Anything that we "throw away" stays with us, often coming back to haunt us. Consider the tons of toxic, factory-produced waste dumped into our rivers, streams, and oceans every day. This manmade, nonbiodegradable waste is carried into the open sea and is often eaten by fish and other small creatures. The fish are eaten by animals such as dolphins, whales, and seals—and human beings. Settling in the fat tissues, the toxic material stays in the animals' bodies for life, causing cancer, ulcers, and respiratory diseases which ultimately kill them. Perhaps most frightening (aside from the fact that we also eat the fish and it has the same effect on us) is that female marine mammals pass the toxic waste to their young while the young are being produced, and through milk. Even if these young survive the birth defects caused by toxins, these babies grow up eating contaminated fish, increasing the levels of toxins in their bodies. And so on. Eventually, the level of toxins will become so great that the animals will no longer be able to survive. Mass extinction of sea life will result. This is the case because we insist that industrialization, with all of its waste products, is the way to success. I, for one, am not willing to live in a world without oceanic life. But that's not even an option because the planet cannot survive without a living sea. People don't realize how important a healthy, thriving ocean is to life on land. The entire food chain depends on the tiny organisms called phyto-plankton at the bottom which are eaten by fish, which in turn are eaten by animals including us. If any link of that chain is disturbed, the whole system collapses. As I learn more about the environment and the oceans, about the damage we've caused, I grow more determined to make a difference by practicing conservation and educating others. I just hope we all wake up in time to help our oceans. The consequences of hesitation and ignorance are too frightening for me to imagine.

REACT: Can you spot the different methods Ms. Watkins uses to develop her position? Does she, for example, use any of the following methods?

- **Examples** (proving points with specific references)
- **Narration** (telling mini-stories in support)
- **Classification** (dividing large and complex things into smaller groups)
- **Prediction** (providing possible outcomes)
- **Analysis** (breaking points down)
- **Definition** (distinguishing what certain things are)
- **Comparison** (measuring one thing against something else)

Note below any methods of development that Ms. Watkins clearly seems to use. Be able to cite specific passages to support your choices. Also note anything you might have done differently in this paper. (Afterward, share your results.)

Ms. Watkins opens with some compelling NARRATIVE to hook readers into the essay. A COMPARISON is then made between the garbage in the ocean and the garbage on land to help readers visualize the extent of the problem. What follows is an ANALYSIS of the problem in terms of what the polluted oceans mean to our quality of life. Intermixed with the analysis are a number of disturbing PREDICTIONS.

(What else might have been done?)

More EXPLANATION of how a healthy ocean is important to life on land could have been included.

extend Write freely and rapidly for at least 5 minutes on a subject you feel strongly about. As you write, prompt yourself to use at least three of the methods in the list above.

In Transition

Transitional words between sentences and paragraphs reassure and steer readers along, giving writing a more pleasing flow. Let's see how a professional writer uses transitional words and phrases to link ideas . . . and smooth out the writing.

READ: Here is a passage from an article on allergies in the June 22, 1992, issue of *Time* magazine. The capitalized words in the passage create effective transitions between sentences and between paragraphs. You can learn quite a bit about transitions simply by noticing them and thinking about how they work.

> Acute attacks of asthma occur when the bronchial tubes become partly blocked. FOR REASONS THAT ARE NOT ENTIRELY CLEAR, the lungs are overstimulated by viral infections, allergens or pollutants. The body RESPONDS by activating various defense cells from the immune system. THEIR MOBILIZATION causes the airways to swell. AT THE SAME TIME, the muscles surrounding the airways contract, cutting off airflow. WHEN THAT HAPPENS, asthmatics must inhale an adrenaline-like substance to stop the muscle spasm and reopen their airways.
>
> IF THE ATTACKS RECUR enough times, HOWEVER, the lungs do not return to normal. THEY CONTINUE to act as if they are being invaded by parasites. THIS constant STATE of inflammatory alert damages the bronchial walls, creating scar tissue. AS A RESULT, the airways can no longer clear the mucus that forms deep in the lungs. The ENSUING buildup reduces the flow of air and sets the stage for the next attack.

RESPOND: Write thoughtful answers to the following questions. Afterward, share your answers with a classmate.

1. Do most of the transitional words appear toward the beginnings or the ends of the sentences? Do you think this pattern is a coincidence, or do you see a good reason for it?

Transitional words usually appear near the beginnings of sentences. That way they come as close as possible to the words they echo.

2. What makes the word "responds" a transitional word? If you had to fill in some unwritten words after the word "responds" that would refer to the previous sentence, what would those words be?

The word "responds" looks back to the word "overstimulated." The missing words would be "[responds] to the overstimulation."

3. Study the words "their mobilization": to what words in the previous sentence do they refer?

"activating various defense cells"

4. From what you can observe about transitions in these two paragraphs, write one or two of your own personal "rules for transition."

My Rules for Transition

Rule #1 [Answers will vary.] Use a synonym or noun form to refer to a key word in the previous sentence.

Rule #2 Place transitional words and phrases as close as possible to the words to which they are linked.

Psst! You'll find a complete list of transitions in your handbook. (Refer to "Transitions, Useful linking expressions" in the index.)

extend

Apply what you've learned about transitions in a two-paragraph passage in which you consider the effects that something new (3-D television, stricter requirements for college entrants, the changing employment picture, etc.) would have on you and your peers. Be able to explain to a classmate how you've used transition in your writing.

Like a Train on Smooth Tracks

"I began to see that writing, especially narrative, was not only an affair of sentences, but of paragraphs. Indeed, I thought the paragraph no less important than the sentence . . . Just as the sentence contains one idea in all its fullness, so the paragraph should embrace a distinct episode; and as sentences should follow one another in harmonious sequence, so the paragraphs must fit on to one another like the automatic couplings of railway carriages."

—Winston Churchill, *My Early Life*

The "couplings" Churchill referred to are better known as **transition** or **linking sentences**. They hook ideas together so that writing can flow along, like a train on smooth tracks.

REVIEW: Carefully review the writing scenario that follows. An idea for each of two paragraphs is given. The transition sentence that follows links the two paragraphs. (Transition sentences can come at the end of the first paragraph or at the beginning of the second paragraph.)

Paragraph A Main Idea:

The drive to the concert was a blast from start to finish.

Paragraph B Main Idea:

The concert itself was one disaster after another.

Transition sentence:

As soon as we got to the stadium, however, things took a major-league turn for the worse.

WRITE: Write transition sentences for the following sets of paragraph ideas. Concentrate on the relationship between the main ideas in the paragraphs. Consider using a transition or linking word listed in your handbook in each of your transition sentences. (Refer to "Transitions, Useful linking expressions" in the handbook index for this list.)

A. Working as a waitress at Dog 'n' Spuds was a nightmare.

B. There were unexpected rewards for hanging in there.

Transition sentence: *On the other hand, not every minute at the drive-in was unbearable.*

A. Jesse was not what you would call a hunk.

B. Jesse was a great success as a leading man in school plays.

Transition sentence: Yet Jesse's appearance didn't hinder his acting career.

A. The first lesson the telemarketing salesperson learns is keeping the customer on the line.

B. Various techniques are used to keep customers from hanging up.

Transition sentence: Exactly how to accomplish this is the second lesson.

A. The men in cigarette ads look healthy, robust, and rugged.

B. A number of "Marlboro Men" of the 1950's sued because they developed cancer.

Transition sentence: Despite their great looks, some of these men had health problems.

A. Some English teachers feel obligated to teach the classics.

B. Many young readers find a great deal of satisfaction reading more contemporary titles.

Transition sentence: However, many students may prefer something other than the classics.

SHARE your transition sentences with a classmate. Did you both see the same relationships between paragraph ideas? Did you use the same transition words? Could you make your transition sentences even more effective? More striking? More lively?

Familiar First, New Next

When a sentence begins, readers want to know what it's about. Then they want to know where it's going. When they move to the next sentence, they want to know whether it's going to be about the same thing, or whether it will move on to something new. Sensitive writers try to give their readers clues about such things. As clues, they use *repeated subjects*, *pronouns*, *synonyms*, and *transitional words* or *phrases*.

If you want to help your readers follow your line of thinking, remember these points:

- Shove toward the LEFT—that is, toward the beginning of your sentence—key words that name your topic and any transitional words or phrases that link your sentence to the sentence before it.

- Shove toward the RIGHT—that is, toward the end of your sentence—any words or phrases you want to emphasize because they are new, surprising, or important.

- When you move to the subject of the next sentence, try to echo one of the key words in the previous sentence. (The most obvious word to echo is the SUBJECT of the previous sentence. That keeps you on course.)

Note how the subject is echoed in the following two sentences:

In my culture, CARS are very large and lethal toys.
THEY tempt speed demons like me to play in dangerous ways.

REACT: Find a magazine article or a piece of your own writing to analyze in terms of its direction and flow. (Focus your attention on two or three longer paragraphs.) Points to consider in your analysis:

- Does the writer echo a key word in a previous sentence when he or she moves on to a new thought? (*Underline examples.*)

- Does the writer use specific transitional words or phrases? (*Circle examples.*)

- What is the overall effectiveness or smoothness of the piece? Does it clearly and effectively move from one point to the next? (*Explain*)

- What else might the writer have done to enable the flow of ideas?

- Has the article reinforced or changed your feelings about the construction of writing?

(Answers will vary.)

extend Write freely and reflectively about an experience or a phase in your life (as a team member, as an employee, as a veteran high-school student). Afterward, analyze the direction and flow of your writing. Does it seem to naturally follow the "familiar first, new next" formula? Does it contain specific transitional words or phrases? Are key words echoed from sentence to sentence? What might you do to improve upon this initial writing?

Almost Human

READ: Here's a passage from Elie Wiesel's *Night*. Take special note of his use of personification. (Don't know what personification is? Look it up in your handbook index.)

> I lay down and tried to force myself to sleep, to doze a little, but in vain. God knows what I would not have given for a few moments of sleep. But, deep down, I felt that to sleep would mean to die. And something within me revolted against this death. All round me death was moving in, silently, without violence. It would seize upon some sleeping being, enter into him, and consume him bit by bit. Next to me there was someone trying to wake up his neighbor, his brother, perhaps, or a friend. In vain.

REACT: Here are some questions that will help you react to the passage. (Share responses with a classmate.)

- Where does the personification occur in the passage? (Underline it.)
- What exactly is being personified? Death
- Does the personification seem natural? Believable? (Answers will vary.)
- What other characteristics of this writing do you like? Dislike?
  (Note how the sentences seesaw between "death" and resistance to it.)

WRITE: Try clustering on your own paper with an abstract noun as the nucleus word, perhaps a word like "happiness" or "courage." As you cluster, think in terms of human traits that relate to the noun. After three or four minutes of clustering, write a paragraph in which your abstract noun is in some way personified. (Refer to "Clustering" in the handbook index if you need help getting started.) Share your results.

(Sample start of a cluster)

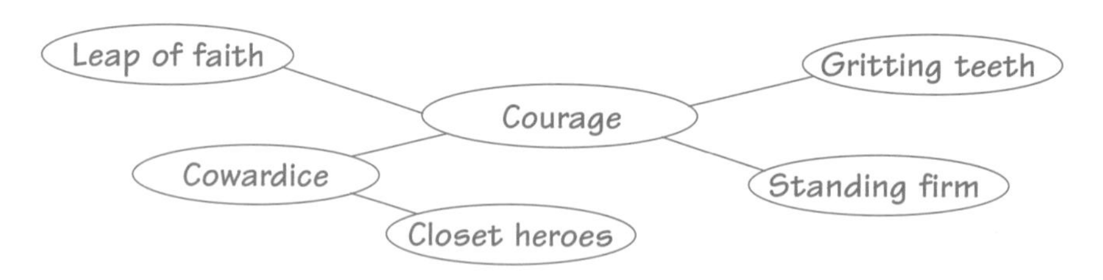

Your handbook lists a number of figures of speech, like personification, that you should practice using in your writing. (Refer to "Figure of speech" in the index for this information.) You've probably worked with metaphors and similes already. How about hyperbole or antithesis?

Metaphor Central

If a piece of your writing needs expanding and clarifying, how are you going to come up with the necessary details? One way is to invent an appropriate **central metaphor** and then s-t-r-e-t-c-h it.

A good place to start your stretching exercise would be the section on "Writing Metaphorically" in your handbook. (Refer to "Writing with style" in the handbook index for this information.) Notice the examples of indirect comparisons—descriptive language that is tied together metaphorically.

- Here is a short paragraph that could use some enrichment:

> The pack of strays would have broken up long ago were it not for the husky that was their leader. She kept the strays in line and always seemed to make the decisions about what to do next. When she stood sniffing the air, she had the bearing of a queen.

- One way to expand and clarify this paragraph metaphorically is to work with the last word, "queen." Notice all the words and phrases in the revised paragraph below that in some way can be associated with a queen or royalty, although the word "queen" is not used—it is the hidden metaphor.

> With a regal sniff, the husky surveyed her whole junkyard kingdom. She enthroned herself on a fallen refrigerator with a sprung door. From there, as the motley terriers and other strays sat up in comic imitation of their leader, she appeared to be thinking about other lots, other packs, other kingdoms. It was because she alone saw beyond the junkyard that she ruled.

REWRITE: Write a different paragraph of your own about the stray dogs, using a circus as a hidden central metaphor. (Compare your results.)

Psst! Stretching metaphors works best for special effects. If this technique is overused, it will draw attention to itself and sound artificial. Sometimes, however, a buried metaphor will work as the central thread of an entire essay.

(Example)

The pack of strays clowned about in the empty lot. Here, under summer's blue big top, a polka-dotted midget waddled near one who walked on stilts. A shaggy mixed-breed waltzed like a trained bear. And at the top of a heap of junk stood the husky, the ringmaster, with eyes that cracked like whips.

extend Find a paragraph or short essay that you've previously written that could be improved if developed around a central metaphor. Revise it accordingly and share your results.

Let me repeat . . .

READ: In this passage from *The Land Remembers*, Ben Logan notes specific images that come to his mind when he thinks of his childhood farm.

> Let the smell of mint touch me. I am kneeling along a little stream, the water numbing my hands as I reach for a trout. I feel the fish arch and struggle. I let go, pulling watercress from the water instead.
>
> Let me see a certain color and I am standing beside the threshing machine, grain cascading through my hands. The seeds we planted when snow was spitting down have multiplied a hundred times, returning in a stream of bright gold, still warm with the sunlight of the fields.
>
> Let me hear an odd whirring. I am deep in the woods, following an elusive sound, looking in vain for a last passenger pigeon, a feathered lightning I have never seen, unwilling to believe no person will ever see one again.

REACT: Ask yourself the following questions as you think about the passage. (Discuss the passage with a classmate. Read it out loud to each other.)

- What three ideas or phrases seem to tie the many images together in this passage?
  Each short paragraph begins "Let me . . ."
- What do these three ideas have in common? How do they differ? Structurally similar
  Different sense emphasized
- What feeling or tone is established in this passage? Does the writing have a matter-of-fact quality to it or is it more poetic and dreamlike? Poetic and dreamlike
- What does the repetition of the three leading ideas contribute to the tone of the passage?
  Sets mood of remembering
- What images or mental pictures do you especially like in the writing?
  (Answers will vary.)

WRITE: Write freely about any subject, but try to begin as many sentences as you can with "Let me." See how long you can keep this going before it becomes tiresome. Afterward, review your writing to see if your "Let me" statements had a positive or negative effect on your writing. (Use your own paper.)

inside info

Much power or beauty in writing comes from the repetition of words, phrases, and ideas. Repetition is also an effective unifying or organizing device, as in the sample passage above.

Real-World Writing

What you want to write and what you actually write often have to be two different things, especially when you write in real-world situations. Your heart might tell you to blow off steam, letting all your strongest feelings show in the words you use. But your head might tell you to calm down, be realistic, focus on results, and watch your language.

Watching your language means controlling your **diction** or tuning your words to the ears of your audience. (For some handbook help on ways to adjust your language to real-world situations, refer to "Diction" in the index.)

WRITE: Consider the following scenario: Bob and Johnny's Ice Cream Co. is accepting applications for individuals to work at the new ice-cream parlor they are opening in your town. Since you need a job (desperately), you decide to write a letter of application. As you write, keep in mind that Bob and Johnny's is a growing, upbeat, socially conscious, all-natural company with an excellent nationwide reputation. They want completely honest, pleasant, and dependable employees. Write a letter showing enthusiasm, honesty, respect for the company, and positive qualities consistent with the company's needs. Address your letter to

Bob and Johnny's Ice Cream Co.
123 Berry Garcia Ln.
Stoughton, ME 01812

Important: As you write, avoid slipping into an inappropriate level of diction.

extend Now write a letter of application to a local ice-cream parlor speaking very, very informally, as if the owner were a close friend. (Compare the two letters.)

Voice Choice

If you listen carefully to the words of a story, a poem, or an essay—especially if it is being read aloud—you will probably hear a voice that seems to speak from the text.

This thing we call "voice" in writing is a result of several choices a writer has to make:

1. Who is doing the telling?
2. Is the teller speaking about something that *had* already happened, something that *has been* happening, something that simply *happened* in the past, or something that is *happening right now*? (In other words, is the overall verb tense in the past perfect, present perfect, simple past, or present tense? Refer to "Tense of verbs" in the handbook index for more information.)
3. Is the teller a participant in the action, an observer, or someone who somehow simply knows about it?
4. What is the teller's attitude toward the subject?

READ: Here is a part of a high-school student's essay about a drug deal he observed. Pay attention to the voice of the narrator:

> I was busy at work when I noticed the whole incident. My workplace opens in the back onto an alley behind the adjacent stores. Approximately twenty-five feet from the rear of the store is a dumpster. When I looked, I saw a man in nice brand-name clothes come from the left and a raggedy man come from the right. They met by the dumpster in clear view. They both looked around, ignoring the door that I was looking through, and looked over each other's packages. The nicely dressed man flipped through the roll of bills he received and nodded. The raggedy man checked his package, and then he also nodded. Both men slipped their packages into their pockets, and after a few quick glances, each went back the way he came. The whole incident took a maximum of forty-five seconds.

REACT: How would you describe the voice of the narrator in this paragraph? Notice these things:

1. The student himself is doing the telling.
2. He tells it in the simple past tense ("was," "noticed," "met," etc.). The present tense verbs he uses apply only to things that are continually the same, even in the present (for example, the workplace "opens" onto an alley).
3. He was an observer, not a participant. He knows and tells only what he saw. He can't tell us about the feelings or thoughts of the drug dealer.
4. He sounds interested, maybe amazed, but otherwise objective and emotionless.

REFLECT: Think about how you would tell this story using a different voice. Here are some options to choose from.

1. Who is talking? Try a plainclothes policeman, one of the drug dealers, an old woman in a second-story room, a dog behind a dumpster.
2. Verb tense: Try the simple present tense, the past tense, or one of the other tenses.
3. Angle: Act as a participant in the action, an observer from a different angle, or someone who heard about the action from someone else.
4. Attitude: Try sounding horrified, amused, angry, relieved, or disgusted.

Write your choices here: (Answers will vary.)

1. one of the drug dealers
2. past tense
3. participant in the action
4. nervous

WRITE: Write a first draft of a story about drug dealing, using the choices above as your guide.

I looked at this ragpicker they sent me, and I couldn't believe what I saw. This guy was a walking billboard: drug deal happening here at 4:00 p.m. Every cop in the precinct must have had his scent. Anyway, I made it quick because an open door down the alley really bothered me. What if somebody was scoping this out? I watched this guy check out the money. What was he thinking? We could check out the goods later. I knew where to find this weasel if there was a problem.

Narrative voice should not be confused with the voice of a verb (see "Voice" in the index of your handbook). "Voice of a verb" refers to whether the verb in a sentence is active or passive—that is, whether the subject of the sentence performs or receives the action.

Reviewing and Revising Texts

Cold Eye and Dirty Hands

READ: One of the most important things you can do to make a piece of writing better is to stand back—not physically, but in your mind. After you've completed an early draft, you must detach yourself from the work and view it with a cold eye. Here are some sentences you can practice saying to yourself so that you can successfully stand back from an early draft with a cold eye:

I didn't write this, a stranger did.
This piece is ancient history.
This is just a chunk of language.
I like this part.
Something crucial is missing here.
Thank goodness, I have another chance.
My best writing is still to come.
I've got a better idea.

REACT: If you have a piece of writing that is still in its early stages of development, turn your cold eye on it and plan a revising strategy. Use the handbook as your guide, referring specifically to the section on revising. See "Revising, Strategies" in the index. When you've finished this cold-eyed strategy session, make a list of "Things to Do" to make your next draft better. (Use the space below or your own paper for your work.)

(The following "Things to Do" could be adapted from the revising strategies.)

- *Read over the assignment.*
- *Check for gaps.*
- *Support main points.*
- *Answer the readers' likely questions.*
- *Organize the ideas in a logical order.*

APPLY: Now you're ready to get dirty hands by working with the messy parts of your writing. First, set aside time for your work: a half hour to three hours is normal for a piece from one to five pages long. Next, gather all of your writing tools. Third, follow your "Things to Do" list and get to work.

Reading as a Writer

When you read as a writer, you ask two sets of questions. The first set relates directly to your understanding of the material (What does this mean? Do I agree?). But the second set includes questions related to the development of the writing:

- What did it take for the writer to do this?
- How would it feel to write a piece like this?
- What is the spirit of this piece?
- How does this work?
- How would I write this differently?
- How might I write this better?

REACT: Read the following excerpt of a student editorial. Then, on your own paper, write out thoughtful answers to any *four* of the writing-related questions listed above. (Share your results.)

We Walk Alike, We Talk Alike, We Look Alike
by Brian Lojeck

You wake up in the morning. You smash your alarm clock to silence the dreaded Klaxon and guzzle down a cold soda to fulfill your nutritional needs. Then you get dressed.

No matter what you wear, you are guaranteed of one thing. You're original. The chances of meeting someone who is wearing the exact same outfit is slim at best. You feel good, right?

Now imagine this: You look into your closet and all of your clothes are blue. Blue shirts, blue pants, blue shoes, blue underwear. Everyone in school is also wearing blue-on-blue-on-blue-on-blue-on-blue. Nice, huh?

That's exactly what a bunch of people who call themselves "The Uniform Committee" want to do to us. They sent out a paper a long time ago to some of us asking if we agreed with the reinstatement of a mandatory uniform in Aviation [High School]. Well, since this is an editorial, you can be assured of one thing: I've got something to say about that.

Before I even go into their reasons, let me warm up with this: How are we supposed to take this Uniform Committee seriously if they didn't even give us their real names? Look at the top of this article. Just below the title you'll find a name, mine to be exact. That way, if someone doesn't like this article they can find me and tell me about it. If I've got the guts to face them after I write this, why didn't they have the guts to face us after they asked about uniforms? Can it be that they know how unpopular the reinstatement of uniforms will be? Can it be they know that it may cost them the respect of the students when word gets out that it's their fault? Yep. Now, for their reasons:

The first reason they gave for supporting the mandatory uniform is to lower clothing costs.

Cool.

(Student answers will vary.)

1. How would it feel to write a piece like this? I think I'd feel breezy, sort of cocky and confident, as if I have all the answers.
2. What is the spirit of this piece? Sarcastic, self-righteous
3. How does this work? First it paints an undesirable picture of the future. Then it demands accountability. Then it begins to tackle the reasons for the committee's idea.
4. How might I write this better? I might drop the cocky tone and show respect for the opposition.

The Write Instincts

READ: Study the short essay of comparison below. Read it over once and react to it instinctively. How does the writing work for you? In what ways? Then read it again in light of what your handbook says about effective writing style.

My sister and I have absolutely opposite personalities. I'm methodical, cautious, organized. Jennifer's impulsive, scattered, and fun-loving. I live for the future. She lives in the moment. When we were kids, I used to exploit these differences in our personalities—using them as a weapon against her. Basically, I teased her to death. For instance, she has always loved food and used to scarf down anything sweet at the speed of light when she was little. Every time we went for a ride in my father's classic 1956 Riviera, something we did most every Sunday, my parents would give us one treat apiece. Usually we'd get a candy bar, sometimes an ice-cream bar. She'd eat her treat in about 10 seconds. I'd peel the wrapper real slow-like, and then eat my treat in stages. The outside of the peanut butter cup first, of course, and then the peanut butter. I'd spend a quarter of an hour on the outside chocolate alone! And of course, she'd have to sit there, and watch me eat the treat she no longer had—hers was eaten, mine was a weapon of torture. One day when she had eaten her Rice Krispie treat, and I was eating mine one Krispie at a time, my parents cured me of my urge to tease. They made me give her half my treat! I'm still the most methodical person I know, but no longer when it comes to dessert.

REACT: How does this writing stack up against the traits or characteristics of an effective style? We've listed a number of common traits below with space to write a brief response to each. Mention strengths as well as weaknesses in the style of the writing. (Work with a classmate if your teacher allows it.)

Originality *Strong—written from writer's unique viewpoint*

Vitality/Life *Strong—interesting words: methodical, scattered, scarf down, one Krispie at a time.*

Weak—cliches or dull words: speed of light, slow-like

Variety Strong—different sentence types and lengths

Simplicity Strong—focus is always evident, doesn't stray from main idea

Accuracy Strong—uses correct spelling, capitalization, etc.

Concreteness Strong—gives precise descriptions: classic 1956 Riviera, Rice Krispie treat

Honesty Strong—conveys writer's not-so-nice attitude: I used to exploit these differences; I teased her to death.

Grace/Movement Could be stronger—combine sentences for smoother description of eating a candy bar

inside info

Remember: Your writing style comes from a series of writing choices you make. It is composed of your words, your sentences, and your paragraphs—nobody else's.

R-R-R-R-Revising

Writing authority Peter Elbow describes the results of first drafts in this way:

". . . a person's best writing is often all mixed up together with his worst. It all feels lousy to him as he's writing, but if he will let himself write it and come back later, he will find some parts of it are excellent. It is as though one's best words come wrapped in one's worst."

READ: Sometimes it's hard to keep an open mind when you read what you have written. You need to put some distance between yourself and your writing.

- Whenever possible, put your writing aside for a day or two.
- Read it out loud.
- Ask others (family, friends, classmates) to read it out loud to you.
- Listen to the language you have used: How does it sound? What does it say?

REACT: These six questions will help you react to your own writing on your second or third read-through:

- What parts of my writing work for me?
- Do all of these parts work together? Are they logical?
- Do all the parts point to one idea? What is the main idea?
- Do the parts say exactly what I want them to say?
- Have I arranged the parts in the best possible order?
- Where do I need to go from here?

REWORK: Reworking your writing means rewriting and refining it until all of the parts work equally well. There is usually plenty of rewriting and refining to do in the early stages of writing.

REFLECT: One of the best ways of keeping track of your reactions as you read, react, and rework is to write comments in the margins of your paper. Margins are the perfect place for you to explore your feelings concerning what you have written. Here are some guidelines:

- Explore your thoughts freely and naturally.
- Keep track of any suggestions for improving your writing.
- Note what you plan to cut, move, explain further, and so on.
- If you are unsure of yourself, write down a question to answer later.

REFINE: Refining is putting the final polish on your written copy. It is shining up both your thoughts and words. Here's what you can do to help:

- Read your paper out loud to make sure that you haven't missed anything.
- Listen for both the sense and the sound of the writing.
- Make your final adjustments. Follow the 5 R's (read, react, rework, reflect, refine) each time you revise. Eventually, the revising process will become a natural part of your thinking.

extend

Select a work in progress and apply the 5-R's strategy. Write your reactions and reflections on another piece of paper.

Cut, Clarify, Condense

Would you like an easy and effective strategy for fixing problems with wording? All you have to do is use the 3 C's of editing.

Editing Code:

CUT [brackets]
If you find a part that's unnecessary or wordy, put brackets around it. If you decide that section is really unneeded, cut it!

CLARIFY
If you see something confusing, unclear, or incomplete in your writing, put a wavy line under that section. You should rethink it, reword it, explain it, or add detail to it.

CONDENSE (parentheses)
If you come across a section of your writing that is wordy or overexplained, put a set of parentheses around it. (Refer to "Wordiness," "Deadwood, sentences," and "Flowery language" in the handbook index for help.)

READ & REACT: Here is a marked portion of a student's in-progress essay using the 3-C's editing code. Rewrite the essay following the coding used. *Hint:* Start by reading the entire paragraph first; then cross out those sections in brackets and consider how to improve the sections in parentheses.

My most memorable experience was the first time I drove my dad's car. I was 15 years old [at the time], and we had just gone up to Saxon, Wisconsin, for the summer. My dad had to go into town [for something], and he let me drive his (pride and joy). (As I was going along, I could see out the corner of my eye that he was trying to be cool, but I could tell that he was [getting] tense) [and uptight]. Every time I would come to a stop, I could see him unconsciously trying (to put the brakes on). As we (were coming into town), we passed Old Dan's Bar. Everything was going great. [What a trip!] Then I noticed that he had his hands on the dashboard to brace himself. As I was watching him, I suddenly drove into a fire hydrant and totaled the front of my father's brand-new Buick. (Dear old Dad almost had a canary). He was so mad at me that he couldn't (say a word). [He was speechless.] After that he decided to turn around and go back to camp. When we got there, he got a Coke from the cooler, and he didn't talk to me until the next day. [Needless to say] the rest of our trip was (a real bummer) for me.

(Revised paragraphs will vary.)

extend Compare your revisions of the above paragraph with a classmate's. What do the two of you agree on? Where do you disagree? Also: Evaluate one of your own essays using the strategy you just learned.

In Short Order

READ & REACT: Carefully read the first draft of "Soft Bones" below. It is the result of an in-class writing activity.

(Students' revisions will vary.)

1 When I was growing up, my parents never quite agreed on my participation in
2 contact sports[.] ~~or on what kinds of physical activity were good or not~~. My mom felt
3 that there were plenty of ways to get hurt ~~in life~~ without deliberately ~~going out to~~
4 ~~do~~ [doing] something that could result in physical injury, like playing tackle football. To
5 make sure I understood where she stood on this issue, my mom sat me down one
6 afternoon and talked about a rare hereditary ailment that ran in her family called
7 "soft bones." [This] ~~It was a~~ condition ~~that~~ made strenuous physical activity really risky,
8 especially for boys. I [imagined] ~~had a picture of~~ my bones twisting like pretzels and hardening
9 in strange positions. ~~Mom just didn't understand about tackling and stuff like that.~~
10 [On the other hand, my] ~~My~~ dad thought ~~of~~ "getting hurt" ~~as~~ [was] something you sort of took for granted. You
11 see, ~~my~~ [D]dad was ~~sort of~~ a definite sports fanatic. ~~My dad started playing ball at an~~
12 ~~early age.~~ From the time I was able to stagger around on my own, he was always
13 throwing some sort of ball at me. ~~And I usually wore NFL "jammies."~~
14 Whether I would play peewee football at age seven became a real bone of
15 contention between my parents. My mother didn't want me to play, while my dad
16 did. This put me in a difficult situation. I wanted to make my dad happy[, but] I didn't
17 want to make my mom unhappy.
18 ~~So,~~ [W]when I told my father I had decided to wait a while before ~~attempting to~~
19 play[ing] organized football, I could tell he was disappointed[.] ~~, but took it pretty well. It~~
20 ~~was~~ [¶A] ~~a~~ couple months later[,] as we were playing on the lawn[,] ~~and~~ [I] twisted my ankle.
21 Worried, I told Dad, "I hope my bones will get back into the right shape okay."
22 ~~Without thinking~~ I blurted out about the "soft bones" that ran in Mom's family and
23 affected males. He looked at me for a second[,] ~~and~~ [then he] started to laugh[.] ~~, and laugh, and~~
24 ~~laugh.~~

REACT: Revise this first draft using the "Revising on the Run" guidelines listed in your handbook. (You'll find this information in the section on revising in the opening chapter.) Make your changes on this sheet. And then if time pemits, rewrite the narrative on your own paper. (Share your results.)

One Form to Another

READ: If you were an alien visitor from another galaxy and had no idea what H_20 was, I would show you not only a glass of liquid water but also an ice cube and a kettle blowing off steam. To get a full idea of what water is, you would have to see it in all its moods or forms.

You can use this same principle to improve or revise your writing. One of the major forms of writing is fiction. Another is poetry. Another is expository prose. Still another is drama. See the chart "A Survey of Writing Forms" in your handbook (listed under "Writing process" in the index) to get an idea of the great many forms available to you.

To get a better appreciation of your writing, try changing it from one form to another. Switching forms will help you develop fresh perspectives and new approaches to your subject that you can apply when you revise.

- Here is a sentence of expository prose describing a house where an old cat-lover lives:

  Cats sun themselves on the fences, peep out the windows, and disappear around corners as I walk by.

- Here is how a professional writer transformed this idea into poetry:

  The house's eye appears to blink
  as a cat in a picture window
  parts a curtain.
  Suddenly, fences sprout
  whiskers, sidewalks run away.
  I am watched from shadows
  as I pass.

- Here is a reworking of the idea (by the same writer) into story form:

  I don't think I was paranoid, though my older sister had called me worse things before.But whenever I passed the neighbor's house where, at last count by my snoopy friends, there lived 24 cats, the feeling of being watched made me twitch and shrug.

- If this writer would transform the writing back into expository prose, the writing would surely be different because of the ideas that had arisen during the excursion into other forms.

WRITE: Write a fairly long sentence (or a short paragraph) about any subject that comes to mind. Then transform it into at least two of the writing forms listed in "A Survey of Writing Forms." Show your work to a writing partner. (For example) The prospect of her second soccer practice made her almost physically sick. She had no experience like the others and knew that she would be cast the fool. That would hurt more than the wind sprints, and more than collisions in a scrimmage. She half-wished that death would rescue her by tomorrow.

Transformation 1 (Letter)

Dear Dad:
I have a confession to make. When you picked me up at practice this afternoon, I hadn't actually been practicing. You saw I was sweaty, but that was from the long, fast walk I took while the team was working out.

Transformation 2 (Song)

Soccer soccer
Gonna hide out in my locker
feeling so sick, oh yeah,
got the competition blues
real bad
I don't think I wanna play . . .

extend Transform one of your compositions (or a good chunk of it) into a new form. Share your experiment with a classmate or your writing group.

Bridging the Gap

Writers need to practice using transitions to get truly adept at moving smoothly and clearly from one point to the next in their writing. Need a list of transitions? Refer to "Transitions, Useful linking expressions" in the handbook index.

READ: The following paragraph contains plenty of good details. But all is not well. The paragraph needs work in the graceful transitions department. (Some of the transitions are too abrupt and noticeable.) Read it carefully and see for yourself.

"One, two; kick, jump; five, six, seven, eight! Oh come on, you look like a bunch of slobs! This is jazz ballet! You're supposed to look graceful, not like soggy pieces of bread! All right, take a quick break!" Miss Nitchka roared. My name is Karen and Miss Nitchka is my jazz ballet disciplinarian. By the sound of it, you'd probably think I'm crazy if I said, "I love jazz, the discipline, the hard work, even the yelling!" Well I do; let me tell you why. To begin with, jazz is fun. I've always loved dancing. I was in gymnastics and I loved it. I wasn't exactly a champion at the tumbling part, but I was absolutely marvelous at the dance floor exercises. Since jazz has a combination of gymnastics—splits, leaps, kicks, high jumps, etc.—and dancing, I took to it. And am I glad I did! Secondly, I love all the hard work, all the sweat. It gives me a sense of accomplishment. I have more confidence in myself because I'm doing something I love and I'm working hard at it. I'm saving discipline and yelling for last because I feel they are the most important. They also have the same meaning. If she didn't yell, we wouldn't work as hard. In fact, we probably wouldn't find much interest in it and would give up. In conclusion, without the discipline we couldn't learn as much, so we wouldn't go on to bigger and better things.

REACT: Circle every transition that draws undue attention to itself. Also note details and ideas that you would like to cut, move, or reword. Then rewrite the paragraph, making sure it reads more smoothly and clearly.

Refining: Sentence Strengthening

When Complex Is Simpler . . .

READ: As you revise, you may want to combine some of your short, simple sentences into more mature, efficient sentences. To join two ideas that are not equal in importance, you may use a **complex sentence.** A complex sentence contains one independent clause and one (or more) dependent clauses. The complex sentence is used to show the relationship of one idea to another.

The complex sentence helps you tell the reader which of the two ideas expressed in the sentence is more important. The more important idea (main idea) is placed in the independent clause; the less important idea is placed in the dependent, or subordinate, clause. Since the purpose of all writing is to communicate ideas clearly, the complex sentence is especially valuable to the writer.

An adverb clause is one kind of subordinate clause. Loosely speaking, it modifies a verb or another modifier in the sentence. It is easier to use adverb clauses effectively when you understand what they do in a sentence and become familiar with the subordinating conjunctions used to introduce them.

- Some subordinating conjunctions are used to introduce adverb clauses of **time:**
  before *after* *when* *until* *since* *while*
- Some subordinating conjunctions are used to introduce adverb clauses telling the **reason why:**
  because *since*
- Some subordinating conjunctions are used to introduce adverb clauses telling the **purpose or result:**
  so *that* *so that* *in order that*
- Some subordinating conjunctions are used to introduce adverb clauses telling the **condition:**
  whereas *if* *unless* *though* *although* *as long as* *while*

COMBINE: Combine each set of simple sentences into a complex sentence by placing the less important idea in an adverb clause. An asterisk (*) is printed after the more important idea in the first few sets. In parentheses after each of your new complex sentences, explain what your adverb clause tells.

1. Eagles will usually kill animals lighter than themselves.
Some fast-moving species have been known to carry off much heavier prey.*

Although eagles will usually kill animals lighter than themselves, some fast-moving species have been known to carry off much heavier prey. (condition)

2. The writhing, talon-pierced carp weighed 13 pounds.
The sea eagle flew low and was almost pulled underwater by its prey.*

Because the writhing, talon-pierced carp weighed 13 pounds, the sea eagle flew low and was almost pulled underwater by its prey. (reason why)

3. The young eagle is heavier than its parents by as much as one pound.*
It leaves the nest.

The young eagle is heavier than its parents by as much as one pound when it leaves the nest. (time)

4. The hunters looked up toward the mountain crest.
They saw an American bald eagle descending with a mule deer fawn in its talons.*

While the hunters looked up toward the mountain crest, they saw an American bald eagle descending with a mule deer fawn in its talons. (time)

5. The lurid and suspicious stories continued to be printed.
Worried mothers lived in fear of their babies being carried off by eagles.*

As long as the lurid and suspicious stories continued to be printed, worried mothers lived in fear of their babies being carried off by eagles. (condition)

6. Arthur Bowland once persuaded a Verreaux's eagle to snatch a 20-pound pack while in flight.
He could test the bird's supposed tremendous strength.

Authur Bowland once persuaded a Verreaux's eagle to snatch a 20-pound pack while in flight so that he could test the bird's supposed tremendous strength. (purpose or result)

7. Scientific tests for muscularity and power will not be a true guide for the species.
They are done with wild, not captive, eagles.

Scientific tests for muscularity and power will not be a true guide for the species unless they are done with wild, not captive, eagles. (condition)

8. Eagles can kill prey four times their own size.
They ordinarily cannot carry a load much over their own body weight.

Although eagles can kill prey four times their own size, they ordinarily cannot carry a load much over their own body weight. (condition)

9. Eagles will usually kill animals half their own weight or less.
They can get away easily with their dinner.

Eagles will usually kill animals half their own weight or less so that they can get away easily with their dinner. (purpose or result)

It's All Relative

Another way to show which idea in a sentence is more important is to use an adjective clause for the less important idea. An adjective clause modifies, or describes, a noun or a pronoun.

Adjective clauses are usually introduced by the **relative pronouns:** *who, whom, whose, which, that*. Such clauses are called "relative clauses." *Who, whom,* and *whose* are used to refer to people. *Which* refers to nonliving objects or to animals. *That* may refer to people, nonliving objects, or animals.

Please note: An adjective clause can also be introduced with the words *when, where,* and *how*.

COMBINE: Combine the following simple sentences into complex sentences by using an adjective clause. Place the less important idea in the adjective clause. An asterisk (*) is printed after the more important idea in the first few groups of simple sentences. You decide which of the two ideas is more important in the rest of the groups.

1. The whale shark is the largest fish in the world.*
The whale shark is found in the warmer areas of the Atlantic, Pacific, and Indian Oceans.

The whale shark, which is found in the warmer areas of the Atlantic, Pacific, and Indian Oceans, is the largest fish in the world.

Note: Commas surround the adjective clause if it is a **nonrestrictive clause** (as in the example above). "Nonrestrictive" means the clause is not required to identify the noun or pronoun. Nonrestrictive clauses give extra information that is not necessary to the basic meaning of the sentence. **Restrictive clauses,** or those clauses that restrict or limit or are required to identify the noun or pronoun, are not set off by commas. (See your handbook for more information and examples.)

2. Dr. Andrew Smith examined the first recorded whale shark specimen in 1828.*
Dr. Smith was a military surgeon with the British army.

Dr. Andrew Smith, who was a military surgeon with the British army, examined the first recorded whale shark specimen in 1828.

3. The fishermen harpooned the shark.
The fishermen had noticed its unusual gray coloration with white spots.*

The fishermen who harpooned the shark had noticed its unusual gray coloration with white spots.

4. The dried skin is preserved in the Museum d'Histoire Naturelle of Paris.*
Dr. Smith originally purchased the dried skin for $30.

The dried skin, which Dr. Smith originally purchased for $30, is preserved in the Museum d'Histoire Naturelle of Paris.

5. In 1868 a young Irish naturalist studied the whale sharks in the Seychelle Islands.*
He had heard the natives speak of a monstrous fish called the "Chagrin."

In 1868 a young Irish naturalist studied the whale sharks in the Seychelle Islands, where he had heard the natives speak of a monstrous fish called the "Chagrin."

6. He saw several specimens.
The specimens exceeded 50 feet in length.

He saw several specimens that exceeded 50 feet in length.

7. Many men reported sharks measuring nearly 70 feet in length.
These men had always been considered trustworthy.

Many men who had always been considered trustworthy reported sharks measuring nearly 70 feet in length.

8. The largest fish ever held in captivity was a whale shark.
It was kept in a small bay rather than in an aquarium.

The largest fish ever held in captivity was a whale shark, which was kept in a small bay rather than in an aquarium.

9. The only other exceptionally large fish is the basking shark.
It compares in size with the whale shark.

The only other exceptionally large fish that compares in size with the whale shark is the basking shark.

10. A fish frightened millions of viewers during the movie *Jaws*.
The fish was a replica of the carnivorous great white shark.

The fish that frightened millions of viewers during the movie Jaws was a replica of the carnivorous great white shark.

Time to Review

How much do you know about using adverb and adjective clauses? How do they help a writer? Do you use them in your own writing? This activity will help you answer these questions. Some important points to remember about adverb and adjective clauses are as follows:

- An **adverb clause** at the beginning of a sentence is set off by a comma; an adverb clause at the end of a sentence is generally not set off by a comma.
- An **adjective clause** that is nonrestrictive is set off by commas; an adjective clause that is restrictive (required) is not set off by commas. (See your handbook for additional information.)

COMBINE: To continue your practice of subordination, combine each of the following sets of simple sentences into one complex sentence by following the directions in parentheses.

1. A. Insects have three pairs of legs, one pair of antennae, and usually one or two pairs of wings.

B. Insects comprise the largest group of arthropods.

(Use B. in a nonrestrictive adjective clause.)

Insects, which comprise the largest group of arthropods, have three pairs of legs, one pair of antennae, and usually one or two pairs of wings.

2. A. It has been suggested that one day insects may inherit the earth.

B. This statement seems exaggerated to us humans.

(Use B. in an adverb clause telling the condition.)

Although this statement seems exaggerated to us humans, it has been suggested that one day insects may inherit the earth.

3. A. This prediction may one day be realized.

B. The insects' small size, great variety, and fast rate of reproduction have made them nearly indestructible.

(Use B. in an adverb clause at the beginning of the sentence.)

Because the insects' small size, great variety, and fast rate of reproduction have made them nearly indestructible, this prediction may one day be realized.

4. A. Farmers like certain pollinating insects.
B. Farmers despise the insects that destroy their crops.
(Use A. in an adverb clause telling condition.)

While farmers like certain pollinating insects, they despise the insects that destroy their crops.

5. A. The insects can be a serious threat to humanity.
B. Some insects carry diseases such as typhus, malaria, and yellow fever.
(Use B. in a restrictive adjective clause.)

The insects that carry diseases such as typhus, malaria, and yellow fever can be a serious threat to humanity.

(Use B. in an adverb clause telling why.)

Because some insects carry diseases such as typhus, malaria, and yellow fever, they can be a serious threat to humanity.

6. A. Butterflies and moths have wings covered with tiny overlapping scales.
B. The scales provide their color.
(Use B. in a nonrestrictive adjective clause.)

Butterflies and moths have wings covered with tiny overlapping scales, which provide their color.

7. A. The worker honeybee will generally die after stinging someone.
B. The barbed stinger stays in the wound, pulling the poison sac and other organs out of the bee.
(Use B. in an adverb clause telling the reason why at the end of the sentence.)

The worker honeybee will generally die after stinging someone because the barbed stinger stays in the wound, pulling the poison sac and other organs out of the bee.

Using Parallel Structure

Parallel structure is the balanced or coordinated arrangement of sentence elements that are equal in importance; in other words, it is the arranging of similar ideas in a similar way. The use of parallel structure can add a sense of rhythm and emphasis to your writing style that makes it more appealing to your reader. (Refer to your handbook for more information on parallel structure.)

REVISE: To better understand parallel structure, look carefully at the sentences below. Each sentence contains two ideas or items that are equal in importance, but are not expressed in equal or parallel form. Those sentence parts that are not parallel and should be are underlined. Substitute a parallel expression in the place of one of those that is underlined. Revise each sentence as necessary so that the new expression fits in well and adds a sense of balance and rhythm to the overall sentence.

1. Swimming is an excellent exercise for strengthening your heart and one that will increase your lung power.

   Swimming is an excellent exercise for strengthening your heart and increasing your lung power.

2. Swim for 10 minutes, dividing the time between the breaststroke, the crawl, and doing the backstroke, and you will have had a good workout.

   Swim for 10 minutes, dividing the time between the breaststroke, the crawl, and the backstroke, and you will have had a good workout.

3. Swimming improves the mobility of major joints and is strengthening for the muscles.

   Swimming improves the mobility of major joints and strengthens the muscles.

4. There is a rather odd myth that swimming in freezing water is beneficial and you will enjoy it.

   There is a rather odd myth that swimming in freezing water is beneficial and enjoyable.

5. At best, plunging into cold water may give you a kick; at worst, you may have a heart attack.

   At best, plunging into cold water may give you a kick; at worst, it may give you a heart attack.

6. Some people get less exercise at the pool than they intend; they talk to friends, tread water, and are hanging onto the side while watching others.

   . . . than they intend; they talk to friends, tread water, and hang onto the side while watching others.

7. Faithful practice will result in a smooth swimming style and your breathing pattern will be efficient.

   Faithful practice will result in a smooth swimming style and an efficient breathing pattern.

8. A steady ten-minute swim would probably comprise a good workout while swimming furiously for three minutes would not.

   . . . a good workout while a furious three-minute swim would not.

COMPLETE: Complete each of the following sentences by adding a word, phrase, or clause that is parallel to the underlined portion of the sentence. (Each addition must be sensible as well as parallel.)

1. Sitting in the middle of his new dormitory room were a suitcase, a box of books, and

   a stereo.

2. He hopes to get a job on campus either working in the library or

   assisting in the lab.

3. This Saturday night some of my friends want to go to the football game, some want to go out for pizza, and some want to go to the movie.

4. This time should really be spent planning for the future, not thinking about the past.

5. We drove all morning to get to the taco stand, and we drove all afternoon

   to get back to our apartment.

Saving the Best for Last

Here's a writing tip you may find useful: by postponing the crucial or main idea until the end of a sentence, you can build tension and draw your reader into the development of your thought. This kind of sentence, known as the **periodic sentence,** packs a nice punch—one that is not easily forgotten. (Refer to "Periodic sentence" in the handbook index for more.)

READ: Read the samples below, paying particular attention to the location of the crucial or main idea (in regular italics).

> ***When the mountains and the pines turned into blue oxen, blue dogs, and blue people,*** *the old couple asked me to spend the night in the hut.*
>
> —from *The Woman Warrior*, Maxine Hong Kingston

> ***In the roads where the teams moved, where the wheels milled the ground and the hooves of the horses beat the ground,*** *the dirt crust broke and the dust formed.*
>
> —from *The Grapes of Wrath*, John Steinbeck

WRITE: Rewrite the following sentences so that the most crucial idea is postponed until the end of the sentence. (Share your results.)

1. The house stood at the top of the hill, surrounded by weeping willows and lilac bushes, punctuating a winding driveway that looked like an upside-down question mark.

   Surrounded by weeping willows and lilac bushes, punctuating a winding driveway that looked like an upside-down question mark, the house stood at the top of the hill.

2. Sean ran headlong into traffic, ignoring his own safety and chasing the renegade dog that held his only baseball.

   Ignoring his own safety, and chasing the renegade dog that held his only baseball, Sean ran headlong into traffic.

Should you go out of your way to use periodic sentences in your writing? No. Should you try to use them often? Same answer. They should be used with care, when it seems right, when an important point demands more dramatic treatment.

Refining: Improving Style

What Makes "Good" Good?

Everyone has his or her own individual tastes. While I really like Mexican food (earthy and healthy), you might like Irish food (homey and hearty) or French food (bon appétit!). I like purple; however, you may go for chartreuse. I really dig blues, but you may prefer heavy metal. With writing style, it's the same. Everyone has opinions about what makes for good writing.

REACT: What do you value in writing? What draws you to certain writers again and again? Is their writing fast paced, or highly descriptive, or a bit hard edged and sarcastic? And what do you strive for when you write? When are you most satisfied with your work? In the space provided below, list five things you like to see in writing (including your own). (You might, for example, enjoy writing that sounds friendly and unpretentious, like one person talking to another person.)

(Lists will vary.)

RECONSIDER: Review your list in light of what the handbook says about the traits of good writing. Turn to the handbook section "Traits of an Effective Style." (Refer to "Writing with style" in the index.) Review this section and note at least two things that you would add to your personal list of traits of effective writing. Share with a classmate the results of your personal inventory.

Though there are certain traits of effective writing that are commonly recognized, each writer's style is different—that uniqueness is the ultimate element of an effective style!

What I Like

READ & REACT: Select a piece of writing—preferably a passage from a magazine article—that you consider to be good in terms of both what it says (content) and how it says it (style). Then in a brief essay try to figure out what makes the writing work for you. Make references to specific words, phrases, and ideas you actually see and hear in the writing. (Attach a copy of the passage to your writing.)

(Answers will vary.)

Points you might want to consider in your writing:

- Does the writer have a clear purpose in mind?
- Does the writing sound sincere and honest? Do you hear a distinctive voice in the writing?
- Is the subject of the writing presented effectively? Is there a form or design to the writing? Does it move logically from one point to the next?
- Does the writer include anecdotes, figures of speech, effective details and examples, etc?
- Does the writing make you react in some way?

Psst! Also refer to your comments in the workshop entitled "What Makes 'Good' Good?" for ideas for your writing.

EXTEND: In a writing of your own, try imitating the style of the passage you selected. (The content of your writing should be original. The way you express your ideas should reflect the sample passage.)

Read as much as you can from a variety of sources if you are truly interested in developing your writing abilities. There's really no other way to expand your writing horizons. You have to see how other people are doing it.

Concise . . . Naturally

READ: User-friendly writing is writing that is concise and natural. "Natural" means it flows along the way we normally think and speak. "Concise" means that none of the words are wasted—they all contribute to the purpose of the writing. None are dead, none are flowery, none are aimless, and none are needlessly repeated. The opposite of natural writing is stilted writing, which is stiff, awkward, impersonal, and forced.

Stilted Thought:

The cool, free breeze in the learning center, which came like a storm in the night, was an extremely exhilarating change from the sultry confines of Ms. Brown's classroom.

Revised for Naturalness and Conciseness:

The cool breeze in the learning center was a refreshing change from Ms. Brown's muggy classroom.

WRITE: The following paragraph is a stilted version of an excerpt from an article that appeared in *Sassy* magazine. Try your hand at rewriting it concisely and naturally. (Use your own paper for your work.)

Unexpectedly and without prior warning, the electric telephone noisily rings and your female parent engages in an emotionally intense conversation with a long-lost kinswoman. The unencumbered, cloying phrase "We would be utterly delighted to visit you" reverberates through your dwelling place. It's the holiday season—time for familial reunions. A certain number of us would sooner spend those vacation days ensconced in an institution of learning than participate in an automobile rendezvous with our siblings and parents. But despite your violent protestations, you will be coerced into sojourning at Uncle Bert's house for Christmas or Hanukkah repast. Thus, you would be well advised to accept the unavoidable and discover a way to take delight in the event.

Without warning, the phone rings and your mom engages in an intense conversation with a long-lost relative. The simple, sugary-sweet phrase, "We'd love to come over," echoes through the house—it's reunion time. Some of us would rather spend those extra days at school than go on any sort of family road trip. But no matter how violently you protest, you will be forced to trek to Uncle Bert's house for Christmas dinner or a Hanukkah party. Face it and cancel the shopping trip with your best friend.

extend Have your teacher read the original paragraph to the class. See how close your paragraph comes to it. (Keep in mind, though, that the point isn't to duplicate—it's to simplify.) You might also want to share what you've written with your classmates.

Smooth, Natural, and Concise

Your handbook lists the main causes of stiltedness (or unnaturalness) in writing and shows you how to overcome this problem. (Refer to "Sentence, Writing effectively" in the index. Once you turn to that section, refer specifically to "Writing Natural Sentences.") Apply what you've learned in the following activity.

READ: Carefully read the following letter to the editor that happens to be full of stilted language. Afterward, note at least five examples of stilted language in the spaces we've provided below. (Work on this with a partner if your teacher allows it.)

To the Editor:

Allow me to register my opposition to the little gasoline-powered contrivance that is commonly referred to as a leaf blower. Most members of our honorable citizenry appear to view it in the aspect of an implement for good lawn grooming and landscape maintenance. But to me it's a big pain in the neck. It blows pollen particles into the air. It blows a whole bunch of dust around. Probably, the unsanitary leavings of pet animals are blown around, too. Gas fumes are not to be ignored, either. Then when I come down with a killer case of an allergic reaction, thanks to the dust and stuff, I can't sleep. The roaring of the leaf blower makes too much noise. I'm ticked. Let's go back to brooms and rakes and similar premodern implements.

Lila

1. Wordiness: Most members of our honorable . . . and landscape maintenance.

2. Deadwood: Let's go back to brooms and rakes and similar premodern implements.

3. Flowery language: the little gasoline-powered contrivance

4. Trite expression: members of our honorable citizenry

5. Euphemism: the unsanitary leavings of pet animals

6. Jargon: an implement for good lawn grooming and landscape maintenance

7. Cliche: But to me it's a big pain in the neck.

extend Remove as many of the symptoms of stiltedness in Lila's letter as you can, and rewrite it so that the main thoughts come through naturally.

Low-Fat Writing

READ: Most writers can leave out a great deal more in their writing than they think. For example, all of the words in parentheses in the following paragraph can be removed or simplified:

At the game (that was played) last night between St. Thomas High and its archrival, Union High, (the players who were considered the best on each team) (were injured) (in the course of the action). Marty Grunwald, (who plays for) St. Thomas, (received an injury to) her shoulder (when she collided) (without warning) with an opposing player (from Union High School). (Regrettably,) (the force of the collision was responsible for) dislocating (her) right (shoulder). (Likewise, in a surprising coincidence), Cassie Ribero from Union High (also suffered a dislocated right shoulder) (in an accidental collision). (The loss of their top players was a disappointment to both teams). [106 words]

When all of the useless words are removed, the thought can be fully expressed in one smooth-reading sentence:

At last night's game between archrivals St. Thomas and Union High Schools, Marty Grunwald and Cassie Ribero, team leaders for their respective schools, both dislocated their right shoulders in collisions with opposing players. [33 words]

REWRITE: With a partner, study the following paragraph adapted from an article in the November 1991 issue of *Scientific American*. Then cut or simplify all of the words and phrases that are unnecessary. Rewrite the paragraph on your own paper. Compare your results with other teams.

Imagine in your mind, if you will, a pinball-type machine that actually propels tiny photons of light instead of the usual steel marble-like objects and that uses things like mirrors to function as bumpers. If you watch very carefully the path taken by a photon as it is fired with considerable force into play, it ricochets off the mirrors as if it were a solid object, like a rock. But if, as all this is going on, you stop observing with your eyes, things begin to get strange and unusual. Unlike a hard, metallic, round steel ball, the photon shatters into many wavelets, each wavelet taking a different route or path through the imaginary machine on which the game is being played.

Teacher's Note: Here is the original paragraph as it appeared in Scientific American:

Imagine a pinball machine that propels photons of light instead of steel marbles and that uses mirrors as bumpers. If you watch the path of a photon as it is fired into play, it ricochets off the mirrors as if it were a solid object. But if you stop observing, things begin to get strange. Unlike a steel ball, the photon shatters into many wavelets, each taking a different route through the machine.

Refining: Editing

Editing Checklist

Have you ever used a shopping or study list? Isn't it helpful to have your thoughts organized? The following checklist should help you each time you review and edit your writing. You might think of it as a "chopping" list, but it's really more: chopping, connecting, rearranging, polishing. . . .

.... **1.** Read your final draft aloud to test it for sense and sound. Better yet, have someone read it aloud to you. Listen carefully as he or she reads. Your writing should read smoothly and naturally. If it doesn't, you have more editing to do.

.... **2.** Does each sentence express a complete thought? Does each paragraph have an overall point or purpose?

.... **3.** Have you used different sentence types and lengths? Are any sentences too long and rambling? Do you use too many short, choppy sentences?

.... **4.** Have you used a variety of sentence beginnings? Watch out for too many sentences that begin with the same pronoun or article (*I*, *My*, *The* . . .).

.... **5.** Check each simple sentence for effective use of modifiers, especially prepositional phrases, participial phrases, and appositives. Have you punctuated these modifiers correctly?

.... **6.** Check your compound sentences. Do they contain two equal ideas, and is the logical relationship between the two ideas expressed by a proper conjunction (*and* versus *but* versus *or* . . .)?

.... **7.** What about your complex sentences? Have you used subordination effectively? Does the independent clause contain the most important idea? Are less important ideas contained in dependent clauses?

.... **8.** Make sure your writing is concise and to the point. Have you omitted jargon, slang, redundancies, and other forms of wordiness?

.... **9.** Is your writing fresh and original? Have you avoided overused words and phrases? If not, substitute nouns, verbs, and adjectives that are specific, vivid, and colorful.

.... **10.** Replace any words or phrases that may be awkward, confusing, or misleading.

extend Add points of your own so the list truly becomes a personal editing checklist. Then put the list to work. Choose a piece of unfinished writing from your folder and work with it, using the checklist as your guide.

Agreement: Subject and Verb

READ & REACT: Study the guidelines for subject and verb agreement in your handbook. In the exercise below, underline the subject and circle the correct verb choice in the parentheses.

1. Half of the dorms on campus (is, are) coed dorms.
2. Most of the students (is, are) upperclassmen.
3. The faculty (present, presents) a freshman orientation to school every year.
4. Some of the students (is, are) commuting to school every day.
5. The campus news (include, includes), among other items, a list of activities for the week.
6. Personal computing is one of the new classes that (is, are) being offered for the first time this semester.
7. None of the freshmen (realize, realizes) where the student union is located.
8. All of the campus organizations (is, are) looking for new members among the incoming freshmen.
9. This is one of the books that (is, are) required for the freshman English course.
10. Mathematics (is, are) a requirement for almost any field of study.
11. The cause of the bad grade (was, were) poor study habits.
12. Of the tests that (is, are) used for evaluating college applicants, the ACT test is used most frequently.
13. Some of the students (request, requests) a specific instructor for each course they take.
14. Business is one of the majors that (is, are) becoming more popular.
15. The reason for the long lines on registration day (was, were) the inefficient methods the school used.
16. Some of the students attending college today (is, are) required to attend all classes.
17. Any of the students missing classes (is, are) required to report the reason for the absence.
18. Statistics (is, are) not as difficult as calculus for most people.
19. The room and time slot that (was, were) assigned to this class have been changed.
20. The increased enrollment for the class (was, were) the reason for these changes.

Agreement: Pronoun and Antecedent

READ & REACT: Study the rules in your handbook concerning agreement of pronouns and antecedents. Then underline the correct pronoun in each of the following sentences. Circle the antecedent.

1. For the job hunter to get the best possible job, (he or she, they) needs to have three or four job offers from which to choose.
2. Everyone looking for a job should be aware of the different methods of searching available to (him or her, them).
3. Every job hunter owes it to (himself or herself, themselves) to become acquainted with all phases of the job-hunting process.
4. Both Ashley and her friend, Shelli, use newspaper ads for new job leads that (she, they) then follow up with a phone call and a letter.
5. Neither Ashley nor Shelli expects to find the perfect job on (her, their) first attempt.
6. Sometimes job hunters try to make (his or her, their) availability known by placing ads about themselves and (his or her, their) job skills in newspapers.
7. Most colleges have especially good placement services because (they, it) understand that finding a good job is the major reason (their, its) students came to college in the first place.
8. Some colleges offer (its, their) students a complete job placement service, including placement help years after the students have graduated.
9. Other college offices, however, think they have done (its, their) job when they place the student once after graduation.
10. The private employment agency charges (its, their) customer only when (he or she, they) get(s) a job.
11. When employers use an executive search firm, (he or she, they) want the firm to hire people presently employed by other companies.
12. Both the employer and the job hunter can send (his or her, their) listings to a clearinghouse.
13. The U.S. government offers all (its, their) citizens a free employment service.
14. Everyone feels nervous during (his or her, their) first job interview.
15. Neither the interviewer nor those being interviewed want (his or her, their) interview(s) to go poorly.

Indefinite Pronoun Reference

A writer must be careful not to confuse the reader with pronoun references that are ambiguous. (*Ambiguous* means *indefinite or unclear*.) Indefinite pronoun reference results when it is not clear which word is being referred to by the pronoun in the sentence.

REACT: In each sentence, circle the pronoun below that is ambiguous or indefinite. Then rewrite each of the sentences so that the error in reference is corrected.

1. As he drove his car up to the service window, it made a strange rattling sound.

   As he drove up to the service window, his car made a strange rattling sound.

2. We moved the car out of the garage so we could wash it.

   So we could wash the car, we moved it out of the garage.

3. Take the apples out of the bowls and wash them.

   Wash the apples after you take them out of the bowls.

4. Sarah put her album on the stereo that she had gotten as a graduation gift.

   Sarah put her album that she had gotten as a graduation gift on the stereo.

5. Jerry asked Jack if he needed a raincoat.

   Jerry asked, "Jack, do I need a raincoat?"

6. The hawk spied the rattlesnake nearing its eggs.

   The hawk spied the rattlesnake nearing the hawk's eggs.

7. When the hail hit the window, it exploded into hundreds of little pieces.

   When it hit the window, the hail exploded into hundreds of little pieces.

extend Conduct a 5-minute minilesson with a classmate or small writing group about another sentence-related problem. Ideally this will be a problem that shows up in your own writing every now and then. (Refer to "Sentence, Writing effectively" in the handbook index for ideas.)

Psst! In your minilesson, identify the problem, show how it can be fixed, and provide at least one sample sentence to be corrected and discussed.

Clear as Mud

READ: You know what happens when you drag your feet along the bottom of a lake. Things become murky and obscure. That's what happens in your reader's brain when you accidentally use misplaced or dangling modifiers. To ensure clarity, you must be able to recognize misplaced modifiers so they can be moved or reworded accordingly. (Refer to "Misplaced modifier" in the handbook index for more information.)

REACT: Each of the sentences below contains a misplaced modifier, a modifier that is incorrectly placed, causing the meaning of the sentence to be confusing or misleading. Locate and underline the misplaced modifier in each sentence. Then revise each sentence by moving the misplaced modifier to its proper location. (Make other changes to the sentence as needed.)

1. The books are piled in stacks for the new students with course-identification numbers. (The phrase "with course-identification numbers" appears to modify "students"; it should modify "stacks.")

The books for the new students are piled in stacks with course-identification numbers.

2. Athletes must train hard to make the Olympic team for many years.

Athletes must train hard for many years to make the Olympic team.

3. When young women began riding bicycles, they were told it was not a feminine thing to do in the 1890's.

When young women began riding bicycles in the 1890's, they were told it was not a feminine thing to do.

4. We will be visiting several four-year colleges that I am considering attending over the summer.

Over the summer, we will be visiting several four-year colleges that I am considering attending.

5. My father has gone to the library every Sunday to check out a book for years.

For years my father has gone to the library every Sunday to check out a book.

REVISE: Many of the sentences below contain a dangling modifier, a modifier that appears to modify the wrong word. Locate and underline the dangling modifier in each sentence. Revise each sentence so that the modifier clearly modifies the word it was intended to modify.

1. After swimming in the lake nearly all afternoon, Bill's mother called him.
   (The phrase "After swimming in the lake nearly all afternoon" appears to modify "Bill's mother"; it is intended to modify "Bill.")

   After swimming in the lake nearly all afternoon, Bill heard his mother call him.

2. While listening to my newest album, someone came to the door.

   While I was listening to my newest album, someone came to the door.

3. Having never ridden on a plane before, the attendant was especially nice to me.

   Because I had never ridden on a plane before, the attendant was especially nice to me.

4. Though only fourteen years old, my father gave me my first driving lesson.

   Though I was only fourteen years old, my father gave me my first driving lesson.

5. After running three laps around the track, the coach signaled us to head for the showers.

   After we ran three laps around the track, the coach signaled us to head for the showers.

6. Coming in late for first-hour class, Mrs. Jones gave me a lecture on common courtesy.

   Because I came in late for first-hour class, Mrs. Jones gave me a lecture on common courtesy.

7. Failing to see the stop sign, the car rammed into the side of an oncoming truck.

   Because the driver failed to see the stop sign, the car rammed into the side of an oncoming truck.

Other Clarity Problems

Careful attention is necessary when revising your rough drafts to make sure each sentence says exactly what you intend it to say. Problems with clarity can result from *incomplete comparisons*, *mixed constructions*, *nonstandard language*, and *double negatives*.

CORRECT: Rewrite each of the sentences to correct the clarity problem. After the revision, identify in parentheses the type of problem you corrected. (Refer to "Sentence, Writing effectively" in the handbook index for help.)

1. I like rock music better than Lawrence Welk. **I like rock music better than I like Lawrence Welk's music. (incomplete comparison)**

2. Jerry enjoys talking to the mailman more than his neighbor.

Jerry enjoys talking to the mailman more than to his neighbor. (incomplete comparison)

3. A "turkey" is when you bowl three strikes in a row.

Bowling three strikes in a row is called a "turkey." (mixed construction)

4. The reason he did not play football is because he had weak ankles.

Because he had weak ankles, he did not play football. (mixed construction)

5. If Martha would of checked the gas gauge before she left, she would not of run out of gas on the freeway.

If Martha would have checked the gas gauge before she left, she would not have run out of gas on the freeway. (nonstandard language)

6. Mark didn't hardly get no help from his brother.

Mark got hardly any help from his brother. (double negative)

7. I gave you better advice than Jim.

I gave you better advice than I gave Jim. (incomplete comparison)

8. You must try and understand other people's feelings and beliefs.

You must try to understand other people's feelings and beliefs. (nonstandard language)

Common Sentence Errors

REACT: Place *RO* in front of each run-on sentence, *CS* in front of each comma splice, *F* in front of each fragment, and *C* in front of each correct sentence. Make any changes necessary to correct each faulty sentence. (For handbook help, see "Sentence, Writing effectively" in the index.)

CS **1.** I never really enjoyed science, math is my favorite class. [;]

CS **2.** By the time we arrived, the show was nearly over, we missed everything but the credits and the cartoon. [and]

RO **3.** Don't touch that chair it has just been painted. [. It]

F **4.** Last summer during our camping trip to Canada. [, I broke my arm.]

C **5.** My room is a real mess, but I like it that way.

CS **6.** Most students would rather goof around than study, most adults went through the same thing when they were in school. [;]

F **7.** The rain which continued for seven straight days. [, which … days, ruined my trip.]

CS **8.** Some run-on sentences are easy to recognize, others are much more difficult. [;]

RO **9.** Maria's mother works at the hospital her father works at the school. [. Her]

RO **10.** John had to go to his violin lesson however he will stop by when he is through. [; however,]

C **11.** Karen enjoys shopping for clothes, especially when someone else is paying for them.

F **12.** After I had squeezed on my stiff, heavy boots. [, I tried to stand up.]

RO **13.** I got an "A" on my English test I've never gotten one before. [.]

CS **14.** Time goes slowly when you are working, it seems to fly when you are playing. [but]

RO **15.** Luis will meet us at the skating rink later he has to go home to pick up his skates. [since]

CS **16.** Never leave your bike outside at night, it might not be there in the morning. [;]

F **17.** Even though we sprayed twice a day with a strong disinfectant. [, the odor remained.]

C **18.** I can't go with you tonight unless you can be back by nine.

CS **19.** The pizza shop is running a special on pizzas this week, for each pizza you buy, you get one free. [;]

Complete and Mature

REACT: Carefully review the following paragraph, correcting any sentence errors as you go along. (You will find examples of sentence fragments, comma splices, and run-on sentences in the paragraph.) Cross out incorrect punctuation marks and add punctuation and capital letters as needed. (Refer to "Sentence, Writing effectively" in the handbook index for help.)

1 As a small child, he had always eaten jelly doughnuts for breakfast. Now,
2 however, at a plump and rather easily winded 29. He has switched over to granola
3 and skim milk. Along with his new eating habits, his looks are also beginning to
4 change. He wears his hair a bit longer in back and thinner on top and his shoes are
5 those flip-flop kind. That are good for lower back pain. He thinks about this as he
6 sits gazing out at the backyard, which the neighbor kid with the nose ring mows every
7 Saturday for a sawbuck. He wonders if the kid knows that a sawbuck is a slang term
8 for ten dollars. Maybe his younger brother Kevin is right in his appraisal, maybe he
9 is old-fashioned and far, far out of step. They had just gone out with their parents
10 the night before, a monthly guilt-abating ritual. Kevin had walked into the restaurant
11 and had scanned his brother's clothes and posture, in addition, he had even seemed
12 to scan his brother's thoughts, with slow-mounting amusement, Kevin had said, "You
13 look so . . . granola." Trying to disguise his obvious embarrassment, the older brother
14 had grabbed his keys and had headed for the Subaru in the parking lot.

extend As you probably know, professional writers occasionally break the rules in their work. (Age and experience have their advantages.) A writer might, for example, purposely use a series of sentence fragments or express a long, rambling idea. Find a passage from a magazine article, an essay, or a novel in which the writer has obviously broken or at least stretched one of the rules regarding the correct use of sentences. Share the passage with your classmates. As a group decide what effect (good or bad) the passage has on the writing as a whole. (Try breaking or stretching the rules yourself in one of your upcoming pieces of writing, but do so carefully and selectively, with a clear purpose and desired effect in mind.)

Refining: Proofreading

Proofreading Checklist

The following guidelines will help you put the finishing touches on your writing before you share it with your readers. (As you use this checklist, add points of your own to truly make it a personal checklist.)

Spelling

1. Have you spelled all your words correctly? Here are some tips:
   - Read your writing backward and aloud—one word at a time—so you focus on each word.
   - Circle each word you are unsure of.
   - For help, consult the list of commonly misspelled words in your handbook. (For additional help, check a dictionary, or ask the "designated speller" in your classroom.)

Punctuation

2. Does each sentence end with a punctuation mark?
3. Are coordinating conjunctions (*and*, *but*, *or*, *so*, etc.) in compound sentences preceded by a comma? Have you used commas to set off items listed in a series, after introductory clauses, and so on?
4. Have you used apostrophes to show possession or to mark contractions?
5. Is all dialogue, or written conversation, properly punctuated?

Capitalization

6. Do all sentences, including dialogue, begin with a capital letter?
7. Have you capitalized the proper names of people, places, and things?

Usage

8. Have you misused any of the commonly mixed pairs of words: *there / their / they're; accept / except*? Refer to the section "Using the Right Word" in your handbook.
9. Have you used any words, phrases, or sentences that may confuse the reader?

Grammar

10. Do your subjects and verbs agree in number?
11. Do your pronouns agree with their antecedents?
12. Have you used any sentence fragments, run-ons, or rambling sentences?

Form

13. Have you chosen an appropriate title if one is needed?
14. Is your paper labeled correctly with the author's name and class?
15. Does the writing form satisfy the requirements of the assignment?

Test Yourself

IDENTIFY: In the following sentences, groups of words with one or more punctuation or usage errors are underlined and numbered in parentheses. Copy the underlined words on the blank spaces making the necessary corrections as you go along. (Be careful to show the exact location of each punctuation mark.)

Plato an (1) ancient Greek philosopher and educator was (2) the first to write about the lost continent of Atlantis. Most scholars agree that Plato book (3) entitled Critias (4) includes only legendary events not (5) real history. In his book, Plato was writing about events that he claimed happened over 9000 (6) years before his own lifetime. When Plato described atlantis he (7) painted a picture of a people of fabulous wealth who ruled over a great and wonderful empire. He said the royal palace was "a marvel to behold for size and beauty. Plato (8) also claimed that the continent of Atlantis sank beneath the sea in one days time. (9)

If Atlantis really existed where (10) was it located? Many places have been candidates for the honor however the (11) following locations are most commonly listed the (12) Atlantic Ocean the (13) Sahara Desert, Crete, Spain, England, Greenland, and Mexico.

Is their lost (14) treasure waiting for someone to discover or (15) was Atlantis only the product of Plato's imagination? Wouldnt it (16) be marvelous if someone found the fabled land of gold and silver where Plato said kings gathered every five years to administer the laws hunt (17) bulls and (18) make sacrifices to the gods? Atlantis has been many things to many people but mostly (19) of all it is what it will always be a (20) mystery.

1. Plato, an
2. educator, was
3. Plato's book,
4. Critias,
5. events, not
6. 9,000
7. Atlantis, he
8. beauty." Plato
9. day's time
10. existed, where
11. honor; however, the
12. listed: the
13. Ocean, the
14. Is there lost
15. discover, or
16. Wouldn't it
17. laws, hunt
18. bulls, and
19. people, but most
20. be: a (OR) be—a

Comma Practice

READ & INSERT: Read and study the handbook rules on using commas. Then insert commas where they are needed in the sentences below. Circle each comma you insert. Some sentences may not need commas.

1. Yesterday in health class, we learned the Heimlich maneuver, a method of clearing a choking person's blocked airway.
2. The Heimlich maneuver not artificial respiration is used to save a choking victim.
3. Unless you act to save him or her a victim of food choking will die of strangulation in four minutes.
4. When using the Heimlich maneuver you exert pressure that pushes the diaphragm up compresses the air in the lungs and expels the object blocking the airway.
5. A friend of mine who had apparently paid attention to her first-aid class saved the life of a choking victim.
6. The victim who had been eating steak was forever grateful that my friend had learned the Heimlich maneuver.
7. That is why it is important for everyone to know how to perform this maneuver or to get quick professional help.
8. Whenever you think a situation is life threatening don't hesitate to call an ambulance or the rescue squad.
9. After calling for emergency help be prepared to state your name the injured person's name the address or place where the injured person is located and a brief description of what happened.
10. This is necessary so that the emergency personnel know exactly what they have to do when they arrive.
11. Remember that your objective to help save a life can be better accomplished when you remain calm and follow suggested procedures.

extend Commas are used to separate a *vocative* from the rest of the sentence. Do you know what that means? If not, find out by referring to your handbook.

Using Commas

INSERT: Insert commas where they are needed in the sentences below and circle each. After consulting your handbook, write the rule (or rules) for each comma you insert.

1. Although the brain requires 25 percent of all oxygen used by the body, it comprises only 2 percent of a person's total body weight.

Use a comma after an introductory adverb clause.

2. Did you know, John, that a whale's heart beats only nine times a minute?

Use commas to separate a vocative from the rest of the sentence.

3. Hey, please turn the music down! I'm trying to get some sleep!

Use a comma after an interjection.

4. If it would make you feel any better, I'd be happy to come along and drive you home from the dentist's office.

Use a comma after an introductory adverb clause.

5. "One-fourth of the 206 bones in the human body," explained Mr. Brown, our biology teacher, "are located in the feet."

Use commas to set off the exact words of a speaker and to enclose an appositive.

6. Although it is a mind-boggling fact, the body does indeed have 70,000 miles of blood vessels.

Use a comma after an introductory clause and to separate a series of numbers.

7. James Rudan, D.D.S., will be extracting all of my wisdom teeth.

Use commas to enclose a title or initials after a surname.

8. It is the female bee, not the male, that does all the work in and around the hive.

Use commas to separate contrasted elements from the rest of the sentence.

9. I have taken science courses all through high school, and I expect to major in chemistry at the University of Wisconsin-Madison; my classes will begin September 4, 1995.

Use a comma between two independent clauses joined by a coordinating conjunction and to set off items in a date.

10. Sarah, who is planning to major in psychology, has already enrolled at the University of Maryland.

Use commas to enclose nonrestrictive clauses.

11. The tiny, delicate hummingbird weighs less than a penny and is the only bird, believe it or not, that can fly backward.

Use commas to separate adjectives that equally modify the same noun and to set off a phrase that interrupts the movement of a sentence.

12. The hummingbird has a body temperature of 111 degrees Fahrenheit, beats its wings more than 75 times a second, and builds a nest the size of a walnut.

Use commas to separate individual phrases in a series.

Black Holes

INSERT: Place commas and semicolons where they are needed in the paragraphs below. Circle punctuation marks you add. (Remember to refer to your handbook if you have any questions about the rules for using commas and semicolons.)

1 One of the most remarkable and brilliant scientists of our time is 50-year-old
2 Stephen Hawking—physics professor author and theorist. His studies concerning
3 the nature of the universe and black holes have advanced our understanding of space.
4 More importantly Dr. Hawking has done more than any other physicist in describing
5 and detailing his life's work in language understood by the average person. In short
6 he has brought the outer limits of the universe "down to earth."
7 These accomplishments alone merit our praise and respect that Dr. Hawking
8 has accomplished them despite disabling personal setbacks is almost
9 incomprehensible. In 1962 when he was only 20 years old Stephen Hawking learned
10 he had amyotrophic lateral sclerosis or ALS. ALS gradually destroys the nerves and
11 muscles needed for moving. Doctors told him that he would probably die before he
12 finished his doctoral degree however Stephen didn't let their prognosis stop him.
13 With the support of fellow Cambridge student Jane Wilde whom he later married he
14 continued his studies and received his Ph.D.
15 During the course of his doctoral work Dr. Hawking became interested in the
16 work of scientist Roger Penrose an early theorist in the study of black holes. Black
17 holes are spaces that Penrose and Hawking believe exist in space. These spaces
18 possibly formed when a star burns itself out and collapses are areas in which gravity
19 is extremely strong anything pulled into the black hole cannot get out. Even time
20 stops!

21 Stephen Hawking's work on black holes and the nature of the universe was
22 published in a book entitled *A Brief History of Time: From the Big Bang to Black*
23 *Holes*. The book was written for people who do not have a scientific background. It
24 is a remarkable book. What makes it even more remarkable is that it was written
25 by a man unable to move his arms and hands to write, unable to speak, and unable
26 to communicate normally. The book is a testament to one person's determination to
27 succeed, to be heard, and to overcome personal tragedy.

extend One semicolon rule in your handbook states, "A semicolon is used to separate groups of words or phrases that already contain commas." Provide an example sentence illustrating this rule without looking in your handbook until after your sentence is written. Then refer to the handbook to check your work.

Using Semicolons

READ & INSERT: Read and study the semicolon rules in your handbook. Afterward, insert semicolons where they are needed in the following sentences. Circle your answers. (Some sentences may not need a semicolon.)

1. Lightning had struck the old willow tree one too many times; now and then one could hear an ominous cracking sound.
2. Before the morning was out, Dad noticed an ever-widening crack in the trunk; it seemed inevitable that the tree would soon fall on the roof unless it was cut down.
3. The tree began to split on a Saturday after a strong, furious windstorm the night before; and Dad knew that getting fast, dependable, and reasonably priced tree service on the weekend would be a difficult job.
4. He called number after number from the phone book and finally found someone willing to come and look at the old willow.
5. We had always loved that willow tree; it saddened everyone to talk of cutting it down.
6. Mom asked the man several questions about bracing the tree; however, he was forced to speak honestly with her about the necessity of taking the tree down.
7. The willow certainly held fond memories for us; nevertheless, we could not risk the property damage and personal injury the fast-splitting tree might cause.
8. As the work began and progressed, our small yard seemed to brim with workers, neighbors, and family members; ladders, power saws, and ropes; leaves, branches, and pieces of the willow's trunk.
9. Finally the job was finished; the tree had been safely cut down.
10. We no longer look out the back door to see our stately, old willow tree; instead, we see the back of our neighbor's not-so-stately garage.

Psst! Remember: When two independent clauses are connected with a conjunctive adverb (*however*, *also*, *moreover, etc.*), include a semicolon before it and a comma after it.

Using Colons

REVIEW & INSERT: Review the colon rules in your handbook. Then insert colons where they are needed below. (Some sentences may not need a colon.) Circle the punctuation marks you add.

1. Rob has sent for information about the universities in these states: Wisconsin, Illinois, California, and Florida.
2. Dear Registrar:

   Please send me your latest catalog. I am also interested in . . .
3. One question is very important to anyone seeking a college education: How much is it going to cost?
4. Rob made his decision after carefully considering the information about tuition, housing, programs, and financial aid.
5. Here is another important, two-part question for prospective college students to ask: Will I receive a quality education, and will the degree I earn be recognized as valid in the career area I have chosen?
6. My father had important advice he never tired of repeating: "These days, you've got to get a good education."
7. As a college freshman, Rob plans to take courses in several subjects: history, English, geography, chemistry, and math.
8. Freshmen soon learn that you sometimes have to leave your noisy dormitory in search of two important ingredients for productive studying: peace and quiet.
9. It is no wonder that during final exam time the college libraries are filled with students doing one thing: studying.
10. All things considered, the freshman year can be exciting, challenging, and fun.

extend Identify and learn one colon rule in the handbook that wasn't covered in this activity.

Punctuating for Style

IDENTIFY: Carefully read the short essay below. Then, on the lines that follow the essay, explain the specific function of each underlined punctuation mark—a dash, a hyphen, or a set of quotation marks. (Consult your handbook for help.)

Along with the fitness and exercise craze that has swept America have come sore muscles, pulled tendons, and torn ligaments. Many of these injuries could be avoided if proper warm-up and conditioning routines were followed. Most beginners start out exercising too hard and too fast. A thorough warm-up before any exercising is a must. The warm-up serves two important <u>functions—stretching</u> the muscles in preparation for a workout and getting the heart pumping.

The stretch should begin at the top of the body and work slowly down to the ankles. The routine should consist of basic stretches such as head rotations to relax the neck, arm circles to loosen the shoulders, and trunk rotations to stretch the back and stomach muscles. Stretching out the leg muscles is also very important as most exercising involves much use of the legs. Toe touches, calf stretches, and ankle <u>rotations—these</u> are just some of the exercises that can be used to loosen the leg muscles. It is important to remember that these are <u>muscle-stretching</u> exercises. Stretching does not mean bouncing or jerking the muscles. Such action could easily lead to pulls, sprains, or tears.

The second half of the warm-up consists of getting the heart ready for a full workout. This can be done with any of a number of activities such as jumping jacks, jogging, or even running in place. You must remember to start out slowly and increase your pace gradually until the body feels ready to begin the full-scale workout. Throughout the warm-up period, you should try to breathe regularly. There is a tendency for beginners either to hold their breath during certain exercises or to greatly increase <u>breathing—both</u> are serious mistakes.

Another common mistake beginners often make is to stop exercising suddenly. Warming <u>"down"</u> after a workout is just as important as warming up. This final phase can consist of the same stretching exercises used in the warm-up. A warm-down, or cooldown as some call it, gradually returns the body to a normal state. This helps prevent muscle injuries and brings the heartbeat back to its normal rate.

1. A dash may be used to emphasize a word, series, phrase, or clause.
2. A dash is used to set off an introductory series from the main clause.
3. Use a hyphen to join two or more words serving as a single adjective.
4. A dash is used to indicate a sudden break or change in the sentence.
5. Quotation marks may be used to point to a word used in a special way.

extend Identify and learn one rule in your handbook for using dashes, hyphens, or quotation marks that wasn't covered in this activity.

Using the Right Word

SELECT: As you carefully read through the following sentences, underline the correct word in each set of parentheses. (Refer to "Usage, mixed pairs" in the handbook index for help.)

1. Elisha attended the (annual, perennial) career fair at the local college.
2. She and her classmates had to (accept, except) (their, there, they're) invitations four weeks in advance in order to attend the fair.
3. (Already, All ready) the (amount, number) of people attending was (all together, altogether) too many.
4. Even though the (sight, site) of the fair was a large auditorium, (their, there) was hardly room for all those who came.
5. Elisha found she had no (personal, personnel) interest in the main speaker's topic, "Let astrology be (your, you're) career guide."
6. (Among, Between) the speakers at the fair were some very eminent members of the business community.
7. Still, (there, their, they're) were (fewer, less) speakers (than, then) Elisha anticipated.
8. At one point, Elisha had to (chose, choose) (between, among) visiting a college recruiter and a vocational counselor.
9. The vocational counselor presented her material (good, well) (accept, except) for those few times she was (to, too, two) (quiet, quite).
10. The booths of the college representatives were set up (beside, besides) the vocational representatives' booths.
11. (Further, Farther) down were the booths of the two-year and specialty schools.
12. The (continuous, continual) activity made Elisha very tired; still, she had to (compliment, complement) the organizers on a job well done.

All Right Alright

CORRECT: Correct any usage errors below by drawing a line through each word that is used incorrectly and writing the correct form above it. There are a total of 15 usage errors in the passage. (Two of these errors have been corrected for you.)

1 The ~~berth~~ birth of my baby sister Tasha had a strange ~~affect~~ effect on my mother. Until
2 that "blessed" day, my mother had always been a calm, ~~excepting~~ accepting person. She
3 endured my pranks and teasings as a matter of ~~coarse~~ course; it was the territory that came
4 with having a son. The day Tasha was born, however, my world came tumbling down.
5 The first indication I had that things ~~wood~~ would never be the same was my mother's
6 command to wash my face and hands before dinner. Dirty hands and face had always
7 been ~~excepted~~ accepted as a young boy's ~~write~~ right. Now, everything was different. I never ~~new~~ knew from
8 one minute to the next which old habit would come before the examination
9 ~~bored~~ board. After the "Clean Appendages Act" came the "~~Healthy~~ Healthful Foods Declaration."
10 Twinkies, pizza, and corn dogs were outlawed; salads, fish, and fruit were ~~adapted~~ adopted as
11 our dietary mainstays. Nothing was sacred. My Nike high-tops suddenly
12 inherited new white shoelaces. My favorite ~~blew~~ blue jeans disappeared.
13 I tried blaming Tasha, but she hardly looked the criminal type. It was hard to
14 be mad at nine pounds of diapers, dribble, and baby powder. I finally asked my father
15 what he thought had happened to Mom. He smiled and ruffled my hair. "~~Its~~ It's not the
16 first time this has happened," he replied. "You should have ~~scene~~ seen her when you were
17 born. We had to carry our shoes in the house and tiptoe even when you were awake.
18 Lawrence, eventually things will return to normal."

Unsinkable!

CORRECT: Proofread the essay below. Draw a line through any errors you find in capitalization, numbers, abbreviations, punctuation, spelling, and usage. Write the correction above each error. Add (and circle) punctuation as necessary. (*Hint:* Numbers are used frequently in this piece. Refer to the rules on "Numbers" in your handbook.)

1 About 450 miles off the coast of Newfoundland in 12,000 feet of water, scientists
2 have recently discovered the remains of the great ocean liner the SS Titanic. The
3 seventy-three year search for the Titanic, which went down in what is considered the
4 worlds' greatest sea disaster has been a challengeing one. It concluded finally in
5 September 1985. Because of this discovary interest in this legendary ship is stronger
6 then ever.
7 In part this interest may be due to the titanics reputation. When it was first
8 launched in 1912, the british steamer was the largest ship in the world. An incredible
9 882 ft. long and 175 ft. high, The Titanic was comparable to 4 city blocks in length
10 and 11 stories in hieght. It was proclaimed the most expensive most luxurious ship
11 ever built. It was said to be "unsinkable".
12 The later claim was the result of special features. The Titanic was equiped with
13 a double bottom and the hull was divided into 16 separate watertight compartments.
14 These added features, it was felt, would make the Titanic unsinkable.
15 Despite its reputation, the mighty Titanic did sink; and on its maiden voyage
16 too. Carrying approximatly 2200 passengers and over $420,000 worth of cargo, the
17 Titanic set sail from England in April, 1912, bound for New York. Just a few days
18 out of port, however on the night of April 14 the Titanic collided with an iceberg in
19 the north atlantic, ripping a 300 ft. gash along its starboard side. The mighty
20 "floating palace" sunk in a matter of 2 1/2 hours, taking with it all of its cargo and
21 1522 of its passengers.

Practical Writing

Letter of Application and Résumé

Letter of Application and Résumé

There's a lot you need to know about writing résumés and letters of application. It's important stuff—you'll need to know how to write these well if you expect to get any kind of job, let alone one you enjoy. And there are very few things more important than finding a job you can live with all day, five days a week.

Before we go on, you should know that there are two basic things you absolutely must do when writing a letter of application: You must be brief, and you must sell yourself. These things are harder to do than you might imagine. However, if you beat around the bush, or if you're bashful, chances are someone else will get the job you wanted.

READ the handbook section called "Writing to Get a Job." (Refer to "Résumé writing" in the index to find this information.) Then answer the questions below.

- What is the purpose of a cover letter or letter of application?

  A cover letter or letter of application introduces someone to a prospective employer, often accompanies a résumé, and seeks a job interview.

- What is a résumé? *A résumé is a short summary of a job applicant's skills, knowledge, and previous responsibilities.*

- Name three things that are always included in a résumé:

  Personal data, education, work experience

- Why do you need to send a cover letter with a résumé?

  It introduces you to the employer and highlights information on your résumé.

- What should you request in a cover letter? *An interview*

after words

Get into small groups and discuss what you've read in this handbook section. Then talk about what types of jobs you are each planning to pursue after high school. How are you going to get these jobs? Whom will you apply to? What skills do you have that make you suited to the jobs you want to get? Treat this discussion as an informal preliminary to job hunting. Sometimes talking your plans over with someone can help clarify those plans and create enthusiasm.

The Cover Letter

Writing letters of application and résumés is a very structured activity. There is clearly a right and wrong way of doing it, and there is a distinctly practical end in mind—getting the job you desire.

READ: With that in mind, read over the "The Letter of Application" section in your handbook. (See "Résumé writing" in the index to find this information.)

REVIEW the following cover letter, checking it against the handbook guidelines. Review it carefully. Even a simple error in a letter of application can create a bad first impression you won't soon overcome.

Jennifer Ott
401 N. Fraternity Lane
Whitewater, WI 53190
May 15, 1995

Mr. Clove Vendajo
Warner, Smith and Vendajo
1093 Fawn Oak Drive
Milwaukee, WI 53124

Dear R. Venndajo:

I would like to apply for the summer internship your company advertised in the University of Wisconsin-Whitewater's Placement Office.

A successful marketing firm such as yours relies on fresh ideas and an awareness of cultural trends. I feel I can offer these things to your company. I am a junior in UW-W's Marketing program and have had great success in all my business-related classes. I'm also young and ambitious, with my finger on the pulse of the Pepsi generation.

I will call you at 10:00 a.m. on Wednesday, May 24, to set up an appointment for an interview. I look forward to meeting you and discussing my qualifications with you in person.

Sincerely,

Jennifer Ott

Jennifer Ott

Use correct salutation form and correct spelling of name (Dear Mr. Vendajo:).

Mention work experience with advertising and commercials.

Don't use trite or overused expressions ("finger on the pulse," "Pepsi generation").

Don't begin so many sentences with "I."

EDIT the letter above, following the guidelines your handbook outlines. You can also refer to the résumé on the next page, which goes with this cover letter. Use the margins provided to note the changes you would make to this letter. Work with a partner if your teacher allows it, and then review the résumé on the next page.

READ "Writing a Résumé" in your handbook; then review the résumé below. Look at the content as well as the format of the résumé. How effectively does this writer present herself?

JENNIFER OTT

401 N. Fraternity Lane 414-555-6293
Whitewater, WI 53190

JOB OBJECTIVE
Summer Internship with marketing firm

EDUCATION
UW-W Marketing major, Finance minor. Currently a junior with 3.2 g.p.a. overall, 3.8 in major

Our Mother of Sorrows High School
Lake Geneva, WI 53147
Graduated valedictorian

EXPERIENCE
1993-present President of the Junior Business Buddies of America, Whitewater chapter

1992-1993 WKMY, UW-W radio station
Worked as an advertising coordinator, selecting and arranging air time for the station's commercials

AWARDS
Graduated valedictorian from my high school

Awarded first prize in the UW-W Business School's "Marketing Management" contest

Took second prize in the Marketing Department's writing contest for a profile of WKMY I wrote for the Dean's Advisory Council

PERSONAL INFORMATION
Born 9/20/74, have lived in southeastern Wisconsin all of my life, and enjoy white-water rafting

Make the cover letter on page 252 into an independent letter of application. You will need to consider the information found in the résumé above as well as the basic format and purpose of the cover letter. The trick is to rewrite the cover letter so it includes the résumé information. Use the model "Letter of Application" in the handbook for help.

Compare the résumés on the following two pages; then answer the questions that follow.

Résumé

Name: Roger B. Smedley

Address: Missoula, Montana

Social Security No. Don't have one.

Date of Birth: April 19, 1969

Education:

School	Year Graduated	Degrees
Freeman Jr. High	1987	
Freeman High		

Work Experience:

Company	Position	From	To
Missoula Messenger	Paper carrier	1988	90 or 91
Dunnock's Store	Bagger and Carryout Boy	Now	

Career Goal: I want a job that pays a lot of money and has good benefits

References:

Roger B. Smedly, Sr. Missoula and Palm Springs (retired) father

Jack Smedley Portland, Oregon brother

KATHY S. WILSON
1711 Bluebird Lane
Union Grove, WI 53182
(414) 784-9931

CAREER OBJECTIVE

Full-time secretary/receptionist where attention to detail, initiative, friendliness, and reliability are desired.

EXPERIENCE

J I Case Company, 700 State Street, Racine, WI 53000
1991-92 school year
Duties: It was my responsibility to maintain personnel records. I also did general clerical work including typing, answering telephones, making copies, and helping with mailings.

Reason for Leaving: End of High School Co-op Program for 1991-92 term.

Dairy Queen, 1600 Durand Avenue, Union Grove, WI 53012
April 1991-August 1992

Duties: I prepared orders for customers and ran the cash register.

EDUCATION

High School Graduate—attended Union High School, Union Grove, WI, from August 1988 to June 1992.

Emphasis on business education:
Accounting, Typing, Shorthand, Office Co-op, Office Machines, and Office Procedures (A's and B's in all classes)

I was a member of the National Honor Society and vice president of FBLA (Future Business Leaders of America). I graduated in the top 10% of my class.

PERSONAL DATA

Born in 1974. Excellent health. I enjoy baseball, bowling, ice skating, and swimming. References furnished upon request.

1. What do we know about Roger's education? Very little, except that he attended Freeman Junior High and High School.

2. Accuracy and completeness are extremely important in a résumé. Decide which of the two résumés is more complete and accurate; then cite three examples on the lines below that prove your point.

a. Kathy Wilson's résumé contains precise information about her duties at each of her former jobs.

b. Her résumé also gives her full address and a telephone number where she can be reached.

c. You can see at a glance that she took several business courses during high school.

3. Which basic rule does Roger break in his statement of his goal? Don't emphasize what "you" want in a job; stress how you fit into "their" needs.

4. Why are Kathy's references more acceptable than Roger's? It is not proper to include references on the same sheet as the résumé; rather, have them available on a separate sheet in case they are requested.

5. Which applicant is more likely to be called for an interview? Why? Kathy Wilson—Her résumé clearly informs you of her qualifications for a secretary/receptionist position.

Preparing Your Résumé

1. Make a list of your accomplishments. Do not limit yourself! Include your accomplishments in and out of the classroom. If you've successfully completed a marathon, or if you've planned, prepared, and served a meal for twelve guests, these are valid accomplishments to list.

   Note to teacher: The questions to be answered in this discussion are "Do certain accomplishments indicate skills that are marketable? What accomplishments indicate job-related skills?"

2. Make a list of your positive personal characteristics.

   Note to teacher: Discuss the marketability of characteristics such as patience, problem-solving ability, ability to get along with others, etc. Discuss jobs that would require each of the characteristics presented.

3. Make a list of your work experience. Include full- and part-time jobs, as well as jobs you've had to do at school, at home, or for any organization you belong to. Include special skills, volunteer activities, and clubs or groups you've belonged to.

4. Make a list of your goals for the future.

Writing Your Résumé

Writing your own résumé can be an exciting process of self-discovery. Carefully recall all your skills, work experiences, and accomplishments on the data sheet below. Do not limit yourself on this first draft. List everything you think might be useful.

Name: ....

Social Security Number: ....

Address: ....

....

Availability: ....
(Part-time, after 4:00 p.m., etc.)

Phone: ....

Work Experience: (jobs, where, when, title, description, supervisor, reason for leaving)

....

....

....

....

....

....

Education: (schools, diplomas, grades, grade point average, current status)

....

....

....

....

....

....

Special Skills and Assets: (typing speed, computer training, awards, community activities, clubs or hobbies, volunteer work)

Job or Career Objective: (summer, part-time, full-time)

References: (name, title, position, address)*

*List your references on this worksheet; do not, however, include them on an actual résumé. Simply state, "References: Available upon request."

As a final exercise, prepare an actual résumé that you could use to apply for a job, either real or fictional. Remember to include in the résumé the appropriate qualifications that will convince the employer to hire you for this specific job.

Requesting a Letter of Recommendation

A crucial part of any college application or job search is the recommendation letter. Why? When a teacher or an employer recommends you for a college program, an apprenticeship, or a job, he or she is saying, "This person is fit to do the work."

How do you get this fitness certificate? By doing good work for someone, of course, but also by writing a courteous and clear letter requesting a recommendation.

While you may request a recommendation letter over the phone, it's a good idea to follow up with a letter. Why? See if you can think of at least two reasons. For help, read in your handbook "The Advantages of a Written Message." (See "Business letters" in the index.)

READ the following request letter written by a student returning to school after an absence of some years. Read this example from Ms. Nero's point of view.

July 12, 1996

Miss or Mrs. Janet Nero
Physics teacher
Western Kentucky Technical College
Hopkinsville, KY 42240

Dear Janet:

How's it goin? Things are pretty hot here, but I'm surviving. I hope you are too. Are you still teaching physics? You were my favorite teacher at WKTC.

I was in your physics class about six years ago or thereabouts. I dropped out after two years but I'm thinking of going back to school at Lexington Technical College. I'm writing this letter to ask if you would please, please write a letter of recommendation for me? I'd appreciate it a great deal! Thanks!

Your affectionate past student,

Dick Drool

SHARE your reactions to this letter with a classmate. Would you want to write a recommendation for Mr. Drool? Why or why not?

Writing the Request Letter

As with most business letters, a letter of request should follow a direct, three-part structure:

- The introduction should provide basic background information and the purpose of the request.
- The body should provide additional details and explanations.
- The closing should present a clear call for action.

READ through the letter and explanation below to see this three-part structure in action.

March 3, 1995

Ms. Gail Scott
Electronics Teacher
Leacock High School
Cary, MI 39054

Dear Ms. Scott:

The introductory paragraph provides background information and states the purpose of the request.

As a senior, I've begun applying to colleges that offer electronics and electrical engineering programs. Because you encouraged me to pursue, as you called it, "a shocking career in electricity," I'm writing to ask if you would write a letter recommending me for the electrical engineering program at Harrisburg Technical College.

The next two paragraphs provide pertinent details.

As you may recall, in your Advanced Electronics class, 1993-94, I consistently received A's on my projects and tests. You remarked on my term project that I had a strong grasp of both electronics principles and the hands-on design of circuit systems.

In order to strengthen my understanding of electronics, I took Advanced Physics this year. I have maintained a 3.2 average. During the past two years, I've also worked part-time at Radio Shack, run cross-country, and participated in the Math Club.

The writer closes with a call for action.

Please send a letter by April 10, 1995, to Professor Charles Reisman, Electrical Engineering Program Coordinator, recommending me for the program at Harrisburg. I've enclosed a pre-addressed, stamped envelope for your convenience. Please call at 278-8549 if you need further information. Your recommendation for the program will mean a lot because you have closely observed my work in electronics.

Sincerely,

Timothy Bartels

Timothy Bartels

WRITE: Select one of the two options below and write a letter requesting a recommendation.

1. You wish to apply for a summer job that requires a recommendation. Write a letter to a current or former employer.
2. Your college (or apprenticeship) application form requires a recommendation. Write a letter to a former or current teacher requesting a letter of recommendation.

Impromptu Writing

In Perspective

When you are involved in an impromptu-writing activity, your goal is to compose a clear, unified piece of writing within a limited amount of time. As you probably know, these writing activities can vary greatly from one situation to the next.

In one situation, you might be provided with a very open-ended writing prompt: *React to the following quotation . . .* or *write about an experience that really caused you to think.*

For another impromptu writing, you might be presented with a more clearly defined scenario like this one: *Discuss a school-related problem in a form suitable for the school newspaper.*

In still another situation, you might be provided with a rather task-specific assignment related to course material: *The Reverend Mr. Collins and Wickham (in* Pride and Prejudice*) possess highly undesirable character traits. Address these undesirable traits in a two-paragraph essay.* (Sounds almost like an essay-test question, right?)

So how, you may ask, can anyone be ready for a writing activity that is assigned in class, leaving little or no time to prepare? Good question. You can, of course, keep up with all of your content-area reading and note taking so you're always ready to write on the spot in any one of your classes. (Make sure to pick up on any clues that a teacher might provide beforehand, like "Be prepared to . . .") You can also draw upon all of your other experiences as a writer, especially your understanding of three basic forms—the paragraph, the traditional essay, and the essay-test answer.

Our best advice is this: Develop a good working knowledge of impromptu writing so, no matter what the assignment or situation, you are able to put together an effective piece of writing with little or no warning. The activities in this extended unit will help you develop that working knowledge.

REACT: Put your personal impromptu-writing experience in perspective by answering the following questions. (Share the results of your work.)

- Describe your most recent impromptu-writing experience. (What was the assignment and how did you carry it out?)

- What other experiences have you had in the past year or two related to impromptu writing? (Have you been involved in a writing assessment or competency test, AP English or history class, writing for college/technical school placement, etc.?) Briefly describe a few of these experiences.

- What writing and thinking skills generally come into play during impromptu writing? (On a related note, what makes impromptu writing different from most other forms of writing?)

- What are your strengths and weaknesses as an impromptu writer?

  Strengths:

  Weaknesses:

- Are there any sections in the handbook that would be helpful to review before your next impromptu writing?

- Can you think of any real-world situations in which someone might be asked (or need) to write something on the spot within a limited amount of time?

after words

Suppose your teacher asked you to create two prompts for impromptu writing—one related to something you are currently studying in English class and a second one related to your course work in another class.

- What writing prompt would work well in your English class?

- What quotation, news brief, poem, or scenario would make a good writing prompt in another class?

Impromptu Inventory

The following inventory can be used in conjunction with the "In Perspective" activity you just completed, or on its own as a quick evaluation of your impromptu-writing experiences. (Discuss your responses to these questions with your classmates.)

1. How often are you asked to do impromptu writings?

Once a week *Twice a week* *Once a month* *Almost never*

2. How do you feel about impromptu writing?

Valuable *Necessary* *A waste* *Not sure*

3. How well do you feel you do on impromptu essays?

Very well *Pretty well* *Okay* *Not too well*

4. Do you take some time to think about the question before you begin writing?

Always *Usually* *Sometimes* *Never*

5. Do you write a focus or thesis statement before you begin writing?

Always *Usually* *Sometimes* *Never*

6. Do you make a brief outline or plan before you write?

Always *Usually* *Sometimes* *Never*

7. Do you keep each of your main points clearly in mind when you are writing so that you can tie them all together?

Always *Usually* *Sometimes* *Never*

8. Do you keep track of time when you are writing?

Always *Usually* *Sometimes* *Never*

9. Do you reserve sufficient time for revising?

Always *Usually* *Sometimes* *Never*

10. Do you talk about your impromptu writings with your teachers and classmates in order to improve?

Always *Usually* *Sometimes* *Never*

Basic Steps in the Impromptu-Writing Process

The challenge in impromptu writing is to select the best of what you know and write about it clearly and concisely—all in a limited time frame. Perhaps the most important quality you can bring to impromptu writing is confidence, and confidence develops through experience and understanding.

The academic essay is the most common impromptu form, a form that often seems useful only in high school and college. Today, however, many businesses and organizations (like the armed forces) feel their employees and members should be able to develop functional reports and essays on the spot.

READ & REACT: When it comes to planning and writing the impromptu essay, there are several basic steps a writer should follow. (Read through the following list, making note of steps you find especially valuable and those that you need to work on or learn more about.)

1. Read the question carefully, looking for key words or the central idea.
2. Restate this question (problem, challenge) into a thesis statement.
3. Try listing, clustering, branching, etc., to collect your thoughts and gather details.
4. Review your list, selecting your best details and deciding how they might go together. (You might number your list, with each detail pertaining to the same idea getting the same number.)
5. Arrange your list into a basic working outline.
6. Reword your thesis statement (if necessary) to reflect your working outline.
7. Write, always keeping your overall point (and the time limit) clearly in mind.
8. Leave enough time to (a) read over the entire essay from start to finish and (b) go back and make necessary revisions.

after words → Are there other hints or reminders you would add to this list? What are they? (Share your thoughts with your classmates.)

Writing and Assessment

READ: Now that you understand the steps involved in the impromptu-writing process, you may well be wondering what teachers look for when they evaluate unrehearsed writings. Read on and find out.

First, teachers look at the ***content***, the ideas that the writing is built upon. Does the writer display a good working knowledge of the concepts covered in class (if the writing prompt is directly related to course work)? Does the writer speak from a position of authority on his or her subject (if the writing prompt is more open-ended)?

Second, teachers look at the ***form*** of the writing, the manner in which the ideas are put together. Has the writer formed a clearly defined focus or thesis statement? Does the writer effectively develop his or her focus? Has proper attention been given to accuracy? Is the writing easy to follow and understand?

Remember, though, that a teacher's expectations are generally not the same for impromptu writing as they are for writing that is produced over an extended period of time. (An impromptu essay will never have the spit and polish of a piece developed under more relaxed circumstances.)

Also remember that the purpose of the impromptu writing will have some bearing on the way it is evaluated. For example, content-area teachers are obviously going to place a great deal of emphasis on the concepts and ideas included in the writing. In a schoolwide writing assessment, teachers may place more importance on the form of the writing—the ability to shape a unified essay within a given period of time.

Sample Writing Assessment Guidelines

Listed below you will find the actual directions given to juniors involved in a writing assessment project in a Wisconsin high school. On the following page are the four writing prompts included in this assessment.

READ & REACT: Carefully read through these directions to see if they include any pieces of information you might incorporate into your own impromptu-writing checklist. Also consider which of the writing prompts you would write on. (Discuss your ideas with your writing group.)

1. Write a well-organized composition of two to five paragraphs on one of the four suggested writing prompts. (The number of paragraphs in your essay will depend on the subject you choose to write about.) You have 90 minutes for your work.

2. Use your time wisely. Begin by brainstorming, and then organize your main ideas in a list or semantic map (cluster). Write a first draft using your list or map as a guide. Reserve enough time for revising and, as time permits, writing a final draft.

3. Include a title.

4. Your writing should be a sample of your best work (given the time constraints).

5. Write in ink, preferably black ink. You may use a dictionary, thesaurus, and writing handbook.

6. Work quietly until it's time to turn in your paper. Turn in all of your planning and writing with your final draft on top.

Writing Prompt 1

Suppose your school district is considering a twelve-month school year. Some people say that having three months off in the summer is a waste of time. People also have said that a lot of time is wasted each fall reviewing because students forget over the summer. In addition, the American school year is considerably shorter than the school year of many other countries. The superintendent is your audience. Write a persuasive essay defending or refuting the idea of a twelve-month school year. Include your reasons for taking a particular position and support these reasons with examples.

Writing Prompt 2

"Power should always be distrusted, in whatever hands it is placed." Discuss the truth of these words of Sir William Jones, presenting supporting examples from personal experiences, literature, film, history, and current events. Be specific.

Writing Prompt 3

An old adage says, "Time brings the truth to light." Discuss the truth of these words, presenting examples from some or all of the following: literature, film, history, current events, biography, or personal experience. Be specific.

Writing Prompt 4

"Down in their hearts, wise men know this truth: the only way to help yourself is to help others." Discuss the truth of these words of Elbert Hubbard, presenting examples from some or all of the following: literature, film, history, current events, biography, or personal experience. Be specific.

Spend 10-15 minutes collecting, focusing, and planning your thoughts for one of these writing prompts, as if you were about to develop an impromptu essay. (Share your results.)

Getting Down to Basics: Establishing a Framework for Planning and Writing

READ: "A finished piece of writing is as good as the planning that has gone into it." Maybe so, but then again, maybe not. Sometimes it is your most freely produced creations that turn out best. If, for example, you were asked to describe a significant or humorous experience in your life, little if any planning would be necessary. Other times, careful planning and organizing will be the key to producing an effective piece of writing. If, for instance, you were asked to defend or refute a particular character as a tragic hero, initial planning and organizing would be essential.

REVIEW: In order to determine how much planning you may need to do for an impromptu-writing activity, ask yourself the following types of questions. (Answering questions like these provides you with a basic framework for your writing.)

- What exactly is the writing assignment? What are the key words in the statement or question? (Make sure you understand what is expected of you.)

- How much time do I have to carry out the assignment? (How will you organize your time accordingly?)

- What is the primary purpose of the writing? (Are you expected to inform, explain, describe? Or are you free to establish your own purpose?)

- What specific subject should I write about (if the prompt is open-ended)? (Write about something that meets your approval and the requirements of the assignment.)

- Who is the audience? (The assignment may suggest you write to an audience other than your teacher. This may change the approach you take in your writing.)

- What form will my writing take? (Are you expected to write a paragraph or an essay? Or will you be able to develop your writing in another way?)

- What voice will I use in my writing? (You probably won't have too many options other than an informal or semiformal voice.)

REACT: Let's suppose, in an impromptu-writing activity, you were asked to write about a school-related problem in a form suitable for your school newspaper. Using the chart that follows, establish a basic framework for your writing. (Spend only a few minutes on your framework, as if you were involved in an actual impromptu writing.)

Assignment: Address a school-related problem in a form suitable for your school newspaper.

Subject: ....

....

Purpose: ....

....

Audience: ....

....

Form: ....

....

Voice: ....

....

Helpful Hint: Turn to "A Survey of Writing Forms" in your handbook if you need help creating your framework. (Refer to "Forms, composition" in the index for this information.) This chart lists many different forms of writing according to purpose, audience, and other basic characteristics.

Using your writing framework as your guide, plan and write your article. (Again, approach this writing as if you were involved in an actual impromptu writing. Spend about 35-40 minutes on your work.)

In-Class Impromptu Writing: From Start to Finish

READ & REACT: The following activity takes you through the steps of an actual in-class impromptu-writing activity. As you read through the model response on the next page, make note of the strengths in the writer's work. Also note what you might have done differently. Afterward, share your reactions. (Remember that the writer had limited time to complete her work.)

Discussion:
This is a very task-specific writing prompt, tied directly to course content. A writer is initially faced with two important questions: Who am I going to write about? Will I defend or refute this character as a tragic hero?

Assignment

Defend or *refute* that either Antigone or Creon is a tragic hero in Sophocle's play *Antigone*. Address characteristics of the tragic hero and the three-step tragic pattern in your response. (You may use your books.)

Discussion:
After studying the assignment, suppose a writer decides to defend Creon as a tragic hero. If a basic framework were established for planning, it would look something like this:

Writing Framework

Assignment: (Stated above)
Subject: King Creon as a tragic hero
Purpose: To display an understanding of the tragic figure in Greek drama
Audience: Teacher and classmates
Form: Academic essay
Voice: Semiformal

Discussion:
It is important that the thesis statement and basic outline of ideas reflect a clear understanding of the assignment and establish a manageable starting point for writing. (Note that this outline only addresses the main points the writer plans to cover.)

Planning

Thesis Statement: A close examination of Creon in *Antigone* is a classic study of the tragic hero in action.

Basic Outline of Ideas:

+ *Creon as a tragic hero*
  - larger-than-life figure
  - displays tragic flaws
  - worthy of pity

+ *Creon's actions follow the tragic pattern*
  - breakdown of traditional values
  - tragic consequences of his actions
  - self-realization in the end

One Student's Response

Accepting One's Fate

by Doris Wessel

A close examination of Creon in *Antigone* is a classic study of the tragic hero in action. The simple fact that Creon is king naturally makes him larger than life and heroic in stature. Yet, he is not an excessive individual, neither exceptionally good nor exceptionally bad. He does, however, have several tragic flaws, the worst of which is his excessive pride, or hubris, which makes him a stubborn ruler and leads to his eventual downfall. During the course of the play, he evokes pity from the reader, another characteristic of the tragic hero. The reader is moved when Creon can't fix his mistakes and is left surrounded by death. "Let death come quickly, and be kind to me," (237) Creon says at the end of the play. His weaknesses do not come from any indifferent evil, but more from external forces such as war and fate. Creon's eventual situation prompts the reader to ask, Why do good men suffer? Why can't things work out after an individual repents? But this is not what happens to a tragic hero. He must deal with the harsh consequences of his hubris.

Creon's experiences throughout the play clearly follow the tragic pattern. When the play begins, the breakdown of traditional values has already started. Creon has to deal with the turmoil in the city that resulted from the war between his nephews. In addition, the traditional values of the gods break down when Creon forbids the burying of Polynices. Then Antigone [Creon's daughter] breaks the law and threatens his authority. He responds by banishing her. His world continues to crumble when his son defies him, and he is told that his people are questioning his judgment. Tiresias, the blind prophet, is not afraid to tell Creon what the people have quietly thought all along: that Creon's actions have undeniably been wrong. Creon realizes this when the choragas [leader of the dramatic chorus] agrees with Tiresias, but it is too late to repair the damage that his foolish pride has already done. Antigone is dead. In addition, his son is dead, as is his wife. Just as Tiresias warned him, he has paid for his actions, "corpse for corpse, flesh of [his] own flesh" (227). After these terrible things occur, Creon begins to realize the extent of his mistakes. "I have been rash and foolish. I have killed my son and my wife" (238). He wants to die, but realizes that he can't. He must live with his guilt, a tragic figure who has become a stronger man.

The first paragraph establishes Creon as a tragic hero.

The second paragraph traces the pattern of his tragic actions.

Notice that the essay is balanced, in that each paragraph essentially contains the same amount of information and detail.

Special Note: The writer had 45 minutes to develop her work. Approximately the first 5 to 10 minutes of her time were devoted to analyzing the question and planning her writing. Thirty minutes were devoted to the actual writing. And the final 5 minutes were devoted to basic revising and proofreading. (A few editing changes have been made here to ensure readability.)

Planning an Open-Ended Impromptu Essay

READ & REACT: Suppose you were asked to respond in an in-class writing to the following quotation: "Let there be spaces in your togetherness." This is a very open-ended writing prompt that would require some careful (but quick) planning in order to identify a specific focus or thesis for writing. Here's how that planning might go:

Initial Brainstorming

Let's say you started by identifying situations or relationships in which space is important and followed with a quick listing of ideas related to each situation:

Family	**Friends**	**Couples**
privacy required	free to say no	my own plans
lock on my room	free to disagree	my other friends
room for others	trust	no strings
	suffocating	not a possession
		suffocating

Focusing Your Efforts

During the listing, a possible writing idea should begin to emerge. For example, perhaps the word "suffocating" under "Friends" or "Couples" brings to mind a particular relationship that specifically addresses the issue of space (or lack of it).

The next step would be to establish a focus or thesis statement related to this relationship that could serve as a controlling idea for your writing.

Possible Focus Statement:

.... and I had a great relationship until he (or she) took up too much space in my life.

Developing a Plan

With a specific writing idea in mind, a simple outline or plan for writing should be developed. (You don't have a lot of time, so keep things simple and to the point. You might establish nothing more than a basic frame for your work, a place to start.) For the sample writing idea, all that might be needed is a list of general points or areas to cover:

- how the relationship once was
- when space started to become an issue
- how it began to affect the relationship
- how the lack of space eventually ended things

Completing the Writing

Obviously, the largest segment of time should be devoted to developing the actual writing. (Again, because of time limitations, it's best to stick to your initial focus statement and plan for writing rather than to experiment or change directions.)

WRITE: Select one of the following quotations (or one of your own choosing) as a starting point for a 45-minute impromptu writing. Follow the basic steps described on the previous page. (Use the space below for your initial brainstorming and planning. Complete your writing on your own paper.)

- *The hardest thing to learn in life is which bridge to cross and which to burn.*
- *Happiness is not a state to arrive at, but a manner of traveling.*
- *There are many truths that cannot be realized until personal experience has brought them home.*

Initial Brainstorming

Focusing Your Efforts

Developing a Plan

Planning a Response to a Scenario

READ & REACT: Plan and write a response to the following scenario, working within the time limitations of a normal class period (approximately 45 minutes). Use the space provided below for initial brainstorming, focusing, and planning. Complete your writing on your own paper.

THINK ABOUT: Imagine a society where violence is glorified as a massive entertainment machine spewing forth film after film loaded with blood-spilling, brain-exploding violence. Imagine a society where every 12 or so minutes of TV is spiced with flashy ads reminding people of the things they can never be or have, unless they take them by force. Imagine a society where compassion is considered a weakness and greed a strength, where "getting away with it" makes you a folk hero, and where the law applies only to those unfortunate enough to lack the funds, prestige, or gumption to lie their way around guilt. Now, imagine this society reacting with shock to the actions of its youth, stating that guns, drugs, and greed are the problem. Our children, so ready to kill, are merely the reflection of what we have taught them and tolerated.

WRITE ABOUT: You've just read about some of the elements that make a society bad and unproductive. For this writing, imagine a perfect society, one that really works for everyone. What three things would be essential to make this new society work? Explain each of your main points.

Initial Brainstorming

Focusing Your Efforts

Developing a Plan

Instant Solutions

The only way to truly improve your impromptu-writing skills is to practice them, and that means practicing them beyond the classroom. Luckily, there are a number of activities that will help you sharpen your impromptu skills for present and future use.

Among the most popular strategies are the writing-to-learn activities, which can be used in or out of class, with or without your teacher's prompting. (Many of these are listed in your handbook.)

One such activity is the **instant solution**. By thinking and writing about solutions to at least one common problem a day, you can strengthen your power to think and write on an impromptu basis. See how you do with the problem described below.

READ & REACT: Read the problem. Then write an impromptu "instant solution" to the problem. (Use the strategies you've picked up along the way to help you gather and arrange your thoughts.)

Problem: You have just found out that you are the winner of a special election for president of the student council; you have also just found out that you are supposed to give a short presentation in about 15 minutes to the faculty advisors. They want to know what topics you would like covered at the next meeting and why. Write your presentation below. You have 15 minutes. (No, make that 10. It will take you 5 minutes to walk to the meeting room.)

Solution: ....

Unsent Letters

Another writing-to-learn activity is the unsent letter. An unsent letter can be written to any person on any topic and allows you, the writer, to become personally involved with the subject. You can write about what you know (or don't know) to someone else, real or imagined.

READ: Just to get you started, read and react to the following unsent letter, which shares one student's thoughts on the impact of an important invention on our lives.

Dear Mister Thomas Alva Edison,

Years ago, you got the first light bulb to light up. That moment was a huge step forward in brightening our days and nights. When I realized all the things I would be unable to do if you hadn't kept trying thousands of materials for the filaments of light bulbs, I decided I wanted to say thank you. Let me tell you about what we now do with lights and electricity. Perhaps one of my favorite uses of lights is the decoration of Christmas trees. Tiny, colorful bulbs are strung around the tree. Glass ornaments reflect the bulbs' colored rays of light to create a magical glow. Many a time I've found myself staring into the twinkling lights of the tree. Many people decorate their houses with the same kind of lights. It is hard to imagine the holiday season without lights, and we have you to thank for that.

I wish you could ride in a plane coming into Chicago late at night. Thousands of lights on buildings, cars, and houses create an earthbound galaxy. Mr. Edison, I believe that a city at night is a worthy tribute to you and your hard work. Streetlights provide the light people need to drive anywhere during the night. Stoplights are a modification of streetlights. Red, green, and yellow glowing circles tell us when to stop, go, and yield. It helps to control the flow of traffic and avoid confusion.

Every night we use plenty of lights inside our homes as well. Doing homework would be impossible without a lamp at my desk. My mother can see to make supper at any time. Night-lights, little bulbs that plug into sockets, help "scare away monsters" for young children. And if something goes bump in the night, we can get up and turn the lights on to see what is going on.

People don't always like to have lights glaring and flooding a room, however. In fact, at restaurants, lights are dimmed to add a soft ambiance to the dining atmosphere. Movie theaters slowly turn the lights down to darkness as the movies begin. Many of the things we do today are dependent on light. When there is a blackout, people seem disabled. Today, if someone has a good idea, we say a light bulb turned on in his or her head. What a perfect analogy, for your light bulb was a great idea! Your invention, Mr. Edison, has given so much to the world. You light up my life!

Heather Bachman

WRITE: Now write your own unsent letter to a famous inventor, scientist, or someone else who has made a positive contribution to our way of life.

Sharpening Your Writing and Learning Skills

READ & APPLY: Writing regularly about new concepts and ideas helps you internalize this information. Put in another way, writing helps you make new concepts and ideas part of your own thinking. That is why writing is considered such an important learning tool.

Self-Help Strategy

Here's a simple strategy that you can employ at any time to help you think and write about your course work in any class. Not only will this activity help you better understand new concepts and ideas, but it will also help you become more proficient at planning and writing essays on the spot.

1. HIGHLIGHT ● Underline a series of important points in your class notes (or notes from your reading) related to a particular unit under study.
2. QUESTION ● Write one or two questions related in some way to the points you have noted.
3. PROPOSE ● Turn one of the questions into a focus or thesis statement.
   - Could the Confederacy have prolonged or even won the Civil War with a few strong alliances in Europe? (a question)
   - The Confederacy could have prolonged or even won the Civil War with a few strong alliances in Europe. (a question turned into a thesis statement)
4. SUPPORT ● List a few main points in support of, as well as against, your thesis.
5. WRITE ● Develop your thesis in a freely written essay, incorporating ideas as they come to mind—or according to any basic planning you may have done.

inside info

This activity proves especially helpful when you are preparing for essay and placement tests, debates, discussions, and so on.

Revising on the Run

READ: Carefully read this first draft of an impromptu writing. Make note of strengths and weaknesses in the writing as you go along.

1 The day I graduated from high school, I think I bolted out of that school door like
2 buckshot. I had just turned 18, I was free—school bells were behind me. I wasn't thinking
3 so much about my future as I was about being free of my past. I really didn't know what
4 was involved in being an adult, and I really didn't care much—I just wanted to get busy.
5 Voting, I now realize, is something everyone in this country can and must do.
6 When I was just 18, I didn't think much about voting. But when I got out on my
7 own and started trying to make a life for myself, I realized just how much young
8 adults need to make their voices heard. In college, I found that financial aid was
9 being cut by the state, and I needed to work full-time to pay my tuition. That didn't
10 do much for my grades. Then the college I was attending wanted to cut enrollment
11 to save money on teachers. So they put me on probation. Nobody seemed to care that I
12 was working my butt off working and studying at the same time. I was very
13 frustrated, but I fought back. I joined student government and expressed my opinion
14 on enrollment, probation, and financial aid to the college's administration. I also
15 started voting in state and local elections, always supporting candidates who supported
16 increased funding for education. I think I made a difference. I not only got through
17 college, I helped make that college a better place to study and prepare for a career.
18 At least it's better than it was.
19 Now I'm in my late 20's. I worry about health insurance, and renters' rights,
20 and overcrowded preschools. I know that who I vote for, whether for my town's mayor
21 or for the president, will make a difference in my everyday life. I have to live with
22 the decisions elected officials make, and so do you. And sometimes the decisions they
23 make can really mess up your life. Don't wait until those decisions start making
24 your life difficult to start voting. Get informed and vote now.

[1-4] Cut first paragraph. [5] Cut this sentence. (The idea is addressed later.) [6] Rewrite the sentence to make it clearer. [10-11] Combine the two sentences. [11-12] Rewrite the sentence beginning with "Nobody" for word choice and appropriateness. [12] Begin a new paragraph to reflect the change in direction (from problem to solution) in the essay. [15] Change "supporting" to avoid repetition. [18] Cut "At least it's better than it was." (redundant) [22-23] Cut "And sometimes . . . your life." (redudant) [24] Cut "to start voting." (awkward repetition) Note: Please keep in mind that your students' rewrites will vary. Special Note: Give your students a specified period of time to complete their rewrites (no more than 15 or 20 minutes).

REACT: Suppose this is your completed draft of an impromptu essay, and you have only 15-20 minutes to work with it. You decide to apply the guidelines for "Revising on the Run" to get the most out of the writing within your limited time. After you make the necessary changes, write the revised version of the essay on your own paper. Work quickly, but carefully. (Share your results.)

In any impromptu or timed writing, work as efficiently as possible. In his book *Writing from Scratch: The Essay* (Hamilton Press, 1987), John Clark Pratt suggests using 10 percent of your time for planning, 80 percent for drafting and revising, and 10 percent for proofreading.

Reviewing Strategy

READ: In "Revising on the Run," you practiced a reviewing and revising strategy that works well when you have very limited time to make changes. The checklist that follows looks more closely at the reviewing process in an impromptu activity. Use these questions to help you determine what to keep and what to cut in your writing.

1. Did I begin with a clear restatement of the question or prompt?
2. Have I addressed the prompt completely, providing examples where and when necessary?
3. Does my essay read smoothly from start to finish? Is it easy to follow?
4. Can I quickly and clearly locate each of the main points in my essay?
5. Have I said something interesting, original, or worthwhile?
6. Have I read through my final essay for overall sense and clarity?

Reflecting Upon Your Work

APPLY: Reflect upon your work for one of the previous impromptu-writing activities in this unit by answering the following questions. (Use your responses as a starting point for a discussion of your impromptu-writing experiences.)

1. Did I have trouble with any phase of the process? Which one(s)?
2. Did I need more time?
3. How could I have used my time more wisely?
4. Did I address all the key points of the question or writing prompt?
5. What is the strongest point in my writing, and what is the weakest?
6. What suggestions does my teacher have?
7. How can I improve my overall essay next time?

Additional Prompts

The prompts listed below (and on the following pages) are simply suggestions of what you might choose to write about for ongoing impromptu practice.

Think and Write About . . .

- news stories
- world problems
- local problems
- notable people
- occupations and professions
- nature
- education and learning
- places and events
- art or music
- food and drink
- cars and travel
- language and communication
- manners and morals
- laws and justice
- social concerns
- customs and habits
- money and costs
- government and politics
- the media

Read and Respond to . . .

- short articles from magazines or newspapers
- song lyrics and poems
- quips, quotes, or short stories
- classroom literature

Watch (Listen) and Respond to . . .

- news broadcasts
- interviews
- music videos
- short films
- recited poetry

Analyze and Write About . . .

- unusual statistics or data
- quotations
- proverbs
- cliches
- euphemisms

Describe . . .

- a favorite photograph
- a flock of birds in flight
- a person who is totally organized
- a person who is great to work with
- someone who has an unusual hobby or collection
- someone who has influenced you
- someone who is one of a kind
- someone you met once or knew briefly
- a high-school dance (or other event)

Compare . . .

- original/imitation
- middle school/high school
- winter/summer
- like/love
- mother/father
- one class to another
- 60's/90's
- musicians or musical groups
- movies or TV programs
- old friends/new friends
- bad days/good days
- alligator/crocodile
- wisdom/knowledge
- opinion/belief

Cause and Effect . . .

- What causes tornadoes?
- What causes rainbows?
- What causes misunderstandings?
- What causes cancer?
- What causes sunburn?
- What causes violence?
- What causes prejudice?
- What causes pain?
- What causes war?
- Why are there schools?
- Why are there towns?
- Why do we worship sports stars?
- Why do we feel anger?

Explain . . .

- how .... works
- how .... is measured
- how .... is made
- how to train ....
- how to find ....
- how to judge ....
- how to win at ....
- how to play ....
- how to use ....
- how to arrange ....
- how to prevent ....
- how to eliminate ....
- how to treat ....
- how to build ....
- how to repair ....
- how to take ....
- how to appreciate ....
- how to run ....
- how to kick ....

Classify . . .

- kinds of courage
- kinds of bridges
- kinds of rock music
- kinds of students
- kinds of assignments
- kinds of friends
- kinds of jobs
- kinds of laughter
- kinds of moods
- kinds of art
- kinds of windows
- kinds of parks
- kinds of vacations
- kinds of magazines
- kinds of TV programs
- kinds of neighbors
- kinds of prayer
- kinds of ads

Argue (for or against) . . .

- television in the courtroom
- final exams
- year-round school
- a large military
- free health care
- higher gas taxes
- smoking in public places

Define . . .

- Democrat/Republican
- liberal/conservative
- alcoholic
- bureaucracy
- loyalty
- pride
- happiness
- style
- mirage
- pollution
- victim
- friend
- fear
- beauty
- luck
- soul
- freedom
- carpetbagger
- syndrome
- normal
- euphemism
- clinic
- grass roots
- sacrifice
- manifest destiny
- photosynthesis
- osmosis
- pacifist
- bandwagon
- hypocrisy
- hippie/yuppie
- prima donna
- senioritis
- taboo
- ethnic

College Entrance Essays

The following prompts were taken from actual entrance essays required by the universities listed. They should provide you with a good idea of the kind of impromptus you might be asked to write.

Northwestern University, Evanston, Illinois

- Explain why one of the best days of your life has had continuing importance to you as a young adult.
- How have your experiences as a teenager significantly differed from those of your friends? Include comparisons.
- Coping with a serious problem or challenge may help to establish a person's true moral or ethical character. Have you faced such a situation? What was the outcome?
- A Northwestern student recently said, "Education, at its best, changes the way you think or makes you think in different directions." Describe how an academic or intellectual experience has stimulated your participation in independent research, study or reading, work in the arts, science projects, etc.

Notre Dame, South Bend, Indiana

- Tell about a particular book, play, film, piece of music, dance performance, scientific theory or experiment, or work of art that has influenced you.
- Select a technological innovation of this century and discuss its effects on your family, local community, or nation.
- Which of your talents, interests, or activities means the most to you? Why?

Washington University, St. Louis, Missouri

- Choose one memorable or significant hour from your life that gives an understanding of who you are.
- Choose one of your most humorous or embarrassing experiences and describe it in detail.
- In the movie *The Wizard of Oz*, everyone remembers the scene in which Dorothy and the Scarecrow have to choose which path to take when the yellow brick road splits in two. Describe what might have happened if they'd chosen the other path.

Literary License

- Explore a real-life lesson you see in a well-known children's story, such as "Little Red Riding Hood," "Goldilocks and the Three Bears," or another of your own choosing.
- Take a brief quote from a literary work you have read recently and expand on whatever insight it gave you, how it rings true for you, or how you see it being important to you in the future.
- Explain how the values represented in a recent work of literature (novel, play, short story, poem) either reflect or counter your own values.
- You are a stand-in for a character in a short story. How will *you* respond in that situation? With the other characters? How will your presence change the final outcome of the story?
- Works of literature often depict conflicts between parent (or parent figure) and son or daughter. From your reading, describe a parent/child conflict and tell how the conflict is resolved.
- People are sometimes blind to truth. From your reading, explain how a character refuses to recognize the truth.
- Separation from loved ones can be a painful experience. Describe a literary character that experiences such isolation. Explain the reason for the separation and the effects of the separation.
- Rebellion is a normal part of life. Be specific about describing a character's rebellion in a literary work. Whom or what does the person rebel against? What is the outcome?
- Characters in literature have hopes and dreams just like we do. Discuss a character with a dream or goal and to what extent the goal is attained.

Think Tank

- What has not been invented that you think would contribute the most to making life better for the greatest number of people?
- Describe one thing that you could do to promote peace, either as an individual or as a member of a larger group.
- What could parents be taught about parenting that would make families better in this country? How might this be achieved?
- In regard to many problems, education is held up as a large part of the answer. Do you agree that lack of education is often a major part of most problems? Explain.
- How could the potential benefits of television be maximized?
- Is there a reason for the seeming upsurge of prejudice in the world today? Explain.
- Is there a problem (situation, person, etc.) in your life for which you could devise a strategy that would lead to eventual improvement or a solution?
- What problems will censorship solve?
- What is the biggest or most significant problem you have ever solved? Did you reach your solution by design or by accident?
- What best prepares someone to become a problem solver? What is education's role in this process?

WRITE: Respond to the following quip by carefully analyzing it, by relating it to a personal experience, by . . .

Quip of the Week

When he arrived for the interview, he was escorted to an office by a genial woman he assumed was a secretary. They began chatting, and because she seemed so open and friendly, he decided he could find out what the job involved by asking the secretary questions. The conversation went smoothly, and after an hour, fear and trepidation had been replaced by enthusiasm about the position. He was about to ask some questions about the coming interview when the woman informed him that the job was his. The pleasant woman had been the employer; the pleasant conversation had been the interview.

WRITE: Respond to the following statistics by commenting on them as a whole or by focusing your attention on one or two specific statistics.

Stats of the Week

DATABASE

- People killed at Hiroshima and Nagasaki (est.): **200,000**
- Total number of nuclear weapons manufactured by the Soviet Union and the United States: **115,000**
- Nuclear weapons dismantled each year by Russia and the United States: **2,000-2,500 each** Weapons that still exist: nearly **50,000**
- U.S. spending next year on upgrades and prototypes of nuclear arms: **$2 billion;** on environment at weapon sites: **$5.3 billion**
- Percentage of the world's energy supplied by nuclear reactors: **17%** Americans who support continued use of nuclear power but want no more plants built: **48%;** who want more plants: **32%;** who want the plants closed: **15%**

WRITE: Find an article in a newspaper or magazine that uses a number of statistics to prove its point. Attach a copy of the article in the space below. Exchange papers with a classmate and write about each other's "Stats of the Week."

Stats of the Week

WRITE: Respond to the following quotation by writing whatever comes into your mind when you read it.

Quotation of the Week

"It is never too late to give up your prejudices."
—Henry David Thoreau

WRITE: Find a quotation you feel is worth thinking about and write it in the box below. Exchange your quotation with a classmate and write about the one you receive.

Quotation of the Week

Writing Summaries

The Abstract

The abstract is a shortened form of a passage using the important words of the passage itself and working these words as simply as possible into sentences.

First, you underline the important words, as in the example below:

> This nation has recently developed a new national pastime: diet mania, or counting calories. Many of us do count them, but not everyone understands what it is we're counting. By definition, a calorie is a measure of heat: the amount of heat required to raise the temperature of one gram of water by one degree centigrade. At this very moment you are generating that same kind of heat; you are burning calories. You have been since you were born, and you will continue to every day of your life. Our bodies can be thought of as biochemical machines that burn the food we eat for fuel; the amount of burning that takes place is measured in calories. How much energy is produced by the burning of calories is determined by how active we are. Just sitting and resting, we expend about a calorie a minute. That means that just to stay alive, our body machines must burn 1,440 calories per day. The more active we are, the more calories we will burn up.

Then you write the abstract by joining the underlined words of the passage into sentences. Note that as few words as possible are added. The original passage contained 172 words; the abstract contains only 53 words, or fewer than one-third as many.

> This nation has developed a new pastime: counting calories. A calorie is a measure of the amount of heat you generate. Our bodies burn fuel (food) that is measured in calories. The energy we produce by burning calories is determined by our activity. Just to stay alive, we must burn 1,440 calories a day.

UNDERLINE: Try your hand at writing an abstract of the passage below. Begin by underlining the key words.

The occasional appearance of comets amongst the heavenly bodies has puzzled men for thousands of years. The first stargazers thought they were distant planets. Aristotle and the astronomers of his time (384-322 B.C.) theorized that they were the results of air escaping from the earth's atmosphere and catching fire; it wasn't until the Renaissance (15th and 16th centuries) that men of science realized that comets were unique heavenly bodies. Even then, however, the long-standing myth that the appearance of a comet meant impending disaster persisted. A comet is, in fact, a gaseous body of small mass with enormous volume that can be seen only occasionally from earth. The head of a comet is sometimes only several hundred miles in diameter while the tail often surpasses a million miles in length. The chances of a comet causing a disaster are very remote, although a comet could conceivably collide with the earth causing considerable damage.

WRITE: Now, see if you can create an abstract for this passage with approximately half as many words as the original while retaining all the important ideas.

The appearance of comets has long puzzled man. At first, they were thought to be distant planets; later, Aristotle theorized that comets resulted when gas escaping from the earth's atmosphere caught fire. It was during the Renaissance that comets were properly identified as unique heavenly bodies; however, the myth of comets forecasting disaster persisted. In fact, a comet is a gaseous body with a head of several hundred miles and a tail of approximately a million miles. Comets pose no real threat to our planet.

The Index